JUST BILL

Just Bill

SMALL TOWN LIFE IN NEBRASKA

PALMER MCGREW

Opus One Studios
8641 Elm Street, Suite 1154
McLean, VA 22101
www.opusonestudios.com

ISBN: 978-1-09835-100-7

Cover and Interior Design by Brent Spears

Dedication & Acknowledgements

To my fellow veterans, many of whom inspired parts of this book, and to the Code of Support Foundation, which makes sure that all veterans get the support they need and, through their service and sacrifice, have earned.

I am indebted to the following people who over the years have shared their stories with me. Many of them will recognize their influence in Just Bill:

Bill Boyle
Chuck Hansult
Jim Hinds
Ken Johnson
Pete Kusek
Randy Lindgren
Terry Murtaugh
Lee Prawitz
Herb Puscheck
John Reppert
John & Dianne Roosma
John Shimerda
Cliff Shoemaker
Don Siebenaler
Roger Waddell & His Sister
(And others I, regrettably, may have forgotten)

Table of Contents

"We'll stop in a small town and learn the history and stories, feel the ground and capture the spirit. Then we'll turn it into our own story that will live inside our history to carry with us, always. Because stories are more important than things."

— Victoria Erickson

Foreward

WHAT THE PEOPLE LIVING in small towns in Nebraska need most is an audience. For the most part, they are intelligent, creative, interesting people, but their lives are narrowly bounded by surrounding cornfields and feedlots. They have many shrewd observations on life, but they only have the same small audience to tell them to. After a while, they end up talking about ((gasp!)) television "reality" shows.

Not that in New York or San Francisco the daily topics of discussion are more erudite than the latest NFL game or *Dancing with the Stars.* That seems to be the focus of many urban lives as well, but at least in the big city something dramatic happens at least once a day.

Not so in our little town, a made up one named Blackjack. It is supposedly named after Black Jack Pershing, but two words in the name proved cumbersome to the inhabitants, so it was made into one, leading to years of jokes about it being a gambling Mecca.

Notable events seldom occur in such little towns. For one thing, there just aren't a lot of people there to do things you want to talk about. And then there is the fact that everyone knows you, or almost everyone, and anything you do is likely to be quickly reported to your friends and neighbors. Someone famous likes to say, "It takes a village..." The gist of which is that in villages everyone is watching, and whatever they have to say about you is likely to be said over and over for years. It does cause one to be somewhat cautious.

Since I lived much of my life in the vicinity of the very large city of New York and the very important city of Washington, D.C., my small town friends were apt to say how they envied my opportunities.

One said, "You can go to the opera any time you want."

I suppose that is true, even though I had never actually gone to the opera when he said that. Whereas, when I lived for several years in a pretty small town in Minnesota, whenever the Minneapolis Symphony came to play, everyone attended the concert. So I'm not at all convinced that opportunity somehow equals realization. For some reason, it often works out just the other way around. When we lived in New York, though, I was a young teen; it was my job to take visiting Nebraska relatives to the Statue of Liberty and the Empire State Building. Most New Yorkers had never been to either.

A friend of mine moved from my neighborhood in Lincoln, the state capital, to a small Nebraska town, and I went many times to visit him there. I was entranced by the differences I could easily observe, even as a teenager.

Later, I found that I had many friends from rural Nebraska, and I asked them to tell me their stories. Some did, and those stories are found here, slightly "enhanced" in some cases. Some of these stories you could make up, but you would not be likely to.

As my wife's aunt liked to say, "People are funnier than anybody." People will actually do things you could never imagine, until they do them.

What surprised me, though, was how some of my rural Nebraska friends have no stories to tell me at all. Of course, they do have them; it's just that they don't find them interesting or amusing.

I suppose that's why a guy who never actually lived in a small Nebraska town came to write about one. To me, it was not just what it was; it was something unknown to most of us with its good and bad sides—both of them amusing, or at least interesting, to those of us who don't live those lives on a daily basis.

Fewer and fewer people in this country live in small towns. Small towns have ceased to fulfill any function that can't be fulfilled as well or better in a larger community. Soon, if not now, you could live in a totally remote location and lead your life quite adequately via the internet or its successor. The lifestyle depicted here is slowly disappearing, and that's too bad.

Even in my childhood neighborhood on the East Side of Lincoln, there were neighbors watching me whenever I was out of the house and giving me parental advice if I didn't act in a way they found acceptable. My favorite example was Mrs. Murray, who liked to sit on her porch and comment on everything the neighbor kids did. We all knew that her own offspring, in their late teens and early 20s, were poor examples for us to follow, and we doubted that she had anything worthwhile to tell us. But, she was there, watching, and that was what mattered. In small towns, everyone is a Mrs. Murray on her front porch.

Prologue

Hi, I'm Ralph Anderson. This is my story.

For some reason, I hadn't thought about actually getting a job until my senior-senior year at Bison State. I say "senior-senior year" because it was kind of difficult to tell what year I was in. It might be better called "Year Five out of Four." I was still trying to pass freshman math, but it didn't seem likely to happen that year either. To my surprise and consternation, however, I got a D at the end of the year (oops!), and realized that I was going to have to leave college and go to work. I seriously doubted that my parents would let me just hang around the house for the rest of my life.

I suppose that sounds pretty lame. I'm not dumb, and I'm not lazy. I just never got into the hang of studying. I could get by without much effort, and let's be honest, I kind of liked it there. College was a lot of fun!

As for getting a job, one of the problems was that I had a GPA of around 2.0, and you can't get a job with that. Another problem was that, at some point, faced with declaring a major while having no idea of what I wanted to do, I had become a journalism major. There aren't that many big papers in Nebraska, and the journalism majors with 4.0s were gobbling up all the jobs there were.

I had worked at Runzas flipping burgers and frying fries for a couple of summers, and I thought I could always do that if I had to. I might still be doing that today, if my dad hadn't come up with an idea. He had a friend who knew a small-town publisher, and he arranged for me to be introduced to her.

Well, I got the job, and now I'm a "reporter." In my first three weeks on the job, I have managed to screw up in every assignment she's given me. I wish I had paid more attention in all those journalism classes.

Oh, Jeez! She's calling for me again.

Part 1

Who was Bill Just?

CHAPTER 1

The Blackjack Press, May 14, 2006

THE PUBLISHER'S NAME WAS Irma Fritzling. Everyone at *The Blackjack Press* calls her Mrs. Fritz. No one on the staff called her Irma. Of course, I did, and on the first day on the job too. I'm not going to do that again!

It's funny how employees seem to have their own rules, and they enforce them. Mrs. Fritz said nothing to me about my gaffe, but the rest of the staff, such as it is, let me know "the rules."

The office was very small, essentially two rooms—one for Mrs. Fritz and one for the printing operation. I had to work somewhere else, unless Mrs. Fritz was out, which was often.

When she called me in from the sidewalk, where I was chatting with townspeople, hoping to learn something, I went in to see what she wanted, and she waved me over to her desk and motioned to the empty chair beside it for me to sit down.

It was the first time I had seen her today, so I had to check to see what outrageous outfit she had on. Today, she's wearing red, as usual, but it was a pantsuit so the red went all the way down to her red toenails. You could never miss her, even on the darkest night. She dressed in bright clothes, always, and since she's about as round as she is tall, that's a lot of brightness

"Have you written that obituary I assigned you?" she asked.

Oh, right, we print this afternoon, I thought. *Nuts!*

I've been dreading this moment. Every time I've turned in an article she has found lots of stuff wrong with it. I know she only hired me because I would work so cheaply that she could hardly say "no." But still, I think she expected I would be a better reporter, with my degree in journalism in just five years, after all.

I handed her the copy I had written. It read:

> William Just, a long-time pillar of the community, passed away yesterday of natural causes. He leaves no family, but a multitude of friends mourn his passing. He was 69. A memorial service will be conducted at Peace Lutheran Church on Saturday, at 11 a.m.

While Mrs. Fritz was reading it, I was trying not to pass out from the fumes from her expensive perfume. *Did she bathe in that stuff?* Then she sighed. And suddenly she looked older than her 50-some years. I think she knew I wouldn't be able to write that obit and was testing me to see if I had the gumption to get the facts and do it justice. My problem was, I really didn't know how to find stuff out. Everyone in this little town knew everyone else, and I didn't know anyone or anything. This journalism stuff was harder than I thought.

Yesterday, I overheard Mrs. Fritz talking on the phone, and she was telling someone that I had "such a nice smile" that she had to hire me. I decided it was time to turn on the smile again.

It didn't work. She paused a second, admired the smile, and said, "Uh, well… this won't cut it, Ralph. Bill was our hometown hero, and we'll have to do a lot more than this for him. But it's not all your fault. The guy was always a sort of mystery around here. I'll write it for this week's paper, but now your job is to find out as much as you can for an article next week that will do him justice. So get started on it right now."

Up until then, I had been embarrassed, but now I was getting scared. I couldn't seem to do anything right, and now the whole town would be sitting in judgment on how well I could write up their "hero."

I decided to try a tactic that I sometimes used with my mother. "How can I find anything out about this guy if he's such a mystery?" I asked, giving her the little puppy dog look I had honed to perfection at sorority parties. It worked really well there. Not here, though.

Come to think of it, it never worked on my mother, either.

Irma Fritzling was well known for her patience. No one could remember a time when she showed any real annoyance. She was known to be a placid, almost stoic figure in the community, despite her flamboyant dresses and bright red Caddy convertible. My question did seem to annoy her though, and she showed just the tiniest irritation in answering.

She spoke calmly and with just a touch of kindness in her voice. *Or was that sarcasm?* "Look, kid, you have a college degree in this stuff. I don't. All I've ever done is run a paper for 9 years, and go broke doing it. You just go ahead and get started on it, and come to me with questions when you have them."

I really wanted to ask a lot of questions right then, but I sensed that this was not the time. I nodded my assent and walked out of the office to the sidewalk without any idea of what to do next.

Essentially, all that I knew about the man was his age, that he was dead, and that he must have some connection to the Lutheran Church where the funeral is going to be. *So, what the hell?* I thought, *I'll go there first.*

I needed to ask where the church was, since I had only been in town for a little over two weeks, but I thought I'd ask someone outside *The Press* offices to be safe.

Irma, I mean Mrs. Fritz, had decided to write the brief obituary on one of the town's best-known and loved citizens. I figured she could do it from her own memories of him, so it wasn't that great a challenge. However, I know she wished that she could just be the publisher for once, instead of the writer, editor, reporter, sales manager, proofreader, and purchasing agent. Sometimes she was the janitor too. *Am I her only hope? Scary!*

My father had told me a lot about her, which he must have learned from his friend, whose name I've forgotten, so I guess I can't write him a thank you note. She inherited the paper when her husband died suddenly of a heart attack years ago. She had been left with three boys to bring up, and her only source of income was the paper. As little as she wanted to run it, she had no choice. Small town papers at that time were selling for peanuts, if you could get anything at all. The times they are a'changin' now, with Gannett out there, buying every little paper it can get, but now she has ink in her veins. Everyone says you couldn't get her to sell for any amount of money.

Up until her husband's death, she had contented herself by being the most outrageous dresser in town—some say the most outrageous character in town. She always loved bright colors, especially reds, and often wore bright red dresses accented by matching shoes, purse, lipstick, and nails. That was before she discovered other colors of nail polish, such as black. She thinks black nails go very nicely with her red dresses, and I'm not going to say anything different. I've learned a few things already, such as: If in doubt, keep your mouth shut.

Mrs. Fritz is shaped like an apple, so the red outfits seem quite appropriate. She can be spotted coming from the far side of town, either on foot, a rarity, or in her big, red Caddy. I hope someday she'll let me drive it, but I'm not holding my breath.

I, on the other hand, try to be as inconspicuous as possible, which is not easy when you're driving a 28-year old Camaro, painted bright yellow and rust. Well, the rust color isn't actually paint.

CHAPTER 2

1955 – Bill Comes to Town

KENNY HAD BEEN WORKING in the frozen food locker for over an hour, and the old jacket that was kept there for such a purpose was no longer effective. He stepped out into the parking lot to warm up, even though he knew it would just be harder to go back in once he was warm.

The locker was a fixture in this rural community. Farmers brought in chickens and sometimes steer carcasses by the pickup-load for storage. In those days, almost no one had a freezer in his own house, and those who did still couldn't handle that much meat. The locker was located behind "The Ideal," a restaurant that had been an ice cream parlor when Kenny's dad, Johnny Jackson, had bought it.

Johnny, like so many guys without much education but lots of native smarts, had cruised through the Great Depression by doing anything that would pay. He had worked most of that time as a milkman in Lincoln. One of the good things about being a milkman was that you were done by early afternoon, leaving you hours to work for yourself. Johnny had made the best of that. He would buy something old, a car maybe, fix it up and sell it, and then buy another one, each one a little better than the one before. He would demand ration stamps, especially for tires, when he bought a car, and those were worth gold. In this way, he managed to save a fair amount of money at a time when most folks were finding it a struggle just to eat.

After the war ended, Johnny noticed that times were radically different. Everyone had money, so it was almost impossible to do the deals he had thrived on. The young returning vets were getting the good jobs, and Johnny was sure he would be fired soon. He took his savings out and went looking for an opportunity in a small town. He found it in Blackjack.

Most of the time, when Kenny wasn't in school, he was working in the Ideal Dairy Bar, usually just odd jobs and swatting flies. He loved working behind the counter, but his dad thought that the girls were not just better at it, but that the customers came in to ogle the girls, not the pimple-faced teenage boy. He was wrong. A lot of the young lady customers came in specifically to be seen by and talked to by the cute teenage boy, who was pushing his way up past 6 feet.

Today, Kenny had been given his least favorite job. Two farmers had brought in their chickens. The chickens were dead, but still feathered and all body parts intact. Someone had to de-feather them, cut them up, put them on trays, freeze them, and put them in the proper lockers.

Kenny was no good with the feathering, but his grandmother, who had lived her whole life on a farm until now, was a pro. She had a huge pot of water boiling on the stove in their little apartment upstairs, into which she dunked them to loosen the feathers, and then quickly and magically, pulled the feathers off in great handfuls. The apartment would have feathers floating in it for days afterward.

Being an inventive and playful teen, Kenny made a game out of cutting up chickens. He would place a chicken on the cutting block and take a huge butcher knife in his right hand, swing the weapon high above his head, and with a loud "Eee-yah!" bring it swinging down on the poor dead bird. Feet would fly off and lodge behind barrels of cleaning materials or the compressor for the freezer. Some of them would not be found until they stank so bad that Johnny had to go looking for the source.

Kenny moseyed into the sunshine for extra warmth. It didn't usually get really hot in Nebraska in the summer. Nineties were unusual. The sun felt good to the chicken devastator.

Another boy walked up timidly and said, "Hi."

Kenny knew every kid anywhere near his age in Blackjack, and he had never seen this guy before. The boy looked respectable, if a little rumpled and covered with bites. His clothes seemed to be well worn, but there was nothing unusual about that.

"Hi," he said back, "I'm Ken."

"Bill," was the curt reply.

"New in town?"

"Yeah… and need a job."

"How old are you?"

"About 17," Bill said.

"What does 'about' mean?" Kenny asked, with a naïve sound in his voice that made it possible for him to ask any question without making anyone mad.

"Okay, I'm 17."

"What can you do?"

"Anything."

Kenny eyed this new guy a little suspiciously. New kids didn't just show up in town. Where had he come from? He had a scruffy appearance, or maybe the right word was disheveled, as if he had slept in those clothes and needed a comb for his tousled brown hair. His pockets were bulging with something soft, and Kenny guessed it might be underwear and socks. This guy was probably a run-away, and he sympathized with that.

Looking him over a second time, Kenny noted that he was about five nine or ten, sandy haired, a little teen acne, and crooked teeth, but he was pleasant looking nonetheless.

Kenny wanted desperately to get out of the freezer, so he took Bill in to meet his father, who was stacking boxes of chocolate syrup in the storeroom behind the counter.

"Hey, Dad," Kenny began, "I've got a friend who needs a job, and I think we should hire him."

Johnny was dressed in his usual shirt, slacks, and white apron, letting everyone know he was the proprietor of this combination frozen-food locker and dairy bar. His receding hairline did nothing to detract from his rugged handsomeness. "To do what?" Johnny asked.

"Well, for now, he could help me with all those chickens, and I need to do some homework this afternoon, anyway, so after he gets the hang of it…"

"You just want to get out of that freezer," Johnny broke in.

"Oh, no, it's not that," Kenny lied, "but he really needs the work, and I really need to study."

Johnny turned around and saw Bill standing there looking hopeful. Johnny tried to act like he was strict, but he had a big, soft heart. He liked the looks of this new kid. "You'll have to train him."

"Oh, sure, I know that."

"And I want you to spend one hour with him to make sure he knows everything he has to do."

"Okay, Dad!" Kenny said with enthusiasm. He was getting out of the freezer.

As they walked to the back of the building, Kenny asked Bill, "Do you know how to clean and cut up a chicken?"

Bill smiled, "Sure do."

"Good, that's the first part, and as long as I'm standing around training you, I'll help you with that. Grab that coat, and I'll show you the lockers the chickens have to go into."

They stepped into the huge freezer with its hundreds of large, locked storage bins, most with names on them, and nearly empty at this time of the year. He showed Bill the two bins that belonged to the farmers whose chickens they were taking care of. Then they retreated out to the long table where they cut up the chickens.

"I'll watch, and you cut up a chicken," Kenny said.

Bill did it expertly.

"Well, that part of your training is done, and you got an A," Kenny said. "The next thing you do…" He talked him through the process. It took about a minute. Then the two of them worked together for another 20 minutes, and Kenny figured that was almost an hour. He went upstairs to the apartment and got out his math textbook, into which he inserted the latest Batman comic book.

When the chickens were all processed, Bill called up the stairs, and Kenny came down. "Okay, show me what you've done," he told Bill.

"You'll have to go into the freezer," Bill said, having already figured out why Kenny wanted him hired.

Since the chickens had been cleaned and divested of everything not edible, frozen, and placed into the correct bins, Kenny was pleased. "Good job," he told Bill. "Now let's get you some pay."

Johnny was chatting with some customers seated at a booth in the restaurant section. This was part of his marketing strategy. Most places didn't have time to talk to customers and didn't develop personal relationships with them, but Johnny, still a new guy in town, worked at the relationship thing.

Kenny interrupted, "Uh, Dad, we've got a new employee to pay."

Johnny told his customers, "Kenny has taken over hiring around here, and now he wants me to pay the people he's hired. I'll be back in a minute."

They walked back to the counter, which served as Johnny's office and desk. Johnny pulled out his ledger and asked, "What's your name?"

"Just Bill," Bill answered.

It's still not clear whether Johnny misunderstood him or was playing his little joke, but he entered "Bill Just" on the payroll sheet. From then on, so far as anyone in Blackjack knew, Bill's name was Bill Just.

Kenny had the rest of the afternoon free, not that there was much afternoon left. He took Bill around town and introduced him to some other kids their age and pointed out some places of possible employment. Bill was a convincing interviewee and had several part-time jobs lined up by dark. Being unhampered by the need to attend school made him a valuable part-timer.

When it came time to go home for supper, Kenny asked, "Where do you live?"

"Well, I just got here, but don't worry about me. I'll be all right. And listen, thanks for everything, okay? You've really been a great help to me, and I won't forget it."

As Kenny walked back toward The Ideal, he wondered what that meant, "I won't forget it."

CHAPTER 3

Peace Lutheran Church

WHEN I PULLED UP to the church, my first thought was that it was certainly an odd-looking structure, especially for a church. From the parking lot, I could only see one door, so I walked over and pushed it open. Once I was inside, the church looked more normal, but it had an oddly familiar but un-church-like smell. Even I knew that Lutheran churches smell like coffee being made, which it almost always is.

I was in the sanctuary, and no one else was in there at the time. I had to look around for someone, maybe in an office somewhere. There was a door at the front of the room beside the altar, and when I tried that one, I found myself in a long hallway with office and classroom doors along one side.

Now I could see why I had smelled something funny. The building was made out of bales of straw! In the sanctuary, they were covered with some kind of material, but back here, they were bare straw. I wondered about the mouse population, but decided to wait until some other day to ask about that.

At the first door, I looked in and saw a woman working away on an old computer. *Probably the church secretary*, I thought. I tapped lightly on the door and entered. The woman continued working for another minute or so before she looked up, surprised.

"Oh, dear," she said. "I'm sorry. Have you been here long?"

"No, no," I answered, "I just got here a minute ago. I'm new in town, and I work as a reporter for *The Press*. I'm writing an obituary on Bill Just, and I need some information about him. Can you help me?"

Roberta, that was her name, as I found out in a few minutes, looked me over carefully. She was forty-ish with bleach-blond hair and was dressed in a yellow pantsuit accented with a bright multi-colored scarf and too much makeup. Some might have considered her outfit inappropriate for work, especially in a church, but the way she dressed apparently didn't stop her from carefully inspecting my attire. I would guess that she had learned to tell a lot about people from their clothes. Farmers probably came in wearing overalls and work shirts, the tradesmen in work pants and shirts, and the local businessmen in short-sleeve shirts and dime store ties. I was wearing a polo shirt and khaki slacks. Did she think, *Maybe a college student?* It would be a good guess since these are my college clothes.

"And your name, honey?" she asked.

"Oh, sure," I stammered, "I'm Ralph Anderson from Crooked Creek."

"So you're from Crooked Creek, are you?" Roberta said softly, smiling. "Well, Ralph from Crooked Creek, we aren't supposed to give out a lot of personal information on members. The Privacy Act, you know. Do you have something proving you work for *The Press*?"

"I guess not," I said. "But you could call Mrs. Fritz at the paper; she'll vouch for me."

And, she'll know I'm out doing my job, I thought.

Roberta smiled. "If you know to call her Mrs. Fritz, I guess that's proof enough. What do you want to know?"

"Anything," I said. " I have one week to write a big article about him."

"Sakes!" exclaimed Roberta. "Anyone in this town can tell you everything about Bill. But I can tell you something interesting. He built this church. Did you know that? Maybe you did. Is that why you're here?"

"Nope, I sure didn't know that. Please, tell me about that."

"Well, like most things about Bill, this is both a little bit rumor and a little bit fact. It seems he was out walking one day, when he passed this place. He walked all the time or rode a bike. Only owned an old Chevy truck for emergencies. It probably wouldn't have made it to Coleridge."

She pronounced it "Chivy," just like almost everyone in Nebraska does. If you want people in Nebraska to know you come from someplace else, say "Chevrolet" or "roof" with an "oo" sound. We say *ruhf*, sounding like "hoof." Call pop a soft drink, or worse, a soda, and we'll assume you're from New York City.

Roberta went on, "We had tried to build, but between the time we raised the money and got ready to build, the prices had shot up so much we couldn't afford it. We had graded the land and poured the slab, but the church council figured out they couldn't afford to put up the building. So, when Bill came by, he saw the site with the floor and no building. He checked around to find out what it was and learned about our problem."

I decided it was time for an "uh-huh" or something, so I said, "Oh."

Roberta continued, "He didn't go to church here. In fact, I don't think he went to church anywhere, but he came in to see Pastor and asked if he could help. He had been in the library and had read about building with bales of straw. He had also seen lots of straw in the fields and realized that most of it would just be burned off or disked in. He guessed there might be enough around so that farmers might be willing to cut it, bale it, and donate the bales to the church. So, the next thing you know, he headed up a work party, stacking straw bales in just the right way. Then we put the roof on it, covered the walls, and ta-da! A church."

Now I was writing furiously on my notepad. This was a great story. I sensed that I had a lot more to learn about Bill Just.

"Do you mean that there is no other support than the bales," I asked incredulously.

"Oh, no, there's a post and beam structure there. You should have seen it when you came through the sanctuary," Roberta said, looking at me closely to see if I might be blind.

"Sure, of course," I said, attempting to make it look as if I already knew that. "I think I'd better get going. Thank you so much, umm…"

"Call me Roberta, honey. And come back anytime. We want our boy Bill to be remembered right. He was a good man, a very good man."

"I'll bet he was," I assured her.

I said goodbye, made my way out through the sanctuary, cranked up the bucket of rust, and headed for the town library.

CHAPTER 4

The Library

THE BLACKJACK LIBRARY WAS another place I hadn't been before. I had seen it, of course, just behind the Court House. In its new, modern-looking brick building, it looks out of place in the square. The Court House was tan sandstone; the other buildings were painted white.

I felt silly parking in front of the library. I was only a block and half from *The Press* offices and had just learned that Bill Just walked everywhere. I thought, *Sure, I could have walked, but I just drove all the way back from the church.* I can rationalize just about anything.

When I entered, the first thing that caught my attention was the bank of four computers, all occupied by teenagers, who seemed to be doing their homework, messaging friends, or playing computer games. These must be the kids who don't have texting on their cell phones.

A librarian hailed me as I walked by her desk.

"May I help you?" she asked, smiling.

I said, "I was told that Bill Just learned about building with bales of hay or straw in this library. I wondered if you could tell me about that and if you could help me find the source he may have used for building the church." I had just asked a good question of a potential source of information. Five years of college had not been completely wasted on me.

17

"Are you planning to build something out of hay bales?" she asked, somewhat surprised, and curious since she had never seen me before.

"Oh, no," I said, "I'm Ralph Anderson. I started working for *The Press* two weeks ago, and I'm supposed to write an article about Bill Just. I was told he built the Lutheran Church out of straw bales, and I want to learn more about that. More about him too."

"Glad to meet you, Ralph," she said. "I'm Mary Dubchek, the head librarian here. I'd be happy to help you on both of those problems. I'm free now. I have three other librarians who come in part time, and they can help you if I'm not here for any reason. At this time of day, just after school lets out in the afternoon, there has to be two of us working, since the place fills up with high school students, and some younger ones as well. With another librarian here, I can leave the desk to help you."

I said, "Oh, thanks."

I was trying to guess how old Mary was. She was certainly much older than I, but it was hard to tell her age. She was not physically attractive looking at all, but she seemed to have a sweet disposition and I already liked her. Maybe if she had something different done to her hair…? She was dressed in a pants suit, flowered top, and solid black bottoms. She seemed to use the same perfume as Roberta at the church… *Or was hers still in my nose?*

Mary went on, "Bill spent hours in here almost every week. You could say he was our best customer. He didn't own a television set or get the newspaper, so he came here to read all the time. He liked it in here, so he was usually here until closing time. Now let me see… What was the magazine he found that in?"

She went to her computer and searched on building materials, straw, and hay. She looked over a number of hits and picked three that were of the proper vintage and printed them out for me. All the while, she was talking.

"Bill was such a gentleman. Ask anyone, and they'll tell you of something he did for him. And he seemed to know a lot too. We think that was because of all the time he spent in our library, of course, but maybe not. We don't think he had much formal education, but he was smart and he read, like I told you,"

I sat down to read the articles on building with straw bales, not hay bales. I wasn't entirely sure what the difference was. Thinking about it for the first time in my life, I thought that hay was something animals ate, whereas straw was some sort of plant waste most useful for putting over grass seed or in bales on "hay wagons."

I also remembered my grandfather joking about his time in the Army saying, "Some of those kids were such hicks that they didn't know their left foot from their right, so the sergeant would put some hay on one foot and straw on the other and call out not, "Right, Left," but, "Hayfoot, Strawfoot." I had supposed the joke was that hay and straw were really the same thing. Now I found out I was wrong about that.

As I read, I hoped I would get another lead. I was surprised to find that there was already a straw bale church in Nebraska, built before the one in Blackjack. It had been built many years before in Arthur, and it was something of a tourist attraction.

Mary pointed me toward the *Green Building Encyclopedia* on the Internet. There, I learned that as far back as 1896 a schoolhouse had been built in Bayard out of straw bales with a straw roof. It hadn't lasted this long, of course, but the Arthur church was still around. I wondered if Bill had gone to see it.

The *Encyclopedia* estimated that as many as 5 million 2000-square foot homes could be built from straw that now was just burned in the fields and, also, that the greatest advantage of the straw was as an insulator. Straw bale buildings, as few as there are, require much less heating and cooling than conventional buildings.

Another article stated that rice straw was even more suited for building material and using it for that would solve a worldwide problem. It is almost impossible to get rid of rice straw. It doesn't deteriorate or compost, so it lasts almost forever. Now it is usually burned, but the smoke is toxic. Despite all the advantages of using rice straw for a building material, no one wants it, and it has to be destroyed, regardless of the consequences. Does that make any sense to anyone?

There's no rice straw around here, anyway. I sure would have loved to have met Bill and asked him how he had discovered this or come up with the idea.

Before I left the library, I would ask Mary to give me some ideas of other people to interview. After all, she had said, "Ask anyone," but I didn't know anyone to ask.

Mary seemed pleased that I was reading diligently, and she walked up to the table where I was sitting. She told me, "You should spend some time reading up on Nebraska and the surrounding area," because that's something that Bill Just had done often. She put down a big stack of materials in front of me, and I turned my attention to those. While I was doing that, she made a list of people I might interview.

I really learned a lot. I had been born in Nebraska and educated in its schools. I had been taught to revere the pioneers who settled the state. I thought I knew the history. But I was so fascinated by what I was reading there that I stayed until closing and in fact, a half-hour after normal closing time.

I learned that as the white man came to America he had to compete with the natives for use of the land. Of course, I already knew that. I was raised on cowboy and Indian movies, but what I hadn't known was how that competition took place. Starting from the arrival of the first settlers, disputes between cultures resulted in murderous raids by both sides. Coming to the new land was fraught with peril, and life expectancies were short.

George Washington, who was deeply involved, as a young British officer in pushing the frontier westward, was convinced that the solution lay in separating the cultures, but he also realized that he couldn't stop white men from pushing west into territory promised to the natives.

That pattern continued unabated until whites occupied the whole land, all the way to the Pacific. Over and over again, the United States government promised land to the Indians to keep them peaceful, but could not prevent its white citizens from moving onto that land.

The first explorers into the area that became Nebraska described it as a vast desert, useless to anyone. The government, having commissioned the study, was happy to cede it in perpetuity to the Indians, even calling it Indian Territory.

Although the government attempted to prevent settling in the Indian Territory, westward expansion continued nearly unchecked. Thousands were crossing the plains toward California, Oregon, or Utah annually, and they needed supplies. Traders moved in along the trails to sell them high-priced necessities. Many of the travelers ran out of willpower or ability to continue and stopped along the way. Others saw the "vast desert" as valuable farmland.

Finally, it was the railroads that broke the territory open to white settlement. The famous Union Pacific rail line that ran from Omaha to California needed revenue along the way. It needed both passengers and cargo. With its tremendous influence in Congress, it got the Kansas-Nebraska Territory, Indian Territory, opened to settlement.

The Indians justly felt betrayed. Many Americans now feel guilty about the way white men treated the Indians, signing treaties and breaking them over and over, but the end result was inevitable. Indian culture, a hunter/gatherer culture, could not compete with European agricultural and industrial culture. I read an extract from Jared Diamond's bestselling book laid open in front of me by my new friend, the librarian; the Europeans conquered, because they had the "guns, germs, and steel."

Tens of thousands of Indians died from smallpox and measles, caught from white men who were at least partially immune. That increased the rate at which the whites could dispossess the Indians of the land. Disease wiped out whole tribes, eliminating most of the resistance.

The remaining Indians alternated between acceptance of the settlers and anger. They might remain peaceful for years, living among the whites and trading with them, but every now and then, they would get mad enough to attack and kill any settlers they found. Settling in Nebraska was a risky proposition.

To obtain land, you could either buy it from the railroad or homestead it if it was in the government's control. Either way, you had to go out to it, live on it, and work the land. Any passing Indian tribe could have you any time it wanted. Homesteaders often encountered Indians, often establishing friendly relations. Sometime later, those same Indians might come along and kill them.

If that weren't bad enough, the "vast desert" often lived up to its reputation. The soil was rich, and if you got lucky, you raised enough to get through the bad times. Most settlers weren't that lucky. It is estimated that about one third of those who tried to settle there succeeded. Winters were harsh; summers were too. Rain was plentiful, sometimes. Swarms of grasshoppers, prairie fires, and hail and dust storms all combined to drive you out.

The first act of settling was "sod busting"— Plowing through a layer of grass roots that had built up for centuries required backbreaking labor and specialized tools. Many would-be farmers never got past that stage. When they did, they died of "prairie fever." Life was tough, and only the very toughest survived.

It was a romantic era all over the world, and the American West was the most romantic place on the globe, or so it seemed. In reality, it was a grim place of disease, hunger, death, and opportunity.

The business of Nebraska was, and remains, farming, but only a small fraction of those who settled there came to farm. The others wanted to make money from the farmers. I could relate to that. I had no desire to be a farmer, either.

There are no statistics to show what all those folks wanted to do, but you can get a good idea by what they did after they arrived. Of particular interest to me was the number of newspapers they founded. Every settlement had at least one newspaper, often more. Sometimes there were multiple English-language newspapers, plus others in German, Swedish, or Czech. I wondered how anyone could make a living that way, and *The Press* was a good example of how tough that still was. In addition, merchants, druggists, doctors, lawyers, bankers, and jewelers, to name a few, flowed into the territory to try to make their fortunes.

Many of today's Nebraskans are descended from the successful pioneers, and I surmised that maybe that is why his little state boasted one of the country's best football teams. The Nebraska team was based on big, strong, tough linemen from small farming towns. Their ancestors were the ones tough enough to make it in this harsh place.

At 9:30, Mary insisted that I had to let her lock up. She checked out a bunch of history and geography books to me, handed me a list of people to talk to about Bill Just, and locked the door behind me.

CHAPTER 5

Mary Dubchek

I SPENT ENOUGH TIME with Mary to learn a great deal about her and her life up to now. Mary had shown me her library, the place where Bill Just got his education. I was finding out that Mary and the library were a single entity.

When people think of the Blackjack Library, they think first of Mary. She is always there, usually at the desk, jumping up eagerly to help anyone who walks in. She is the soul of the library—a place that might not exist without her.

These days, you can find most of what you want on the internet from home. You may go to the library to do it, but only because Mary has made sure there are four modern computers on high-speed data links there. Plus, she's there to help you. If you are a teenager and it's after school, you might be there, because that's where the other 9th and 10th graders are. That's due to Mary, also.

The library is her life. She's not happy that her life is that way. It just is, and she makes the best of it. It's not her fault that she takes after her father or that her father most resembled a frog. She has never even had a date, much less someone romantically interested in her.

She realized that this would be her fate about her junior year in high school. She had a bad crush on a boy in her class, who was not especially popular, good looking, or smart. He was just a nice boy who often spoke to her before class began, and she misinterpreted that as stronger interest. Her mistake was telling her friends that she "liked" him, meaning that she was interested in him. Of course, they told everyone. The boys started teasing him mercilessly, and the object of her affection told her to leave him alone. That hard lesson was enough to scare her away from any more romantic ideas.

Bill Just was the best male friend she had ever had. He was single too, and that may have given his friendship with her a romantic appearance. However, there was never a hint of interest in that on Bill's side that she could detect. Then, after he more or less adopted a family of a mother and two kids, he looked more and more like their property.

She mourned the life she had always envisioned for herself—husband, children, house with picket fence—but she made up her mind to be happy and productive no matter what.

A few days after first meeting me, I took her to lunch as a reward for being so helpful to me on the Bill Just story and some others I was working on. Mary was old enough to be my mother, and sometimes she acted a lot like a mother to me. I kind of liked that.

Mary was dressed that day in a blouse and skirt, a fairly short skirt at that, and her round legs stuck down from the hem of her skirt like stumps of a major tree.

After large pieces of Dutch apple pie for dessert, I asked her, "How did you get into the library business, Mary?"

She said, "After high school, I attended the community college with no idea of what I wanted to do. Up till then, I thought I could be a concert pianist, if only my fingers would grow long enough. But, alas, they never did. See?" She held up her hand, showing her stubby, fleshy fingers.

"I love to read, and I always got A's in English all through school. But what do English majors do? I thought about grading a hundred freshman themes into the wee hours of the morning, and I decided I needed a major that didn't lead to teaching."

"And you picked becoming a librarian?"

Mary answered, "Not at first. Then I got a student job in the college library, and I liked working there. That was what pushed me into library science. I transferred to the University of Lincoln for my final two years, got my degree, and then came back home to Blackjack and got a job in the little library here."

I said, "I think it's a good thing you did. You run a wonderful library for a town like this.'"

"Well, thanks, Ralph," Mary said, blushing. "I'm glad you came here too. You've already done some great pieces in the paper, and that's pretty special in a jerkwater town like this.'"

"I don't know, Mary," I said. "This town may be small, but 'jerkwater'? I don't think so, and you and your library are my main reason for saying that."

CHAPTER 6

Blackjack, Nebraska

THE NEXT DAY I was back in the library asking questions. Mary called over two high school girls, who were giggling over some email on one of her computers. She introduced them to me.

"Ralph Anderson, this is Tina, and this is Wendy. They don't seem to be working on homework or research right now. Are you, girls?"

((Giggles.))

"So, I thought they could give you a little history of Blackjack. All right, girls?"

"Okay…" Tina laughed. "But what do we tell him?"

Mary smiled at them. "You'll think of something."

Wendy appeared to me to be the more serious of the two young ladies. She was nicely attired in a blouse and sweater, still looking neat after a full school day. She furrowed her brow and began to speak slowly and thoughtfully.

"When Nebraska was settled around the middle of the nineteenth century, small towns such as Blackjack were, like, real important to the pioneers. They were places to get supplies, connect to the government for things like homesteads, something that most of them had, and things like that."

27

"Oh, yeah!" Tina chimed in, "I remember now."

Tina was in jeans and a tee shirt with a rude message on the front, and despite an elaborate hairdo, she gave off an essence of grape pop, probably because of the huge wad of chewing gum in her mouth.

She went on, "The railroad ran out of money when they got to Black-jack, or whatever it was called then. The town sprang up at the end of the little railroad. You could still see the tracks when my parents were younger. We'd be driving to someplace and my dad would point them out, and he'd go, "That's where the train ran that started our little town.""

"That's right," Wendy said. "When the railroad company ran out of capital to lay more track, all the settlers coming west on it were dumped right here. The state put their land office here. Merchants built stores to sell farm implements and supplies to the new farmers, banks opened, newspapers sprang into being, a school opened, and a jail was built."

Tina was getting into it now. "And the courthouse… There's a good story about the courthouse, Wendy. Should we tell him?"

"Please do," I said.

Tina decided she was the storyteller. "Well, the first courthouse was built in Jackson, the next town to the east, even though all the court business was going on here, so one night a bunch of guys went over there and stole all the records and brought them here. The problem was that they had to ford a crick, and all the old records got soaked, so there aren't any records from before that time."

"Right," Wendy said, "and in a few years, a stone County Court House was built that still stands today. Later, the railroad moved on to the West, but Blackjack continued to thrive by serving the farmers in the surrounding area."

"It doesn't seem to be thriving so much now," I observed.

"That's right," Tina went on. "Stuff happens. ((Giggles)) Cars, for example."

Wendy went on more seriously, "The automobile changed everything. With a car or truck, a farmer could drive to Bison, where there were big stores and more of everything."

"There are, like, malls there," Tina said.

Wendy went on, ignoring her friend, "Little by little, all the small town withered away."

"But Blackjack is still here," I said, stating the obvious.

Tina responded, "We're a, you know, bedroom community now. Industries come and go all the time. Once, when the railroad was here, the town was a shipping point. Then, the railroad died. The land office was no longer needed and closed. Grain elevators moved to be near active railroad tracks. Blackjack almost ceased to exist."

I decided that Tina, for all of her outward silliness, was the truly bright one.

She paused and thought for a second, then continued, "Our town had several names over its first fifty years, but after World War I, it was renamed Blackjack in honor of General Pershing, who once taught ROTC at the university. We take a lot of kidding about that since folks from surrounding towns claim we're a gambling Mecca.""

So," I summed up, "there's no business in Blackjack now. Is that right?

"Not exactly," Wendy answered. "Businesses still try to make a go of it and hire workers, but not many survive for long. Now a new ethanol plant has been hiring, and everyone wonders how long that will last. There was a 'call center' in the old drug store on Main. It employed from 10 to 20 people, depending on workload, who called phone company customers all over the country who were late paying their bills. My mom worked there, until they started laying off."

Tina chimed in, "Agriculture is still the only, like, permanent business in this area, and that is getting harder and harder for the family farmer to make a living at."

Wendy said, "Tina's right. I think small town Nebraska is dying. How long will Blackjack last? No one knows. There are always rumors of folks leaving Omaha and Denver to live in small towns and work from home, but who would leave those places for a town with no theaters, no hotels, no real restaurants, one small grocery store, and the nearest Wal-Mart a twenty-minute drive?"

At that point, Mary passed by the table where we were sitting, and said, "Of course, the residents of Blackjack don't see it that way. We love the wide-open spaces, the scarcity of traffic, the sweet-smelling air, and the friendliness of our neighbors. Many of them would tell you that if it hadn't been for Bill Just, the town would have folded up years ago."

I noticed that the girls were looking anxiously at the computer they had been using. A tall boy was starting to read their latest instant message. "You'd better go back to your computer. Thanks a lot, ladies."

They both blushed a little, but they jumped up and ran the three or four steps to the computer, where they slipped between the boy and the screen.

The girls had been helpful in a number of ways. I shared their pessimism about the future of small towns. Out in ranch country, they still served an important role, but they could be spaced far apart now. There had to be some center of social and economic support, and it needed to be just close enough to the ranches for the kids to get to school and back in the same day.

One of the great advantages of growing up in a small town, I had learned from friends in college, was that you not only had to do everything, but you could do everything. A kid growing up there learned how to do almost every job that came along, either on the farm or ranch, at school, or in 4H. It paid to have friends from places like that. They knew how to get things done.

I turned to thank Mary, but she had slipped away too. I sat back down and wrote out notes from that conversation. Here I was, a college graduate, learning stuff from high school girls… and liking it!

CHAPTER 7

The Driver

A FEW DAYS AFTER first working in the frozen food locker, Bill showed up at The Ideal looking for work again. Johnny saw him walking in and asked, "Do you have a driver's license?"

Bill lied, "Sure do."

He had been driving a tractor on the farm for years, but he hadn't gotten his license when he turned 16, since no one back there cared about it and his dad would have had a storming fit if he'd asked for time to go to town and take the test.

Johnny said, "Come with me." He took Bill out to an old pickup truck that was always parked at the restaurant and told him what a wonderful thing it was.

"It's a '38 Ford, but it's got a '51 Ford rebuilt engine in it. It runs great. Look at this."

He popped open the hood and pointed Bill toward the engine that looked a lot like a truck engine to Bill.

Johnny told him, "Now, what I want you to do is this. There are two large boxes by the back door. Those go to the post office. Just tell them they're from me, and they'll ship them and call me to pay for them later. Then go to Mrs. Hamm's house and pick up pies. She'll have four pies ready. Be careful with those and bring them straight here. I'll need them by lunchtime. Then go out to the Stringer farm and pick up a load of chickens for freezing. Bring them back here and take care of them. Stringer has a large locker here, and that's where you'll put them when you get them cut up and frozen. Any questions?"

Bill said, "I don't know where any of those places are. Can you give me some directions?"

Johnny laughed at himself. "Sure, sorry. It's a small town, and I'm used to everyone knowing where everything is."

Bill put the packages in the truck, climbed into the cab, and started the truck. He was surprised to find a gearshift and a clutch. He had never driven a truck with manual shift before. The one truck on the family farm had an automatic, and the ancient tractor he had driven only had one forward gear. He tried to remember what the positions of the gears were, but had only a vague idea. He got it into third, thinking it was in first, and lurched forward. Johnny was standing there watching and wondering what was going on. Before Johnny could stop him, Bill lurched out of the parking lot and went bucking down the street.

The post office was two blocks away. Bill was surprised he hadn't seen it in his three days in town. He was curious about how this would work out, and when he got to the head of the short line, he told the postmaster, "Johnny Jackson sent me with these packages to mail."

The postmaster looked at the return addresses, apparently checking to see if they were indeed from Johnny. He told Bill, "Okay, just leave them here with me." That was all there was to it.

Mrs. Hamm's was about the same distance in the opposite direction. They didn't even have numbers on the houses in Blackjack then, so he looked for the yellow house with the gray front porch on Oak Street. All the east-west streets were named after trees.

As he drove through town, he was stalling, bucking, and lurching. The small town was busy this time of day, and he had to stop at the two stoplights in town, more because there was traffic coming across than the red light, which he would have run without hesitation if he could have. Stopping required starting from a dead stop again, which he couldn't very well do in third. Once, he got it into reverse and almost backed into a car behind him. Soon people stopped on the sidewalks and watched his progress. He was the entertainment in Blackjack that day.

But, even with his ineptness with the gears, he managed to get to Mrs. Hamm's in a few minutes. He walked to the front door and rang the doorbell. Mrs. Hamm was a short, plump woman of about 60 or 70; he couldn't tell. She was in a classic cotton dress, and her hair had recently been done at a beauty shop.

She simply said, "Yes?"

"Johnny Jackson of The Ideal sent me for pies," Bill replied.

"Oh, sure, honey! Come right on in..." The whole house smelled of hot pies. Bill, who hadn't had much to eat lately, salivated. She led him to the kitchen, where she had four pies on cooling racks. "How are you going to carry these in that old truck?"

Bill hadn't thought of that. "How does Johnny do that?" he asked.

"I think he puts two on the seat next to him, and maybe two on the floor," she said.

Bill tried that, and it worked pretty well, but with the lurching in third gear the pies on the floor slid around and some of the crust around the edges got knocked off. He drove back to the Ideal and carried them in, wishing he could have a piece right then.

Finding the Stringer farm was another story. Finding farms was always an adventure, even though Bill had grown up in farm country. The description of the road to turn onto from the highway was just a vague one. He passed it three times before he recognized it. It was a dirt road, deeply rutted. Luckily, it was dry now. He bumped down it until he crossed the third section of the road, where he turned left, and it was the third farmhouse on the right. Once again, he passed it before he realized it.

In the way of the typical farmer, Mr. Stringer was not to be found when Bill finally got to the farm. He looked around for a few minutes and decided to try the house.

Mrs. Stringer was working in the kitchen and told him, "You go down by the silo, and that's where you can find the Mister."

Bill knew farms better than anything, and he hated them. He had grown up on a farm about 30 miles away. His father was a stern Dane, who never showed the slightest affection for anyone, especially his son. He required full days of hard work starting at five. Much of the year it was dark for the next hour or two and bitterly cold in the winter. Still, the boy was required to do the same boring chores every day without fail before he could go to the kitchen for a meager breakfast. If he took more than ten minutes eating his breakfast, his father punished him. When he was little, that often meant a whipping with a belt. When he got big enough to fight back, that changed to added work well into the night. The only escape was school, but his father pulled him out of school when he turned sixteen. He said he needed him to work full time on the farm.

Bill had been an excellent student and dared to dream of graduating from college and becoming a lawyer or businessman. His father said that ninth grade was all the education you needed to farm; in fact, it was more than you needed.

Bill had learned a lot in school that his father had never learned. Much of it was from the other kids who talked about how things were done on their farms. Bill's dad seldomly talked to other farmers, or anyone for that matter. Bill tried to convince him to track crops, prices, weather, and all sorts of things that might have made the farm more money. His dad would have none of it.

His attitude was, "I always growed corn, and I always will."

The farm was fairly typical for central Nebraska. They milked 8 cows twice a day, ran a cream separator, cooled the milk in water that was pumped from a well, and put the milk cans out by the road in the morning. They usually had about 30 chickens running around the yard. They searched for eggs every morning, and the hens obliged by laying most of them in nests in the hen house. They raised most of their own feed—mostly corn, but a little millet and maybe two acres of soybeans.

Bill's father didn't even want electricity when the government made it available in '48. He didn't want to pay for something he was getting mostly free from his windmill, even though it was a 32-volt system. They heated the house with a corncob stove, but the only hot water was on the stove and the "plumbing" was mostly outside. It was a cold walk to the outhouse in the winter. They were tough and resourceful people, as were most of the people on farms in that state.

Bill didn't know that his father was failing, health-wise, because the taciturn old man never told anyone. Bill might have done things differently if he had known his father was about to die. A few months after his sixteenth birthday, Bill walked out the kitchen door, took the milk cans out to the road, and kept walking, until he reached Blackjack. He had only heard of Blackjack, never having been there, and it wasn't his destination. He had Lincoln or Omaha or Denver in mind. But, when he reached Blackjack, he needed to make some money before he could continue on.

Now, here he was, on a farm again, if only for a few minutes, until he could drive away with a load of chickens. He went down to the silo and found Stringer transferring a load of green-feed from a wagon. The conveyor was so noisy that it took him a few minutes to get the farmer's attention. Back home he had learned, the hard way, not to interrupt his father by tugging on a sleeve or anything like that. He was always rewarded for such activity with a swift backhand to the head. After standing around waiting for Mr. Stringer to look around, he finally walked around into his field of vision.

Stringer turned off the conveyor belt, and it got quiet enough to talk. "Well, what have we here?" he asked.

Bill told him, "Johnny Jackson sent me for some chickens for the locker."

Stringer was a carbon copy Nebraska farmer. He was a large man, not real tall, but tall enough and "husky." A belly protruded over his jeans belt, but there was no doubting his strength. His hands were the size of boxing gloves. He smiled at Bill and answered pleasantly. He was a lot friendlier than Bill had expected. Bill was just learning that Nebraskans are almost invariably friendly. He'd grown up among them, but his perception was so colored by his own family that he thought the friendly folk he met other places were the exceptions.

"Back that truck up here next to the barn," Stringer told him.

Uh-oh… Bill thought, *Back it up?*

He decided it was time for honesty. "Uh, Mr. Stringer, I'm afraid I can hardly make the truck go forward, much less backward. Would you mind backing it?"

"Not at all," Stringer said, with a small smile. He jumped in and had the truck just where he wanted it in ten seconds. Bill wished he had been able to watch more closely to see how he had done it.

Stringer couldn't resist teasing Bill a little. After all, there aren't many opportunities to meet someone new on the farm, and good-natured teasing is a great icebreaker, or so all farmers thought. In the process, he found out how experienced Bill was on the farm.

He asked, "Are you working for Johnny full time or are you looking for some work?"

"I need some work, Mr. Stringer, but I'm afraid the only way I could get here would be to borrow this truck, which I don't know how to drive."

"You got here okay," Stinger said, a little confused.

"I have never driven a stick shift before, and I can't get it into the proper gears."

Stringer smiled. "Climb in! I'll give you a lesson." He talked Bill through shifting to all the gears and stayed with him long enough to make sure he had it right. Then he said, "If you can work one or two days this week, I can come in and pick you up. Would you like to do that?"

Bill had been thinking that he didn't, but Mr. Stringer was so nice, so unlike his father, that he surprised himself and said he would. He told him that he had no work lined up for the next day.

Stringer said, "I'll pick you up at 7:30 at The Ideal."

They loaded the back of the pickup with 120 chickens killed by Stringer earlier that day. Blood was still dripping from some of their necks, and the bed of the pickup was starting to puddle up with chicken blood.

When they were done, Mr. Stringer asked, "Can you get all the way back to town without backing up again?"

"Yes, sir, I can," Bill said, "…unless I get lost."

He drove off, smiling to himself and thinking that Mr. Stringer was a pretty nice guy and that it was going to take the rest of the day to take care of those chickens and clean off the truck. If he was lucky, someone would give him a free supper at The Ideal… and maybe even a piece of Mrs. Hamm's pie.

CHAPTER 8

A Place to Live

THE DAY WHEN BILL met Kenny at The Ideal, Kenny showed him around town, at least the downtown section, and the first place he took him was the "haunted house." It was a tiny house, one street over from the highway, or Main Street, convenient walking distance to almost every place, and just far enough from the highway that the traffic wasn't too noisy.

The boys, Kenny, Bill, and Kenny's friend, Jim Strange, approached the house with great care, checking around them all the time to make sure no one was around. When they got right up next to the front of the house, Kenny said, "Look in the window."

"Why?" Bill reacted instinctively.

"Just do it!" Kenny and Jim whispered together.

Bill looked in the window. "Geez!" he exclaimed. "There's a coffin in there."

"Yeah," Jim told him, "the old man who lives here sleeps in it at night so he'll be in it when he dies."

"How do you know that?" Bill asked.

"Oh," Jim said, brushing his blond hair from his eyes, "everyone knows that."

Jim was a younger boy and much shorter than Bill or Kenny, but he had a self-assurance that made him seem comfortable with the older boys.

"He's right," Kenny said. "He's a witch or something, maybe a vampire. He sleeps in a coffin and probably sucks blood from people's necks."

"No, he doesn't," Jim whispered. "He buys his food at the grocery store, like everyone else. He just wants to die in his coffin, that's all."

"No, there's something weird about him, not just the coffin. Just look at him when he's out of the house. He's really strange," Kenny assured his little audience.

In fact, the old man was already dead and buried, but the boys didn't know that.

The next day, Bill asked Johnny about the house and the coffin. Johnny was amused at the story that the old man slept in the coffin at night, and the fact that the boys didn't realize he was already dead. He told Bill the story, since he seemed to know everything about everyone, including "Old Man Hornbeck."

"In 1941, I think it was, Phillip Hornbeck sold his farm and moved into town. He built that tiny house with just a living room, kitchen, and bedroom—all small rooms. Later, after learning about indoor plumbing, he added a small bathroom. That house sits on a big lot, nearly three quarters of an acre, so there's lots of empty space around him."

Bill asked, "Did he want a lot of land?

"Probably not, but he wanted to stay far away from other people, at least that's my guess. Then, not long after arriving in town, he had a stroke and lost some use of his left arm and the left side of his face. The doctor told him that he could expect more such problems and that he should put his affairs in order."

"That doesn't sound good," Bill commented.

"No, it didn't sound that good to Hornbeck either. He had no family to speak of. He'd managed to get his kids mad at him, and they wanted nothing more to do with him. It wasn't actually his fault. He had probably had mental problems for several years by the time they got fed up with him. Some people said he had never been right, but it was really after his wife died and left him alone on the farm that his insanity came out, or so I hear."

"So he was nuts?"

"Well, that's a matter of opinion, but the majority opinion is that he was.

"After the stroke, he just wanted to die. I don't think he was a religious man, but he still believed in the hereafter and thought that anything had to be better than the present life. His country was at war; many things were rationed; he was sick and almost broke; and he had nothing left he wanted to do. His only entertainment was his radio, but his hearing wasn't so good, so he had to play it real loud in order to hear it. Fortunately, he lived a hundred yards from the nearest neighbor, and even then, they complained of the noise.

"He decided he wanted to be buried in a pine coffin. A man of the land, he had no desire to be responsible for putting a steel box into the ground that might lie there for a hundred years without disintegrating. He went to the lumberyard and asked about hiring a carpenter. He got the names of several, but they all wanted more money than he could afford, so he built his own coffin. He worked on it for weeks, using only a handsaw, a plane, and a hammer. When he finished, he put it into his living room."

"Yeah, I've seen it there," Bill added.

Johnny went on. "He wanted nothing more than to be placed into that coffin and into the ground, but he couldn't die. Having worked hard all his life, he had the heart of a racehorse. The rest of his body was falling apart, but his heart beat on and on.

"He tried to starve himself until he was just a walking skeleton, but the fasting seemed to improve his health, not worsen it. He passed 90 and kept going, much to his regret. He became the male version of a witch for the people here. He looked awful with his bony body and contorted face, and he wasn't quite right in the head. Not to mention, every kid in town had peered through the window and seen the coffin on the table. As you know, the rumor was that he slept in it at night, but no one dared go there at night to see. His house was expected to be haunted, and he was supposed to be the haunter.

"So, finally, just a couple of weeks ago, relief came to poor old Mr. Hornbeck," Johnny sighed.

"What do you mean, relief?"

"By that, I mean he died. His children rallied together after he died, and feeling real guilty, they bought the most expensive coffin at the funeral home for his burial. I don't think they ever went into the house, and the pine coffin still sits in the living room."

Bill said, "That's quite a story. So it's just sitting there vacant? The house?"

"Yep. No one in town wants the house, and no offers have been made for it, so far as I know."

His first night in town, Bill had slept in an abandoned boxcar at the old rail yard and had the bug bites to prove it. He didn't get much sleep that night and knew he had to find someplace better to stay. Now that he knew the story about the Hornbeck house and that no one wanted it, he decided he had a home. After dark, he let himself in.

Of course, the door was locked, although who locked it was a mystery. Bill had seen a large screwdriver in the back of The Ideal, and he went over and picked it up. He used it to jimmy the door, and that was no problem. Inside, it was pretty dark, but he didn't want to turn on any lights, providing there even was electricity. He stumbled around in the dark for a few minutes, but then his eyes adjusted to the darkness and he could start to make things out.

He found the bedroom. The bed was made, but he had no desire to sleep on the same sheets that Hornbeck had probably died on. He found some clean sheets in a closet and remade the bed. Then he looked around some more. In the kitchen was the usual stuff: sink, stove, refrigerator. He looked in the fridge, and there was food in it. He decided not to eat anything that might have spoiled, but some stuff in jars was probably okay. He noticed that the refrigerator was cold and the light went on when he opened the door, so there was electricity. He tried the tap at the sink and water came out. Another good sign.

I'm home, he thought.

The place smelled really bad, which wasn't surprising, considering who had lived and died there, but that was something he could tolerate for the short term. The next morning, he found some cleanser and started scrubbing. He searched the dresser drawers and closets and found a few items of clothing to supplement the few he had brought with him.

A few days later, Minnie, Kenny's mother, asked him if he'd like some of Kenny's outgrown clothes. He took them with immense gratitude, and suddenly he was actually living on his own. None of the men or boys in town seemed to know he was living in the house, but the women did. How that happens is the eternal mystery for men.

It was three weeks before someone saw him going into the house, and the word spread around town that he had moved in. By then, he had friends and a reputation for hard work and trustworthiness. No one cared where he lived. Now he could finally take the coffin out of the living room.

CHAPTER 9

Meet the Sheriff

SOME PEOPLE MIGHT THINK that a small town in the middle of farm country would have little use for a sheriff, other than to pass out a few traffic tickets. That's actually what Jackie McBean thought when he applied for the office after the former sheriff retired. McBean had met and talked to many county sheriffs in his former capacity as an Omaha detective. It seems he just hadn't paid much attention to their problems.

There wasn't a lot of crime in Bryan County; that's a fact. What surprised McBean was how much there actually was and what it consisted of. For example, he had investigated three murders, or at least probable murders, in his five years on the job. Only one was officially ruled a murder, but he was fairly certain the others were. All of those were out in the farm country, where you expected people to be the salt of the earth. Mostly they were, but life on a farm can be lonely and frustrating, and opportunities for social interaction can be few. Some people just never seem to learn how to get along. The smallest annoyance can turn into a bitter feud that never goes away, and then one day, it all boils over and someone gets hurt.

Some of those farmers are dirt poor. All farms are not created equal. Some have better land or better water. Some suffer more from the wind that blows constantly across the prairie. Some farmers just aren't good at farming, and some are just plain unlucky.

During the Second World War, the male population was seriously depleted by the draft, especially the younger male population, and those not off to the war were often the weaker or otherwise less desired, at least by the Armed Forces. Then, when the war ended, the boys came streaming back, but they were changed. "How you gonna keep them down on the farm once they've seen Paree?" the song goes. Those strapping soldiers, sailors, and marines came home to find their girlfriends in the arms of the hated "Jody," the guy who stayed behind. A couple of the Jodys were now mysteriously deceased.

Changes had come in wholesale fashion during the war, and the lingering scars were deep. A munitions plant had opened just on the edge of town and workers had flooded in from the surrounding farms. Twice it blew up, killing and maiming some of the workers, mostly women. When it closed after VJ Day, some of the workers chose to stay in town, rather than go back to the farms. Some settled in Blackjack, and some moved on to Lincoln, Kansas City, or Denver. All in all, it was a different town after the war.

One of the holdovers was a large bar that had been built when the munitions plant was operating. It was a huge bar for a little town, but it had a steady stream of customers, some standing at the door in the morning waiting for it to open. It had an incongruous name for small town Nebraska: The Matador.

What were the causes and what were the effects was the age-old chicken and egg question. Did the bar make the drunks, or did the drunks make the bar? No matter, drunks poured into and out of The Matador all night, and often earlier. If McBean had nothing else to do, he could always go over to The Matador and preemptively restore order.

The first day on the job, McBean was called by a storeowner in Blackjack to come get a boy accused of stealing. When he got to the farm equipment store, he was amazed to see a nice-looking blonde lad of 16, being held at gunpoint by the angry merchant, who was holding a double-barreled shotgun in his hands. The boy had been caught trying to drive off on a tractor that was on display outside. It was grand larceny.

The boy looked like someone you would want to marry your daughter. His family farm was in trouble, and the boy hoped to save the day with a new tractor they couldn't afford. Now this Galahad was probably going to reform school, if not the penitentiary.

Most days, not much happened, but the sheriff stayed plenty busy, even before the drunks came out of The Matador, so it was three or four days before he decided it was time to check up on the new kid who had shown up in town. The boy looked young enough to be truant from school, and the sheriff had no idea where he was sleeping now. He knew he had slept at the old freight yard one night. The deputies had just let him sleep, since he wasn't causing any problems, except that he had no bathroom nearby. The old depot wasn't in service of course. It stayed active as the headquarters for some truckers who often parked in the yard, but the kid wouldn't have known there was a bathroom in there and that it was always unlocked. After that night, he had disappeared, and McBean worried about where he might have landed.

The sheriff didn't actually go searching for him, but he kept his eyes open for him throughout the day. Late in the afternoon, he found him at the feed store unloading a big truck. He approached him casually and said, "Son, I'm the sheriff here, and I like to know who's in my town. Would you stop by and see me when you're done here?"

This was a moment Bill had dreaded. He looked the big sheriff over quickly, while gathering his nerve. The guy was in jeans and a tan shirt. On the shirt pocket was the star. He was the sheriff, all right.

Bill didn't know what might happen, but the one thing he couldn't tolerate would be being sent back to the farm. He was thinking, *I could make a run for it, but I need the money I'm making today. How far could I get before this guy would find me anyway?*

So, he said, "Certainly, Sheriff, where's your office?"

He walked over to the sheriff's office in the basement of the Court House a little after five.

As far as McBean was concerned, the kid had already passed his first two tests: He had been respectful, and he had shown up. McBean knew, of course, after years in police work, that it was guys like this who often used their polished manners and nice looks to con the trusting members of the community, so he was still wary.

"What's your name, son?"

"Bill."

"You got a last name, Bill?"

"Huh?"

"Bill what?"

Bill had thought of this many times, and he was ready. The solution had come to him at The Ideal; he was Bill Just.

"Where you from, Bill Just?"

"I lived on a farm north of here all my life, but I'm on my own now."

"And how old are you?"

"I'm 17, sir."

"Old enough to not have to go to school. Can you prove your age?"

"No, sir, I'm afraid I can't."

"Driver's license?"

Trouble! He had been the main entertainment just two days earlier trying to drive the stick shift pickup through town. By now, everyone in town must have heard about it.

"Not on me, sir. My wallet was stolen."

It was weak, but he hadn't been prepared for that challenge.

Sheriff McBean decided he had learned enough for now. He would get the rest of the story soon enough. He smiled and said, "Well, you'd better get another one if you're going to drive Johnny's truck around. I hear you're a good worker, and everyone seems to like you. If you keep your nose clean you'll have no trouble with me. Do you have a place to stay?"

"Yes, sir, I do… for now, anyway."

McBean was going to ask where, but changed his mind and instead simply said, "Well, good! Welcome to Blackjack."

CHAPTER 10

Water

When I left the library after my first visit there, I went back to my rented room with an armload of reference books. I had to admit to myself that I was confused by what I had learned at the library.

I let myself into the back door of the Lindstrom house with my key, climbed the back stairs to the one-room second floor, and dropped the books onto the bed. I had completely missed eating supper, and I was hungry as a bear at the end of hibernation. I remembered that Mrs. Lindstrom, who tended to treat me like a son, or rather a grandson, had told me to help myself to leftovers from the fridge anytime I wanted. I went back down the steps and into the kitchen, looked in the refrigerator, and found a pork chop and piece of lemon meringue pie. That would do just fine. I calculated that I hadn't eaten a vegetable since leaving home three weeks ago, and I didn't intend to ever eat one again.

I took the food up to my room, along with a glass of milk, even though I loathed 1%, and I plopped down on the bed with the books.

I had always been an indifferent student. I was smart enough to get Bs and Cs without effort, but I had never managed to learn much, it seems. Now I was wishing I had. I had a vague memory of being taught about the water source for Nebraska farmers several times, starting in grade

47

school, but the words meant nothing to me. I didn't plan to be a farmer, so I simply paid no attention.

Something was wrong, though. Everything I had just learned pointed to my native state being a wasteland, but it wasn't. It was a major producer of agricultural products; I was fairly sure of that. Just sit in The Ideal, slurping a malted milkshake, and you could barely think, because of the steady stream of huge farm trucks taking corn, millet, and wheat to an elevator someplace, not to mention chickens, hogs, and beef. What was the word? *Contradictions.*

Where did the water come from? was the question that now bothered me for the first time in my life. I had been around the state a little with my father on pheasant hunting trips and with scouts on camping and canoeing trips. Now I thought about the water I'd seen or, rather, hadn't seen.

Around this part of the state, there was the Republican River. It ran almost along the Kansas border until it meandered down into and through Kansas. Most of the year, you could wade across it and only get your shoes and socks wet. Not much water there, even though they had dammed it at Republican City and made a small reservoir. Or was that the reason it was so shallow beyond the dam?

Once, I had seen its northern equivalent, the Niobrara, which ran along the border with South Dakota. I had even gone canoeing on it once. It was just about deep enough for a canoe, if there wasn't much weight in it. You had to be careful not to stick your paddle in the bottom.

Another river I had canoed in, the Big Blue, was anything but big, most of the time. Every few years, it would flood, and then it would come out of its banks and would be "big" if you counted all the flooded farmland.

Of course, the major river in the state is the Platte, which crosses it from west to east. It is famously "a mile wide and an inch deep." It's fed by melting snow in the Rockies. If there's a big snowfall in the winter, the Platte might have actual water running in it during the spring—not much to count on there.

And, on the eastern border, there's the Missouri, or the "muddy ditch" as some people call it. It carries a fair amount of water, I guess, but it only touches a small part of the state.

From my reading tonight, I now knew that I was only thinking about "surface water." What I would learn about was "ground water."

All this concentration was making my head hurt. I had never studied this hard in college. *So why am I doing it now?* I thought.

"There has to be some reason that Mary started me on the ecology of Nebraska," I grumbled aloud to myself, and I had no better plan at the moment.

Out of habit, I got up and switched on the little TV that the Lindstroms had put in the room for me. It wasn't attached to the cable that the downstairs TV used, so all I could get was one channel from Bison City, but that served to pass the time most every night until I was sleepy enough to turn it and the lights off. All I could get now was a rerun of a CSI episode I had seen before. So I opened a book on Nebraska agriculture. A few minutes later, I turned the TV off. This stuff took more concentration than I was accustomed to spending on research.

I had opened the book to a bookmark placed there by Mary, and the chapter I turned to was about something called the Ogallala Aquifer.

See, I thought, *that's typical. What the hell is an aquifer, anyway? How is anyone supposed to understand stuff if they use obscure terms (I was instantly proud of myself even thinking the word "obscure") that no one knows?*

I nearly closed the book, thinking that I would ask Mary in the morning, but I decided to give it a try on my own first.

There was a map showing the area this thing covered, or actually laid beneath, and it was big. Huge! I looked carefully at the area under Nebraska and saw that almost the entire state laid over this thing, which, I gathered, was full of water. Looking for data on that, I found a statement that some 64,000 square miles of Nebraska laid over this water, or about 83% of the state. I sensed that this might help explain those big farm trucks full of grain and beef.

"There might not be much water on the ground here, but there's a whole bunch of it underneath," I said aloud, now reassured. For once, I was actually doing research and learning from it. If I had had any natural curiosity, I would have read further to see where this thing came from, but I actually had to force myself to keep going.

As I read on, I found that how much value there was in that aquifer thing depended on the date of the source. Older sources spoke of it academically and only alluded to potential. Recent sources boasted about the amount of water being pumped out and the impact on agriculture; a few expressed concern about "depletion." I thought about depletion for a second and dismissed it. *My gosh! That thing's an ocean. How you gonna deplete an ocean?*

My eyelids grew heavy toward midnight, and even though I fought it, I fell asleep still clothed and with the book open on my lap.

CHAPTER 11

Driving Adventures

BILL WAS SOON IN demand at several farms in the area. He knew how to do almost any farm chore. He not only did them well, but he also had ideas about how to do them better.

When Stringer asked him where he learned some of those techniques, he told him, "My dad insisted that everything had to be done his way. I guess I kind of rebelled against that. Well, I couldn't do anything about it, but I thought about it a lot, trying to come up with better ideas. Some of the things I thought of work, and some don't. I'm glad you let me try them out."

Stringer said, "I'm learning some things from you, and you're still wet behind the ears. You go ahead and try your ideas out, but if they aren't working, be smart enough to go back to the ways you were taught, okay?"

"Don't worry, Mr. Stringer. I've had to do that already a few times."

There are lots of jobs on a farm that farmers really hate to do and are happy to hire someone to do for them, such as detassling corn, cleaning chicken coops, baling hay, and working in areas inhabited by wasps or snakes. It was hard, unpleasant work (especially the chicken coop), but it kept Bill in money.

When Johnny found out that Bill was working on the farm, he offered to let him use the pickup truck to get there, provided that he made some deliveries for The Ideal during the day. The timing presented some problems, but Bill was resourceful and made it work. Soon, he became very adept at driving the farm roads—in dry weather.

One day, when he had no farm jobs, he stopped in at The Ideal to see if he could pick up some work there. Johnny asked him to make the usual deliveries and pickups. Bill was happy to do that, since he found that using the truck was paying off for him in different ways, mostly farm jobs. He knew he was good at farm work, and he was getting plenty of it.

When he finished his deliveries and brought the pies in to The Ideal, Kenny, who was working around the place as usual, said, "Hey, Bill, the girls want to take a ride in the truck. What do you say?"

Bill wasn't sure this was part of the deal, but Johnny had overheard and nodded his assent. The "girls" were Sandy, Beth, and Barb, who had worked the morning and afternoon and were now getting off work for the day. They were all about Kenny's age, just a little younger than Bill, and he had gotten to know them over the past few months. They liked to tease him when he was around The Ideal, and he considered them to be a lot of fun to be around.

He got the keys back from Johnny with no idea of where they would go in the truck. Two of the girls crowded into the cab, whispering and giggling, with Bill while Kenny and Beth got into the back.

"Where should we go?" Bill asked the girls in his cab.

Sandy said, "My grandparents had a farm west of town, and I always liked the trip out there. C'mon, I'll show you the way."

So they headed out of town on a dirt road. The trouble was that it had rained three of the last four days and the road was muddy. Bill slipped into the ruts, now full of muddy water, and had trouble making headway, so he tried to climb out of the ruts with little success. At a low spot, the ruts disappeared into a quagmire, and coming out of it, just barely, on the other side, he avoided the ruts, but this was worse. He had to drive in the ruts, or he would bog down.

Concerned with maintaining the little momentum he had, he gunned the engine up a little hill to a wooden bridge that crossed a small stream, made it up to the bridge, and started to slide sideways. He had no control of the truck at all at that point, and it slid right to the middle of the little bridge and stopped. He looked around and found that the truck was stuck across the road and wedged between the sides of the bridge, exactly touching both sides. The bridge, it seemed, was just exactly as wide as the truck was long.

He jumped out to see if he could push the truck off or around, but there didn't seem to be any way to move it, and he had to drive. Kenny reluctantly got out into the muck and pushed, but he couldn't budge it.

Bill said, "I need everyone to push."

Barb said, "I'm not getting out into that mud with these shoes on." Bill looked at the girls' shoes and noticed for the first time that they were all wearing white tennis shoes. No, there was no way they were going to get out, and doubtful that it would do any good anyway. So they sat, wondering what to do.

The girls tried to get some music on the radio, but all they could get were farm reports. No one in the truck seemed to care what the price of corn was that day.

Time passed slowly, and the girls' well-honed teasing skills came to the fore. Never mind that it was one of their ideas to take this road, it was Bill's fault that they were stuck.

Salvation came in the form of a tractor, driven by a farmer, who was going from one of his fields to another. He had to cross that bridge, and couldn't, as long as that truck was sitting there. After opining that kids who didn't know how to drive on dirt roads should stay off them, he hooked a chain to the back of the truck and pulled it off the bridge.

The girls returned to The Ideal with clean shoes and a story to tell about Bill's driving that was told and retold hundreds of times. Bill had to avoid the counter girls when he came for the truck from then on. Fortunately, when school started up in the fall, they could only work in the late afternoons, long after he had completed deliveries. A good thing too, because he got stuck in the mud several more times. Everyone did. He just didn't know that.

For the first few weeks, Bill lived in fear of being recognized by someone and sent back home. He was prepared to keep running if he had to, but he really wanted to work out a life in Blackjack.

The problem was that he was only about fifteen miles from the home farm, and kids his age were getting drivers' licenses and access to cars and trucks. He suspected that they would start adventuring out of the neighborhood as soon as they dared, and all he needed was for one of them to see him in town.

Luckily, his work schedule was sort of working out to make him invisible to outsiders. Early mornings, he often ran errands for Johnny, and then, if Johnny said he could, he would drive the pickup truck out to one of his farm jobs, being out of town until late afternoon. He would look carefully at the crowd in The Ideal when he got back to be sure no one he knew was in there. Folks came from many miles to eat the broasted chicken. It was one of the best cheap meals in the area, if not *the* best. Twice, he thought he recognized a family eating there and managed to stay out of sight while turning the keys over to Johnny or one of the kids working there.

He couldn't attend any high school functions, not just because he wasn't a student there, but because a football game, for example, would attract people from all over the area. Kids in town were always asking him to events at the school, and he had to make excuses. The local kids seemed to understand that he felt awkward at the school since he wasn't a student there, and they may have suspected that he was a run-away, but that was his business as far as they were concerned.

After finishing his day at the Ideal, Bill would go to the library and spend the night there, usually until it closed at nine. Then he'd retreat to his little house with a few books and read until he fell asleep.

Sunday mornings, he had to stay home until the church services were over, since folks came in from the farms to the churches. He was a fugitive.

But, one day, the girls who worked at The Ideal, who were always asking him to things, suggested a ride in the truck to a nearby town, where they thought there was a store they wanted to visit. Bill reluctantly agreed to drive them, if Johnny said it was all right, which he did.

When they pulled into the little town, the first thing Bill noticed was that kids his age were very interested in who was in that truck. This was not a good idea, but now that he was there, what could he do?

He found the store, an old five and dime, still hanging on with meager business. He parked in the back and let the girls out. He stayed in the truck.

A few minutes later, George Lindbeck walked by, saw him, and came trotting up to the driver's door with a huge grin on his face. Bill had to admit that he was thrilled to see one of his best friends from school, but this was a problem.

George yanked the door open and punched Bill on the shoulder by way of expressing young-male-type friendship. Bill grabbed his buddy and gave him a quick hug.

Then, he said, "George, listen. You can't tell anyone where I am, understand?"

"No, I don't," George responded, looking confused.

"Where does everyone think I am?"

"I'd say there are two schools of thought on that. One, that your father killed you and buried you under the barn floor. We've been trying to figure out how to search the farm to see if you're buried there, but we're too scared of your father. And the second is that you ran away, which I guess you did, unless your parents just kicked you out. Which is it?"

"I ran or, rather, walked away. I don't want to go back. I can't go back. You understand, don't you?"

"Sure," George answered. "I only been wondering why you didn't do it a long time ago."

"Yeah, me too, but I had to be old enough and big enough to earn a living."

They talked until the girls came back, and George swore an oath not to tell anyone. Bill figured that would last for a few weeks… maybe.

He realized again that his freedom was egg-shell thin.

CHAPTER 12

The Search for Bill Just, Day 2

MY SECOND DAY OF trying to find out who Bill Just was, I awoke later than usual and bolted from bed. I didn't know exactly what time it was, but the sun streaming through my south-facing window made me think it must be at least eight. I pried my eyes open and saw that I was still dressed in the clothes I had been wearing the day before, the khakis and polo shirt, but I guess I must have removed my shoes at some point during the night. The book I had been studying the night before lay open on the bed, next to an empty plate with a well-gnawed pork chop bone on it.

I felt grungy, so I took a shower and shaved, dressed in clothes virtually indistinguishable from those I had worn the day before, and went down to the kitchen for breakfast. I poured a bowl of sugar-frosted Corn Pops and sat down at the kitchen table. Mrs. Lindstrom must have heard me open the refrigerator, because in a minute she came bustling in to pour me a cup of coffee and play mother, her favorite pastime.

"Good morning, Ralph! Did you sleep well?" she purred.

"Oh, too well, I think, thanks. I was up late reading."

"That's unusual, isn't it?" she asked, with surprise registering on her expressive face.

56

"I have to write an article about Bill Just, who died the day before yesterday."

"Oh my! I heard. We'll all miss him around here."

I perked up. "Did you know him?"

"I think everyone in Blackjack knew him," Mrs. Lindstrom said brightly. She always spoke brightly, even when mourning, apparently.

I pursued my question. "But did you really know him? I have to find out as much as I can about him, and I only have a few days. So far, Mary at the library has me learning about Nebraska and the Ogalallago Reservoir, or whatever it is."

Mrs. Lindstrom smiled benevolently as if I were a third grader. "You must mean the Ogallala Aquifer."

"Yeah, that's it, and I don't know what it has to do with Bill Just."

"I would trust Mary, if I were you. There's not many know as much about things as she does, and especially Bill Just, so whatever she tells you to do, you should do," she advised.

I considered this while crunching a mouthful of Corn Pops. The cereal in my bowl had now turned the milk a golden brown and was now the liquid equivalent of eating sugar with a spoon—just the way I liked it.

Mr. Lindstrom was reading the paper in the living room in front of the television, which was turned to the Weather Channel. It was always turned to the Weather Channel, except on Sunday afternoon when Mr. Lindstrom watched golf on TV, which, I thought, was the equivalent to watching trees grow. When Mr. Lindstrom heard us talking in the kitchen, he padded in, scuffing his slippers on the rug as he walked.

"That damn weather girl is pregnant again, or still… or always? I don't know which," he said. "You know, Ralph, it was Bill who found out that corn was sucking too much water out of the soil and convinced a lot of the farmers to switch to wheat, soybeans, or milo. Saved a few farms, I tell you. You should write about that."

Mrs. Lindstrom explained, "My husband was the county agent before he retired. He knows pretty much everything about crops and water."

Lindstrom didn't object to that description. In fact, he didn't even smile.

"Know how much water a single corn plant transpires into the air every day?" he asked.

"I have no clue," I admitted, also wondering what transpiring was.

"Well, it's a bunch. How much rain do you think falls on a farmer's field in one thunderstorm?"

"I don't know," I had to admit again, feeling ignorant of the basics of farming in my home state.

"Do you know why we have so much rainfall and so much violent weather in the summer here in Nebraska?"

"No, sir, I really don't."

"Well, come on into the living room for a few minutes, and I'll give you a little lesson." With that, he shuffled back into the living room and plopped down in front of the TV, with me following with my nearly empty cereal bowl.

"Well, sir," Lindstrom began, "don't feel bad. Most people couldn't answer those questions, and you'll be a fount of knowledge for them when we're done here. Take some notes."

I had to run upstairs for my notebook and pen. When I returned, I found Lindstrom transfixed by the burgeoning belly of the weather girl.

"Oh, you're back," the erstwhile county agent said after a few seconds. "Climate folks measure rainfall in acre-inches or, in other words, the amount of water that would cover one acre one inch deep. That comes to about 28,000 gallons of water." He said "thousand" just like the announcer on *Wheel of Fortune*: "THOU--------SAND dollars!" Maybe he watches that after the all-day weather report.

He went on, "Try to imagine how much water that is. Now, last week, that thunderstorm we had rained over two inches, so on every acre it covered, it deposited about 56 THOU-SAND gallons of water."

"Wow!" I said, after a slurp of sugary milk, genuinely impressed.

"The point is, the violent weather we get here is important to the farmers. It helps 'em. Hell, they can't grow anything without it, and it hurts them too. Flattens whole fields of wheat sometimes. Are you writing this down?"

I was sitting almost dumbfounded, trying to imagine 56 THOU-

SAND gallons of water. "Oh, wait a second." I scribbled down *28 thou gals per acre.*

"But one corn plant uses as much as a gallon and a half of water every day, and there's one hell of a lot of corn plants per acre. So that farmer needs all that water and probably more if he's growing corn. Get it?"

""Got it," I replied, trying to act professional.

"Good," Lindstrom said. "And a typical thunderstorm is about 15 miles in diameter, so that means it covers about 180 square miles, or over 100,000 acres. Think about all that water falling at one time. I'd do the math, but I'd lose the decimal point. So you do it if you want to know."

"I will," I said. "It must be millions of gallons." That was a pure guess. Remember, it took me five years of college to pass freshman math.

Lindstrom ignored that guess. He knew it was billions, but he wanted me to find that out for myself. "Now, the question is: Why do we have that weather here? That's important, so listen carefully."

"I'm listening," I responded, and I was telling the truth. I hadn't even finished the sugary milk out of my bowl.

Lindstrom looked away from the television to make sure I was indeed listening, and he went on. "Warm, moist air from the Gulf of Mexico comes north most of the summer, and when it does, it collides with cold air from Canada. That usually happens in Kansas or Nebraska, sometimes in Oklahoma or one of the Dakotas, but most often around this part of the country. When that warm, moist air meets the cold air, weather happens. That's why we have so many tornadoes, and they have even more in Kansas."

I wasn't aware that the tornados were happening more here than other places. I just assumed that everyone had them.

"And," Lindstrom ended, "the rest should be obvious to you."

He turned his attention to the weather channel again, on which severe weather warnings were being shown in much of central Kansas, and I made my escape.

Back in my room was a list of people Mary had suggested I interview. First on the list was a Mrs. Adamson, and next to her name was listed her phone number and address. I used my cell phone to call her.

"Why, sure, honey!" Mrs. Adamson said. "Come on over, but give me an hour to fix my hair."

I checked my cell phone to see what time it was. I don't wear a watch. I saw that it was only 8:25 a.m., too early to go back to the library. I looked at the short list again and found the name of a woman named Cecille Gadd. I wondered how to pronounce Cecille, since I had known girls who pronounced it Suh-seal and one who actually pronounced it Cecil. So on the way out, I popped into the kitchen again.

Mrs. L was meticulously washing my bowl and cup by hand in preparation for putting them into the dishwasher. She turned toward me and smiled her motherly smile, while inspecting my clothes, probably to see if I was dressed properly.

"Sess-i-lee," she said. "And that's a good choice. I would like to hear what you find out from her. We're all wondering about her and Bill.'

"What do you mean?" I asked.

"You'll find out, I hope," she replied unhelpfully. "Me…? I don't spread rumors." Something in her smile gave me an indication that she could hardly wait to spread a few facts. Then she added, "In small towns like this one, I suppose you know, folks tell the same stories over and over. You can learn almost anything you want to know just by listening to those stories, but you have to sort out which ones is true. Just because someone's told it a hundred times, don't mean it's true."

I did know that. I had spent much of my life in small towns, and I knew how people treasured their stories and retold them at every opportunity. I remembered the example I had been taught in college. Something really interesting happens in "Smalltown," Nebraska, and it makes the national news. Say, for example, a woman locked her child and her keys in her car, and the baby died from the heat. Or even better, that a man came by and broke the car window to save the child, only to be yelled at by the mother, who was upset that her window was broken. That story might capture imaginations all over the country, but in New York or Chicago or even Lincoln, it would be forgotten the next day. In Smalltown, seven versions of that story would be told and retold and debated for years.

I went to work, calling people to interview.

No one answered at the Gadd phone number, so I made a run over there in my car to see what I could see. I found a typical Midwestern rambler with a neat yard and an old Chevy pickup in the driveway. No one answered the doorbell or my knock, so I checked the time again and decided Mrs. Adamson had spent enough time on her hair, if that's really what she was doing.

On the way over to her house, I swung by *The Press* and picked up a copy of the paper that had come out that morning. It was a little bit like a spy mission, because I didn't really want to have to explain to anyone what I was doing just yet. I turned to the obituary page and found Mrs. Fritz's version of the obituary. It was much more detailed than mine had been, and I was happy to see that it would provide me with a lot of information that might have been hard to find on my own. I put the paper on the front seat of the car for future use. I was glad that I had managed to get in and pick up the paper without meeting Mrs. Fritz. If I had run into her, I might have told her about the hay, the water, and the corn, but I doubted that would impress her very much.

The sugar high from my Corn Pops was already wearing off, probably because of the coffee—something I had never developed a tolerance for. I decided to pull into the drive-thru lane of McDonalds and get a Danish. I had to sit at McDonalds for a couple of minutes, eating, because the drive to my next stop was only going to take about thirty seconds.

Even though all these places in Blackjack were within five blocks of each other, I had managed to spend almost an hour getting to Mrs. Adamson's place. She was waiting for me by the front door when I pulled into the driveway.

It was obvious that she had done her hair. It looked as if she had just come from the beauty shop, and I guessed that she had been there yesterday to get a new shot of blue dye. I didn't understand why women of her vintage wanted blue hair, but the joke in town was that the water tower not far behind the town's only beauty shop was actually full of blue hair dye.

"Mrs. Adamson, I'm Ralph Anderson from *The Press*. As I told you,

I've been assigned to write an article about Bill Just. I understand that you can help me find out about him."

"Yes, of course. I'm Vera Adamson. Call me Vera. Please come in and have a seat. Would you like some coffee? I have a new coffee grinder, and I just ground some beans and put on a pot. It's almost ready. I'd love to hear how you like it."

I knew I couldn't refuse, so I just said "Yes, I would love a cup, but just one, please."

With that, Vera hurried into her kitchen, leaving me sitting by myself in the living room. I reminded myself to look around and notice things, like a good reporter should. I saw that the living room was almost a dead ringer for those of my aunts, who both lived in similar ramblers—very formal furniture, although with a modern appearance, wall-to-wall carpet, light blue, prints of famous impressionist paintings, and one picture of the Nebraska football team of 1995 autographed by Coach Tom Osborne. Doilies covered the arms of every chair and the sofa. A 32" television seemed to be the center of attention in the room.

Vera Adamson returned with a tray of coffee, sugar, cream, and coffee cake. I should have known! *Why had I stopped for that Danish when I was visiting a woman's home in Nebraska?*

Vera asked, "How did you happen to come to Blackjack, Ralph?"

It took me fifteen minutes to turn the conversation to Bill Just.

Vera told me, "I've known Bill, or I guess I should say, I *knew* Bill, almost from the day he came to town. But it was after he came back from the Army that I really got to know him. I was a secretary for Helmer Lindquist in his insurance office. I did that for forty years. Bill had been working for Swanson out at the factory, you know, where he was a glorified secretary hisself. They had told him he would be promoted to be the manager of administration, but that TV dinner fad kind of petered out. They didn't expand like they expected. Hank, that's what we all called Mr. Lindquist, called on Bill one night to sell him some insurance, but after spending an hour with him, he made him a job offer."

"What did Hank want him to do at the agency?" I asked. I knew she was going to tell me, but I figured I ought to be asking questions if this was an interview. That reminded me to start taking notes.

"Just a minute, just a minute... I'm getting there," Vera said, with a smile. "Bill didn't take it right away. He wasn't unhappy at Swanson and still hoped for the promised promotion. After a few more months, though, he figured that he would never get ahead there, so he come over to see if Hank still wanted him."

"Hank was getting real tired of making sales calls every night, and he figured that Bill was just—Oh! That's funny! 'Bill was just.' Anyway, what I mean is that he figured Bill was exactly the fella to take those offen his hands."

I took another sip of coffee and felt a surge of energy as another jolt of caffeine hit my bloodstream. I also noticed that my hand was shaking when I held the coffee cup up to my mouth. Caffeine. I fidgeted in my chair, determined to ask a question and not knowing what I should ask.

"Why do you suppose he picked Bill to hire?" I finally asked.

"Oh, he was so impressed with Bill! He talked about him for days after he had first met him. Well, sir, after Bill come to work for us, Hank spent a few weeks training him in insurance, but Bill had been reading in the library and he had an idea of his own. He had learned about mutual funds there. Lots of farmers around here sell their farms and move into town. In fact, most of this town is made up of those farmers. Well, when they sell the farms, they get lots of money, and Bill figured out they had no idea what to do with it.

"So, he did take the evening calls over for Hank, but during the day, he visited the new arrivals in town, mostly retired farmers, and sold them mutual funds. He could have made a lot of money, and I mean *a lot*, if that's what he wanted. But he had also learned that no-load mutuals did about as well as the ones he was selling, so he helped most of those farmers to buy no-load funds, For those, though, he didn't get no commissions.

"Of course, Hank didn't like that much, but he was making plenty from the insurance, so he didn't interfere. And Bill was helping a lot of people. Word got around, and Bill became sort of a hero to those folk. If they wanted insurance, guess who they went to."

"So, it was good business for Bill…?" I ventured, ever on the alert for a little piece of scandal.

"Yes, it was, but I don't believe that's what Bill wanted so much as to help those old farmers. He got their money put safe away, where it would grow and pay them a steady retirement besides."

I was curious about Bill's motivation. Were there people in this world who helped others at the expense of their own livelihoods? I asked, "Was Bill making money then?"

Vera reached over and patted my hand. "Sure he was. He wasn't getting rich, but he was making more money than most folk in this area. And insurance is a funny business. You sell a policy, and it pays you as long as the policyholder is making payments. That's one reason why Hank wasn't too concerned about Bill selling them no-load funds. Hank had been selling insurance for a long time, and he was getting commissions on hundreds of policies. Pretty soon, Bill would be getting that too."

When I finally left Vera's house, I could hardly sit still. In fact, I had bailed before she was finished, because I was so jumpy and had to go so badly that I just had to get out of there.

No more coffee! I told myself.

As I hurried toward the nearest men's room, I realized that I had a pretty good story already. Put together the no-load mutual fund sales to retired farmers, the switch from corn to wheat or beans, and the straw-bale church, and it was a great story. As I stood in the men's room at McDonalds, draining my bladder, I was thinking that back in college (last month), I would have quit searching and started writing at this point. I could have gotten at least a C, which was good enough for me then. Now, though, I had to face Mrs. Fritz, not to mention the adoring Just fans.

But what was this business Mrs. Lindstrom was so curious about, the business about Bill and Cecille Gadd? I just had to try to run that down for her sake, even if it didn't get into my article.

Small town papers like *The Press* have to be careful what they print about the locals. Locals not only make up their reader base, but their advertising customers too. It was obvious that Bill Just had been a very popular guy in Blackjack and an *exposé* (worth an A plus in college journalism) would anger both the readers and the advertisers and probably put the paper out of business.

How did I know that? you may be wondering. Well, I remembered a class at college on The Business of Journalism, in which I had read about a small town publisher who uncovered a corrupt high school coach and athletic director. The guy was taking kickbacks from sports equipment salesmen and buying inferior equipment at premium prices. One boy had sustained a head injury because of a badly-made football helmet. You would have thought that the town would have risen up in anger at the coach. Instead, it took out its anger on the publisher.

In another case I had studied, a school principal had uncovered a ring of teachers and principals who were sexually abusing girls in their schools. Getting no backing from the school board, she passed this on to the local paper. The principal was fired; the ring continued abusing girls; and the paper went broke.

No, there would be no *exposé* of Bill Just, at least not in *The Press*.

I was unable to reach Cecille Gadd until evening. I decided to go back to the library and see what more I could learn from Mary. She was probably surprised that no one seemed to have said anything to me about her friendship with Bill, but she wasn't going to bring it up. She probably wanted to see what I would find out by myself.

I told Mary about the statement that Bill had been the one who had convinced some farmers to switch crops and his assertion that he had saved some farms in the process.

"I wasn't really aware of that, or I've forgotten it. Bill was into so many things that it was hard to keep up. He read a lot every day and would react to things he learned, so that would be just like him. He could have read that almost anywhere, and he would do something about it."

"Can you point me to some likely sources?" I asked.

"Sure," she said, "give me a few minutes."

While she was on the computer, I walked around the library, looking it over. I found a small section called Blackjack History. I looked at some of the self-published books on the shelves and found *Blackjack – The Early*

Days, and *A History of Blackjack*. I picked them up and carried them back to the desk where Mary was printing out a list from the computer for me.

I asked, "Can I take these out?"

"Not a chance," she said. "Those are the only copies left, and they're staying right here. But… you're free to look at them in the library."

I took the books over to one of the tables and sat down. I discovered immediately that the "early days" were long before Bill Just was born. Still, it was interesting reading, and I made a mental note to return later and take a good look at them.

I was reading articles about plant water usage in agriculture journals and finding a few references to the huge amount of water required by a single corn plant, when a man noisily plunked himself down across from me and snarled, "Do you need to take up the whole table?"

A quick glance across the table revealed a large man, rumpled and gnarly looking.

"Oh, sorry," I reacted, and then realized that I wasn't taking any more room than might reasonably be taken by anyone sitting at the table. Still, I gathered my little stack of magazines into one pile and tried to become invisible. A few minutes later, the man was snarling at someone else over some imagined infraction. I finished my research and returned the magazines to the desk.

"What's with Mr. Personality?" I asked Mary.

"Oh, that's Pete Thorson; pay no attention to him. He likes to think he's mean."

"Can I ask you something?"

Mary answered, "Of course."

"What can you tell me about Cecille Gadd?"

Mary sat silent a moment, and her eyes seemed to be focused on her hands. When she spoke, she phrased her response carefully.

"Cecille is a single mother. She came to town with two small children after a lousy marriage broke up, and she was practically starving. Bill took her into his house as a temporary arrangement until she could get on her feet, and she's still there. She's a sweet lady, and her kids, who are grown now, are delightful. Beyond that, you will have to find out yourself."

I tried to ask the next question as diplomatically as I could. "Why would Mrs. Lindstrom want to know more about Bill and Cecille?"

Mary laughed. "I guess everyone in town would like to know more about that. They lived together for about 30 years, but never married. I guess that's the answer. Everyone would like to know what was going on."

Mary's eyes lit up with an idea, and she said, "You should go by the Court House to see what records there were for Bill Just, " and I mentally kicked myself for not thinking of that. As I left, Mary said, "Come back later, and let's talk about Bill and trees."

"Oh, sure," I responded and walked over to the Court House.

The Court House was an imposing building for such a little town. I climbed the limestone stairs to the front door and entered to find myself in a wide corridor. Offices lined the corridor, and all had titles that meant little to me. Some were obvious, such as the license bureau, but others were less obvious.

I asked the first person I found, who looked as if she worked there, about records. She pointed to the far end of the hall and an office that read *Recorder* on the door. Walking down the corridor, I passed a lawyer, I guessed, escorting a teenage boy to court. I looked at the kid, maybe two or three years younger than me, and thought, *How does a kid like that get into trouble around here?* I made a mental note to find out later. I never had a chance.

When I walked into the Recorder's office, I found four women working there and a handful of lawyers, I assumed, going through records. One of the clerks took me into the vault and showed me how to search for different kinds of records. I spent the rest of the afternoon doing that and only found a deed to the house. No marriage records. A divorce decree for Cecille Gadd had been granted for extreme physical and mental abuse.

I finally reached Cecille on the phone in the evening, and she told me she worked all day, but she could see me the next night at 6. She would meet me at The Ideal.

I went to the library to continue my research. I observed to myself that if I had ever worked this hard in college I could have graduated in four years with a decent GPA—maybe a 4.0.

Mary was at the desk, of course. "Well, Ralph, good to see you back in here. What are you looking for this time?"

"I don't really know," I answered. "I have a free evening, though, so I hope I can make some progress on my article."

"How's it going so far?"

"I'm getting lots of good stuff, and I'm learning a lot, really a lot, about this town and this state. Tell me, Mary: Why did you have me read all that stuff about Nebraska? Does that have something to do with my article?"

"You caught me, Ralph." Mary laughed. "I knew you'd get plenty for your article, but I wanted you, and everyone, for that matter, to learn about their state. I gather you've done a good job of that already. You're a smart guy."

My gosh, someone called me smart!

"Thanks, Mary, not really," I said, "but I appreciate your help, and now I want to know what you think I should do next."

Mary thought for a couple of seconds. "There's a book over in our town history section that you ought to read. You'll have to do it here, though; I can't let it leave the library."

She showed me the book called *Reminiscence of Coming to Nebraska*.

I took it to a quiet table in a back corner. The story I read went about like this:

"We crossed the Missouri River and kept moving west. We passed through Lincoln, which was a new town at that point and very small, and then through Crete and York. Eventually, we came to the place where the Republican River and Turkey Creek come together.

"The only people out there were living alone and long distances from each other. Some were hunting and trapping, some farming, and some running small stores.

"We scouted along the river and found a stake pounded into the ground with a note attached that said it was some town, even had a name, but all that we could find was the stake. Then we met a fellow coming down the river on his horse. He was the earliest settler in this region and had built a shanty out there. He showed us some land in the area that he said was real good, and we liked it. We camped that night, and when we woke up in the morning, we saw some smoke. We knew someone must be around. It turned out to be government scouts from Fort McPherson. We liked the area and decided to file a claim. I brought my wife and child from Iowa, but I did it in the fall and we barely survived the winter.

"In 1873, a few of us were appointed commissioners by the governor to call an election to locate the county seat. We held the election in an old log house. We also elected a county clerk, a sheriff, a judge, and a few more fellas.

"Then a frame building was put up for a hotel and a courthouse."

This was pretty good insight into how the state was originally organized. I wasn't sure why I needed to know this, but I was glad that all that had been done by someone else before I was born.

On the way back to Lindstroms', I thought about how much time I was spending on this, and how little time I had spent on schoolwork in college. No wonder I liked it there so much. But I was beginning to like this place too. And now I knew what the pioneers had to do to get this place going.

CHAPTER 13

Ethnic Choruses

I GOT A FEW more days to write an article about the town's hero, and so far it was going okay, but I still had a lot to learn and a lot of writing to do. I was confident that I could do a good job if everyone left me alone to work on it.

But then, Mrs. Fritz gave me another article to write for the same weekly edition. At least I was going to have a lot of inches in the paper and, I hoped, some bylines. That is, if I could get both of them done.

So, right in the middle of my research on Just, I had to drive over to Pocahontas and take in a concert of some smalltown choruses. *Wow! How exciting!* That's sarcasm in case you didn't know. Irony.

I wondered if Mrs. Fritz somehow found out that I sang in my high school chorus. Because if she thought I actually knew anything about music, well, let's just say that I joined the chorus because it had most of the good-looking girls in it. The teacher made it really easy for the boys to sing their parts and let the girls make most of the music.

Anyway, I climbed into my rattletrap, said a little prayer that it would start, cranked it, and drove the 43 miles, through countryside I had never seen before. I found Pocahontas on the state map without difficulty, and finding it on the ground was even easier. Along the way, I passed signs to Powhatan and Rolfe. My faint recollection of these names was that they were from Jamestown in Virginia. *What the heck are they doing in Nebraska?*

As I drove into town, the first thing I could see was the water tower with faded paint on it that read, *Girl's BBall Champs 1987.* I guess that was the last championship any of their teams had won. I thought that I would repaint the water tower or encourage the kids to paint it, like they did in Blackjack, with the year of the current high school senior class.

Next, I had to find the Masonic Lodge, get a ticket, and see what, if anything, I could find to write about.

First surprise was that the Masonic Lodge is in an old church. I didn't find out why the church was still standing but wasn't an actual church anymore. A real reporter would have found out. Then, I got my first perk: my ticket was complementary. I was a real reporter now; I could get into things for free.

So I wandered around, wondering what to do, but it wasn't long before someone took charge and announced that this was a special treat: a meeting of three choruses, from three different towns. Even I recognized that they were probably going to sing songs from three different nations. We've got the Czechs, the Poles, and the Germans. It was going to be World War II all over again, in song.

The Czechs were the hosts, since it's their hometown, and they introduced the Poles to sing first. Third surprise? They were actually good! They sang two songs in Polish, and I wondered if even they understood the words. The songs were beautiful. Then, they sang two American songs. Stephen Foster, I guessed.

There was great clapping and cheering by the audience, which was mostly the other two choruses or their wives. The choruses turned out to be all males, and made a note to later find out why that was.

Next, the Germans sang, and it was classic German music—once again, well done. They sang *Vater Rhein,* and there wasn't a dry eye in the house, even though probably no one spoke German or cared anything about that river.

Finally the Czechs sang, and it was even better than the other two choruses. I clapped until my hands hurt. Then, the MC said, "Now, here's the moment we've all been waiting for!" As if they had rehearsed it, they all broke out in the Beer Barrel Polka in three languages and, sure enough, someone rolled out a barrel.

It turned out that the barrel was empty, but off to the side, there were three kegs of beer, one for each nationality, and plenty of wurst, kielbasa, brat, and kraut. This was a great party!

The singers could hardly stop singing long enough to eat. Some were singing with mouths full of wurst, spraying crumbs in all directions.

I was finally able to corner the MC and ask him to explain the men's chorus thing. He told me that it was an old European tradition, and the town fathers had hardly built their houses before they formed their first town chorus. Even this type of meeting of choruses was part of the tradition. Originally, he said, the nationalities only sang with other countrymen, but this way was more fun. He also told me this was all fairly common with the Bohemian, German, and Polish towns. For the first time in my short life, I realized I'd been missing something growing up.

The MC told me that the ethnic chorus tradition had almost disappeared . Few thought of themselves as "Bohemians" anymore, or Poles, or Germans. I thought that was a good thing, but those choruses were pretty special.

I asked the directors to line up their choruses, and I took some pictures of them as Mrs. Fritz had told me to do. Ace reporter turned photographer.

Driving home I was pretty excited. I had a wonderful time, and I was pretty sure this was going to be the easiest article I had ever written. I could see a big feature spread in my future!

CHAPTER 14

In the Army Now

BILL AND KENNY HAD become good friends, and Kenny took a real interest in Bill's welfare. When Kenny was approaching graduation from high school and had filled out applications to several colleges, he wondered about Bill's future. Bill was working odd jobs and managing to survive quite nicely. He seemed pleased with his life, and that didn't seem right to Kenny.

One day, Kenny asked, "Bill, what are your plans?"

Bill had to think. "I guess I don't have any plans, Kenny. Why do you ask?"

"Well, do you expect to spend the rest of your life cutting up chickens and cleaning out chicken coops? You're too smart to do that kind of stuff."

Again, Bill had to stop and think. Was that true? Was he too smart for that kind of stuff? Wasn't that one of the reasons he had fled the farm, because he considered himself too smart to simply slave away as his father's assistant?

Bill said, "I can't go off to college like you. I never finished high school. How am I supposed to get better work?"

"Good question, Bill. I don't know, but you might want to think about it. I saw an Army recruiting ad on TV last night. It said you could put away some of your Army pay, and the Army would add to it so that you could go to college when you got out. I'll bet there are other programs like that too."

Bill responded, "I'll have to register for the draft when I turn 18, and I could be drafted. In fact, I probably will, since the Korean War is still going on. Oh, excuse me, I meant 'Police Action'."

Kenny said, "I don't know how draft boards work, but since they have to pick someone and none of those people know you, I'd guess you'll be on the top of the list, all right."

Bill mused, "Yeah, they can fill part of the quota with someone whose parents they don't have to answer to."

Over the next two months, Bill pondered this and his future, and he realized that Kenny had pointed him down a road that offered some potential improvement in his future. On his 18th birthday, he went to the Army recruiting station and enlisted.

Bill had to produce documents to enlist, and the documents had his actual last name on them. So, while in the Army, he was William Larsen, not Bill Just. Three days later, he was at basic training.

The first eight weeks of basic were devoted to three things: making a disciplined soldier out of a civilian, physical conditioning, and teaching all the fundamental skills the Army required. Many of the recruits found the discipline harsh and distasteful. Compared to life with his father, for Bill, this was easy. He had worked hard physically all his life, so he did well in the physical conditioning part. Plus, he was pretty smart, so he picked up the soldier skills readily.

After the first four weeks, his drill sergeant took him aside and said, "Larsen, you are my best recruit. I'm promoting you to acting squad leader. If you keep up the good work, that's your job for the rest of basic."

The next eight weeks were called Advanced Individual Training. Based on aptitude tests and success in basic training, each soldier was assigned a specialty and received training in that field. Bill volunteered for Parachute School and was assigned to the 82d Airborne Division at Fort Bragg, North Carolina. Upon graduation from Jump School, he was assigned as a rifleman.

Later, he was selected for a job in personnel and spent the next two years in that—first, in a Battle Group Headquarters, and then, because of his high skill level, at Division. He was promoted to Specialist 4 and then to Sergeant.

Although Army pay was pretty low, with his higher rank and jump pay, he was able to save money. He took some classes at the Education Center in the evenings, while his buddies were down in Fayetteville, blowing their pay. An education counselor suggested that he take a General Education Development test, which he passed, and he was awarded a high school equivalency.

Bill only had to spend two years on active duty, because he had volunteered for the draft, so technically he had been drafted. He was released from the Army the day after his 20th birthday, with a high school diploma and money in the bank. He was one of the draftees who came out of the Army much better off than he had gone in.

Then he wasn't sure where to go. He probably could have gone to any of the state colleges and eventually graduated. He had thought about that many times, but in the end, he went back to Blackjack. He never could explain why he did that. His friends were gone in one way or another. Many were in college, others in one of the armed services, and the rest married and working. There's an old saying, "You can never go home," but he did. And the funny part was that Blackjack was now what he considered home.

His goal was to come back triumphant. To do that, he had to get a real job. That proved harder than he expected. What he hadn't realized was that there weren't many "real jobs" in Blackjack, and those that existed were filled and others were already waiting for openings.

Kenny came home for Christmas from the university and had a party. Bill was invited, of course. He almost didn't go, but it turned out to be a good thing he did. He saw his old pal, Jim Strange there for the first time since he had come back to town, and Jim asked him where he had been.

"I just got back after two years in the Army," Bill answered.

Jim was surprised. "Oh, rotten luck," he said.

"No," Bill responded, "it was good. I was a clerk/typist and worked mostly as a personnel clerk in the 82d."

"You jumped out of airplanes!"

"Yeah, sure did, but mostly I worked in administration."

"What are you doing now?"

"Looking for a job," Bill said glumly.

Jim thought for a moment, trying to remember what his impression of Bill had been two years before. They had barely known each other since Bill wasn't in school and Jim lived out of town. He decided to ask around. "Check with me later. I may be able to give you a lead."

As luck would have it, the first guy Jim approached was Kenny, now going by "Ken." Ken told him, "He's first rate. Smart, works hard, you would trust him with your wallet."

As the party was breaking up, Bill caught up with Jim on the porch and said, "You told me to check with you."

Jim smiled. "Right. Come on over to the Swanson plant tomorrow and ask for me. I work on the loading dock, but I know the manager real good. I'm purty sure he needs someone in administration."

The next day, Bill had a job—not a great job, but a real one. The next Saturday, he made an offer for the little Hornbeck house and got it for practically nothing.

CHAPTER 15

Trees

MARY HAD BEEN EAGER to tell me something about Bill Just and trees. One day, when I was researching in her library, she brought over a couple of pamphlets to show me. They were about Arbor Day events in years past. She pointed to the inside cover where it read, "Arbor Day Chairman, Bill Just."

Mary asked, "In your research, have you learned much about trees in this state?"

"Actually, no," I answered. I was really getting tired of admitting all the things I didn't know!

"Well, you should have, because it's an important part of our history. When people got here, they expected to have wood to build with. Think of all the things we use wood for today. We build houses and barns out of it; we use it for fence posts; then they built wagons from it... and so on. But there weren't any trees here. This was prairie grassland. It was so bad that people lived in sod houses, which I'm sure you've seen in your research."

"Oh, sure," I said, wondering how I had missed that.

Mary went on, "So, it wasn't long before Nebraskans figured out they would have to grow trees if they were going to have any. When I was at the university, I would go over to the Capitol Building and go up to the top of the tower and look out at the city and the surrounding country. You could see exactly where people had planted trees. Lincoln is like a huge park, and in the summer, you can hardly see houses because of all the trees, but outside of the city, the only trees are around farmhouses.

"Farmers planted trees for shade, mostly, and for windscreens. Look at farms today, and you can find places where farmhouses were once, but are gone now. You can tell because of the trees that were planted around the houses.'

She stopped, having forgotten where she was going with that.

I tried to help. "And Bill…?"

"Oh, right! After a few years here, Bill realized that Blackjack still didn't have many trees. The other towns he visited had plenty, but we didn't. He set out to change that. The Blackjack you see today with all those big oaks, willows, and maples is the product of his efforts. In a few months, you'll see the maples turning red, and the whole town will be a blaze of color. That we owe to Bill. Now, lots of us consider fall the best season because of that."

I interjected, "I thought everyone in Nebraska celebrated Arbor Day by planting a tree."

"That may be true in most places, but it hadn't caught on here until he started his Arbor Day programs. Look, you need to know that for your article, but as an educated Nebraskan, you need to know more than that. You need to learn about the Nebraska National Forest, for example. It's the largest man-planted forest in the country, and it's in the Sandhills, a place where trees don't normally grow, even today. Botanists say that forest is a thriving forest in every way, full of elk, deer, squirrels, rabbits, and all kinds of forest critters. Sit down, and I'll bring you some reference material."

"Geez, I've never worked this hard in my life," I mumbled.

Mary was approaching from my rear with a handful of material and heard my complaint.

"You know why this thing you're doing is important?" she asked.

I thought a second and said, "I'll give you two reasons, and you pick one. The memory of Bill Just… and my job."

Mary laughed. I was already one of her fans, and when she laughed, she looked a lot nicer. "Okay, those *are* two, but this is my reason: You're writing the modern history of this town. When it's printed, a copy is going to go over on the town history shelves for all time. Think of that while you're working so hard."

CHAPTER 16

Pete Thorson

PETE THORSON, THE GUY I met in the library, was a big man. He hadn't always been so big, but as he aged, he kept getting larger. Not that he was ever small. He reached nearly six feet in height while in high school and playing end on the football team. That was an accomplishment for someone who only weighed 155 pounds.

Many small towns in Nebraska have 8-man football teams, and some have 6-man. In Axtell, where Pete grew up, they had an 8-man team. Even at that, it meant that virtually every able-bodied boy in school had to be on the team. In fact, everyone had to be in the band, the chorus, and the student council.

One of the oddities of life in a town with an 8-man team was that the concept of a 50-yard line was foreign. 8-man teams played on a field that was only 80 yards long, so there was no 50-yard line.

Pete could play on the line weighing 155, because he was tough and ferocious. He often blocked the kid opposite him far into the backfield or simply pancaked him, dropping him on his back and, thus, was unable to make a tackle. He didn't know how he did it and his coach didn't either; he just did it.

Sports were important in Pete's life, but not central. He was too small to play for Nebraska, but he was able to make the team at Bison State, although he seldom started.

A lot of the football players there played handball in the off-season, and Pete was the champ of the handball players. The college had no handball courts that it knew of, but for years, football players had known about and used a "court" that may or may not have been built as a handball court. It was about the right dimensions for handball, had the requisite white walls, much scarred and marked by the black handballs of that time, a concrete floor that devoured gym shoes, and no ceiling. The lack of a ceiling was a problem, because that also meant no roof. Someone had laid chicken wire across the top to try to keep the leaves out, but they got in anyway. Warmups consisted of sweeping the place out. You always came with a rake and a broom. In the winter, a snow shovel came in handy too. There was a mysterious presence of coal dust as if at one time the place had been used as a huge coal bin. When you finished playing, your clothes and skin showed a trace of coal dust, and it never completely washed out. Handball everywhere was a game for tough guys, and at Bison, it was a ritual of testosterone.

The players who introduced Pete to the game were some of the toughest guys in that part of the state, and they converted handball into close combat. Pete was the toughest one of all, though, and once he got the hang of the game, and over the pain and swelling in his hands, he rose to the top of their little ladder.

Handball courts are rare in Nebraska, or were when Pete was young, so he had few opportunities to play after college. Still, he entered tournaments for twenty years and did well. In fact, he got better, even though he only played a few times a year. By the time he was forty, he was acknowledged by most to be the best player in the Midwest outside of Chicago. That is, if you played by his rules.

In handball, if one player hinders the other's ability to play the ball, a "hinder" is awarded and the point replayed. If someone calls "hinder," it is automatically replayed. If someone called a hinder while playing Pete, his response was likely to be, "I don't see any blood." Pete considered the only valid hinderance to be if you were knocked unconscious, bleeding profusely, or had a broken bone. Clearly, you could not play the ball in any of those cases, although it might depend on which bone was broken.

No one was tougher than Pete in the handball court, and he found that was helpful in the rest of his life too. He developed an artificial tough demeanor, and that kept others at a safe distance. He liked it that way. He didn't have to deal with people on a personal basis.

Pete's father had been a plumber, carpenter, and all-around handy man, and Pete could have made a good living at any of those jobs, but telling your potential customers how stupid they are proved not to be good for his business.

So now Pete's business was selling cleaning supplies, mostly to schools. That meant he traveled throughout the state and Northern Kansas all summer and some of the spring, when schools were buying supplies for the coming year. He dealt with janitors and principals in hundreds of schools. Those people could and would eat up hours of his time if he let them, but they were discouraged from doing that by his outward gruffness.

Pete had broken nearly every bone in his fingers playing handball. What he may have lacked in skill, he made up in effort. Strangely, after he tore the splints off out of impatience and the bones healed crooked, he found that he had some new shots with tricky spins.

While his crooked fingers improved his handball, they made other things harder. He couldn't tie a tie, for example. No one would have cared if he hadn't worn a tie at all, but for some reason, he did—one tie, the same tie, every day of the year, pre-tied and slipped over his head in the morning. Usually it was not centered so that it draped out from under one of the collar points. It had been covered with gravy spots for years and acquired new ones almost daily.

Pete also wore only three "dress" shirts, if you could call them that. They were wash-and-wear short-sleeved shirts that he washed himself and hung on a hanger to dry. One of them had a large ink spot on the pocket from a leaking ballpoint pen. He wore it every third day, and no one dared say anything about it.

A lot of folks assumed that this gruff old guy was a bachelor, considering how he looked when he left the house each day. That was far from the truth. Pete had a wife and seven kids. You can't get much more married than that.

He was dressed in his standard uniform the day I met him in the library, if his snarling at someone was what passed for meeting him. He later told me that he liked the way I had responded, quickly reducing the area I occupied. He had never seen me before, but he said that he immediately liked me and made a mental note to find out what this boy was doing in town. It might turn out to be useful in some way.

CHAPTER 17

Fire!

THE PAGER BLURTED ITS ring three times before Bill woke up enough to realize what it was. Groggily, he rolled over toward the night table, reached up and fumbled to turn on the lamp, and groped for the pager. He was at a point in his life where he needed glasses, but he was in denial, so he attributed his inability to read the message on the pager to his sleepiness. Suddenly, it became clear to him that it was a fire.

Bill had joined the volunteer fire department immediately after returning to town from the Army. His experience as a sergeant helped convince his fellow firemen that he was a natural leader. Though young and very inexperienced in firefighting, he had been made a lieutenant after only two years.

Bill dressed quickly and hustled to his pickup, clapped the blue flashing light on the top, and drove quickly to the fire station, which, he was amazed to find, was engulfed in flames. It only took a second for him to realize that all the fire-fighting equipment was trapped inside, and even if it hadn't already burned, it was inaccessible.

This was even more embarrassing than the time an old building across the street from the fire hall burned to the ground. All anyone could think of after that was: How could a fire a few feet from the fire hall get so out of hand? Where were the firemen? The truth was less interesting, but nobody really cared about the truth. The truth was that it was a controlled burn to get rid of the old termite palace and for training of the fire department. No matter how many times they told people that, no one bought it.

Now, no one was doing anything so far as Bill could tell. Lots of people were standing around watching, because the best entertainment of the year in Blackjack is a good fire. People will stand around in their pajamas at three in the morning in two feet of snow watching a fire, when they could be snug in bed.

Bill walked over to Doug Jones, who was standing in the street doing nothing but watching the station burn. "Doug, where's Tom?"

Tom Meyer was the Fire Chief, and Bill was surprised that he couldn't locate him. Doug pointed toward a house on the other side of the street. "I think he went over to that house to call New Frankfurt. No way to get to our commo in the fire."

Of course, Bill thought, *our equipment is out of commission, and our communications are in the fire too.* He strode quickly to the house Doug had pointed to and walked in the open front door without knocking. He found Tom on the phone and stood by while Tom talked to the fire chief in New Frankfurt, or "Frank," as most people had come to call it.

Tom was saying, "Well, someone's got to come put this fire out before it burns down the whole town, and we cain't do nothin'."

Bill couldn't hear what the Frank chief was saying, but it was obvious that it was bad news. The New Frankfurt chief was telling Tom, "You remember yesterday I told you I had to do some engine work on the La France? Well, we're doing a complete overhaul on that engine, and it's tore apart and laying all over the bay. I couldn't even tow it there with a team of horses. I was countin' on you to back us up, not t'other way round."

Bill sized up the situation and saw that it would be another hour or more before any other fire company could get to Blackjack. Meanwhile sparks and pieces of burning material were spewing from the fire and drifting around the whole downtown area. He ran out and gathered as many of the firemen as he could find.

"We're not going to get any help on this for a long time. What we have to do now is prevent the rest of the town from burning."

He grabbed three guys and told them, "You three go north along the main street. You three (he pointed at them) go south, and get the owners to get out their hoses and start wetting down their roofs and even the walls, in some cases. If you find no one home or able to do that, you're going to have to do it. Find the hose at the building and do it for them."

He headed back to talk to the chief, but on the way, he looked up at the water tower. He wasn't sure why he looked up, but it may have been just because he was thinking of water and that's where it was. The tower was brightly illuminated by the fire, and when he looked up there, he saw three boys scurrying down the long ladder.

The town water tower looked like a bad patchwork quilt. Every year the senior class painted their class number on it, but they had to sneak up in the middle of the night to do it, and they didn't have time or paint to cover over the previous paint jobs. The boys he saw had probably been up there painting when the fire started. Sure enough, the tower was now displaying the number "63." Oddly, the six was very rounded and the three was a block figure. He guessed that one of the boys had painted the 6 and one the 3 without coordinating style beforehand.

Bill didn't like the odds of the boys getting down unhurt. They seemed to be in a little panic and were trying to get down the long ladder as fast as they could, hoping to get away without being seen. Bill had a fairly good idea who they might be, and he looked around for their fathers. He found one standing there, watching along with the rest of the town.

"George!" Bill yelled. "Your son and his friends are on the water tower. Get on over there and try to talk them down. They look like they're kind of panicky."

George Fedarico started fuming. "I'll get them down all right, but they'll be sorry!"

So Bill said, "George, this is no time to be angry with them. Let's get them down safe first. Tomorrow you can get mad if you want."

At that moment two skyrockets came up from the burning fire house, followed by a rolling explosion, as someone's secret stash of fireworks lit off in twos and threes. Bill shook his head. If there is anything more embarrassing for the fire department than having its own firehouse burn down, it was having the fire fed by illegal fireworks stored there.

Some of the rocket-types were coming dangerously close to the boys as they scurried down the long ladder on the side of the water tower. Now Bill had another problem. They had to get the boys down fast.

Then, one boy, still holding a can of paint in one hand, slipped while dodging a rocket flying past him and fell about two stories. He broke both legs and probably ended his football career, but was otherwise not badly hurt. Now Bill needed an ambulance, but it was caught in the fire too. He explained the problem to the boy's father and helped carry the kid to the bed of the dad's pickup for transportation to the hospital, a twenty-mile ride. Luckily for the boy, he wasn't in great pain yet. That would come a little later.

The teams of roof-wetters that Bill had sent out were working all up and down the street, and no other fires had broken out as yet. Bill headed back to the chief again and found him still on the phone. He pried him loose long enough to tell him about the fireworks and explain what he had done to wet down roofs. Tom nodded his approval and got back on the phone with another fire chief, still trying to get as much help as he could.

Bill figured there wasn't much anyone could do at this point. The station was a goner and all the equipment, besides. Now the only thing anyone could do was put out any new fires that started from this one. He hoped his teams were preventing any new fires.

And they were. By the time the first out-of-town fire company showed up, the fire had burned the station to the ground. There was still plenty of smoldering material to be wetted down, but nothing left to save.

It was a bad night for the fire company. It was even worse than the oft-repeated scenario of a firefighter's chimney fire from burning green wood.

Over the next week, the fire story was the single topic of discussion in

Blackjack. Needless to say, fire authorities from the state capital and city officials convened meetings to discuss the many problems and misfortunes just encountered. A meeting was held with the town council and most of the fire company at the Court House.

All were concerned that this was a black eye for Blackjack.

That was, so far as Bill was concerned, the least of the problems. There was now no fire equipment in town, for starters. He began calling around for used fire trucks.

After Tom had told them what he thought probably lay ahead for them, Doug Jones said, "Tom, I think Bill Just may have saved the whole town last night."

A general murmur from the firemen in the room indicated their agreement.

Bill asked to be allowed to speak. "As a lieutenant in our company, I did what I could, while our chief was getting help from out of town. That's my job, and that's all there is to it."

No one wanted to say to Tom's face that they thought he had been ineffective as chief, but in private discussions, a lot of the guys were saying that maybe Bill ought to be elected chief, despite his relative inexperience.

He wasn't, but Tom retired as chief a few months later. Doug Jones took over, to Bill's great relief. For years thereafter, though, stories of Bill's actions were told and retold with his contribution to saving the town growing with each retelling.

CHAPTER 18

Deadly Serious Business

I TURNED IN MY copy on Bill Just to Mrs. Fritz and went out to find some news or personal interest or advertising or anything to put ink on paper when we went to print. Editors hate blank pages. I stopped by the barbershop as I always did when I needed to find out something going on. I didn't find any action, but I heard someone refer to Rod and Reel. It sounded like he was referring to a couple.

As it turned out, he was, and a spirited discussion followed to inform me of how they came to be called Rod and Reel. Although there wasn't complete agreement, it went about like this:

His name was Rod for Roderick Fisher, an unfortunate choice by his parents, the Fishers, of course. Did they reject Bob, as in bobber? On the adjacent farm lived a cute girl, just a little over a year younger, whose parents had named her Real, pronounced Ray-all, after a heroine in a romance her mother had just read. She was called Real until the day she attended Rod's junior prom as his date. That night she became Reel of Rod and Reel, and it never went away. Had she married anyone else... but no, she married Rod.

I called the Fisher home in town and was greeted by a sleepy voice. It seemed that the Fishers weren't usually up and about at 8:25 in the morning, but Reel was kind enough to ask me over and promised me a cup of coffee and a cinnamon swirl. I arrived there at 8:32. Rod hadn't made it to the kitchen yet.

Judging by Reel's appearance, they must have been in their mid-80s. The house showed a certain lack of close attention. I could see stuff that Reel probably couldn't, such as on countertops and the front of her dress. She was dressed in Midwestern Senior Chic—a flower print dress, hair permed, low-heeled shoes, and the obligatory apron.

She asked me to sit at the table in the kitchen and apologized for not using the dining room table. Through the door, I could see mounds of mail and newspapers on that table and was glad she hadn't tried to clear it off before I got there.

She took an aluminum foil tray full of cinnamon swirls out of the oven, but they were still frozen. She said she must have forgotten to turn on the oven. The coffee was weak.

Rod clumped into the kitchen carrying the daily Lincoln paper. He mumbled a half-hearted greeting to no one in particular and opened the paper to the sports section. He was wearing a flannel shirt, even though the house temperature was nearly 80 out, and his shoes looked like he had farmed in them for forty years. He hadn't shaved for at least three days. He was a big man with huge farmer's hands that looked out of place holding a newspaper instead of driving a combine.

"Rod!" Reel said. "This young man has come to talk to us. Put down that paper!"

"Hmmmph!" Rod responded, continuing to read the paper.

Reel explained, "Rod is a dedicated Cardinals fan. He has to check the scores and box thingies first thing in the morning to see how his precious Cards are doing. Did they win, honey?"

"Box scores," Rod said.

I hadn't thought about what we were going to talk about before I got there, not really having more than a couple of minutes to think. I had no idea what might come from this interview, and now I wondered if anything would. I could write about the names, Rod and Reel, but apparently everyone in town already knew about that.

"What's new with you folks?" I asked, hoping that something would pop up.

"Damn Cards lost to the Reds in the 10th inning" came from behind the paper.

"Nice of you to ask," Reel said cheerily. "Rod and I had a very serious chat about our futures yesterday, and we decided to be cremated upon our passings. Today, I have some forms to fill out. You're going to help me with that. Aren't you, Rod?"

"Nope," Rod said with determination.

"Honey," she said, "we have to make some choices, and I need your help. Did you know they want us to tell them if we have any artificial parts. Of course, you have two artificial knees and one hip. They don't burn up, I guess. I don't know what they do with them."

This was great stuff. Who knew?

Rod suddenly looked alert. "Oh, yeah!" he said. "Dr. Pimpleface, that fourteen year old surgeon, says he wants the last knee back, the one he put in, when I die. Wants to study it or something. Put that down."

"Oh, nuts!" Reel said with a twinkle. "I was planning to use it for a paperweight."

"Make a lousy paperweight anyway," Rod replied and dove back into the sports section. "Cubs won too. Bad day."

"Rod, we have to talk about this; we have decisions to make. It's probably not nice to do this in front of this nice young man (she had clearly forgotten my name), but we have to talk about it."

"Not me," Rod said.

"Yes, you do!" she exhorted.

"No, I don't. We talked about it yesterday, and it made me sad. Don't want to talk about it anymore."

"Why did it make you sad?"

"I don't know."

"Well, neither do I. You're 87 years old, have to take about 50 pills a day, and you know you're going to die someday. Why be sad about it?"

Rod put down the paper with a sigh.

"I guess, because I think you'll be sad. I don't want you to be sad, so I say to myself 'I hope she isn't too sad when I die,' but then I think, 'What if she isn't sad?' That would be sad for me. Of course, I'd be dead and wouldn't know. But then I think of me dying and you not being sad. The kids not being sad. The grandkids not being sad. Tony LaRussa not being sad, for God's sake. The whole Cardinals team not even knowing I died, or caring. Then I get real sad. I don't want to talk about it anymore."

"Wow!" Reel said. "That's the longest speech he's made so far in this century."

I had brought a small tape recorder with me and had set it on the table and turned it on when I first came in. I had meant to mention it to them, but it was probably too late now. And they might not have noticed it, since I don't think either of them could see very well. I was loving this conversation and hoping the recorder was working right.

"Well, honey," she said, oblivious of my presence, "what if I die first?"

"Oh, God!" he cried, letting the sports section slip from his hands. "You wouldn't do that, would you?"

"I might," she said. "Not on purpose or anything, but I might."

"Young fella," he said, looking right into my eyes for the first time, "are you a lawyer or something like that, because I want you to get her to sign a legal document promising not to die before I do."

"No, I'm not," I answered and saw the disappointment on his face.

"He's just being silly," she said to me.

The timer on the stove chimed, and she fetched the heated buns from the oven and placed them on the table.

While she was digging the cinnamon swirls out from the pan, I had a thought.

"Why cremation?" I asked. "Surely land isn't a problem here in Nebraska. Land is what we've got the most of."

Rod lowered the paper, held up his cup for a refill, and stared at me for a few seconds. "The boy's right, mother. Why did we decide to be cremated? The cemetery isn't even half full, and anyway, we've got three plots already paid for."

"Well, we did decide, and just a minute ago, you said you didn't want to talk about it anymore, so let's not go back over old ground," Reel said.

Rod asked, "Where are the kids going to go on Memorial Day if we're just a bunch of ashes. And, anyway, how do you know they'll even be our ashes? What if they just burn up some wood and put the ashes in a jar? How would anyone know?"

"Well, I don't know what you'll do with my ashes, Rod Fisher, but I'm going to put the urn with yours right up there on the mantle. I'll also put some into the ground in our cemetery plot so that I can go out there when I'm lonely and talk to you. I'll bring the sports section and read to you about the Cards."

"Do you think I'll hear you?" Rod asked, with a serious expression on his face.

"Maybe."

"What if I die first and you come out to talk to me a few times, and then you stop coming?"

"Because I died?"

"Maybe, or maybe because you met someone else. If you can talk to my ashes and I can hear you, what would I hear if you had an affair with some other guy?"

"You know, I think you're right," she said. "I don't want to talk about it anymore, either."

I finished my coffee and hurried to the office to write what I thought would be a great story about an old couple facing the inevitable, and I had just enough time to do it. I carried with me a mental image of an artificial knee holding down a pile of papers.

CHAPTER 19

Cecille Gadd

I GOT TO THE Ideal ahead of time. I was hungry, having missed lunch, and I hated being late. The Ideal was filling up with the supper crowd, so I was lucky to get a booth. I really wanted a booth, since I figured that Cecille was more likely to talk candidly if she had some assurance that her words were confined to a booth. Never mind that I was planning to publish them in the paper.

I decided to wait for Cecille before ordering, but I had to eat something, so I ordered some chicken wings and a large Coke. There's nothing like cooking oil and sugar to relieve hunger pangs.

To pass the time, I eavesdropped on the neighboring conversations. I figured that's what reporters are supposed to do, so it would be all right. There were two blue-haired ladies in the booth near me.

One kept saying to the other, "I'm 86 years old."

The other lady replied, "Huh?" the first three times, but the 86-year old was persistent.

A fourth time she said, "I'm 86 years old!"

Her tablemate answered, "I'm from South Dakota."

I quickly looked away so as not to appear to be listening, and I saw her coming in. Cecille actually arrived before the wings, which made me look like a genius. I rose to greet her, surprised at her age, which, from the looks of her, must have been around 60. For some reason, my mental image of her was of a young woman, attractive enough to turn the head of Bill Just, who seemed to be circumspect in all his affairs, except for her.

Not that Cecille was unattractive. She was a tad plump for my taste, but considering her age, she looked pretty good. She was blonde, nicely dressed in a plaid skirt and white blouse, hose and heels, and some lipstick. She hung a light coat on the hook by the booth.

"I guess you must be Ralph Anderson, but how did you recognize me?" she asked.

I didn't know.

"I can't tell you. When you walked in, I just knew it was you. And yes, I am Ralph. Thank you for coming."

"No, it is I who should thank you. Some of the people in this town will say things about Bill and me that they suspect are so, but they don't really know. I frankly welcome the chance to tell you what I can about Bill. He deserves a good write up, and I would like it to be based on truth, not rumors," Cecille said a little bitterly.

I had prepared for this interview carefully. I had written out some questions to make sure I asked them correctly.

"Let's pretend that I never heard of Bill Just or Cecille Hans, OK? Would you—Oh, wait! Here's a menu. I assume you would like to eat while you're here."

"No, I really don't," she replied. "I'll have one of your wings if you offer it to me, and I'll order a ginger ale. I have supper in the fridge at home. I love the food here, but if I eat it, I'll gain five pounds."

I passed the basket of wings to Cecille and summoned a teenage waitress to place her order. I held off ordering my own meal for the time being.

"All right, back to what I was saying. Would you just start at the beginning for me? Who was Bill Just?"

"I'll try. Bill was the nicest man I ever met. He rescued my kids and me when we were down and out after a bad divorce. He let us stay in his house. He said he didn't need the bedrooms we occupied. The idea was that when I got a good job of my own, I would move out. It turned out to be a good deal for both of us. He adored the kids, and they adored him. I contributed to the expenses, such as utilities and repairs, and I did a lot of the cooking and cleaning. When I was at a point where I could move out, Bill asked me to stay."

I thought this was the perfect time to fire my big gun, The Question. "Were you and Bill intimate?"

Cecille looked disappointed in me. "Now, young man, that question is rude, and it's none of your business. I'm not going to discuss it in any way, and if you're going to ask it again, this interview is over."

"I'm sorry," I said softly, giving her my best imitation of naughty puppy eyes, "it's just that everyone in town is asking. You must know that."

"Did you hear what I just said?" she barked. "Last chance, change the subject, or I go." Heads turned in our direction all over the room.

It had started off so well, but things didn't go well after that. I wondered if I should have waited until I had much more material before I asked her the big one. She did agree to think of some of the things Bill had done in and around Blackjack that had so endeared him to the town. She said she would work on it that night.

I wasn't sure she would help me much now. I did find out about her kids, both having graduated from college, but she wouldn't talk about who paid the bills. Finally she said, "Check the VFW," rose, grabbed her coat, and marched out the door.

After she left, I ordered the specialty of The Ideal, the broasted chicken. I had no idea what that meant, and the waitress only told me that they did it in a "broaster." It was good, and I made a mental note to eat there often. It came with chips, the All American Meal. I followed the chicken with a hot fudge sundae. I was still good on my campaign to not consume another vegetable forever.

CHAPTER 20

Rex - The Agency Dog

BILL INHERITED THE INSURANCE agency upon the death of Hank Lindquist and took immediate steps to improve not only its image, but its functioning. He used all the money he had been able to save to make a small addition to the building, and then he borrowed from the Blackjack State Bank to furnish it in a modest but attractive style.

When all the work was completed, upon the advice of Cecille, he held an open house that lasted all day one Saturday in May. Luckily, it was a perfect day, and lots of folks turned out to see the new office and pay their respects to a man now held in very high regard in town. With the weather so nice and for the convenience of the visitors, someone propped the front door open, and it stayed that way until late afternoon.

Cecille kept several crock-pots going with little cocktail wienies in them, and the girls kept busy at the punch bowls, mixing the lime sherbet and ginger ale punch.

No one noticed when it happened, but at some point during the day, a dog wandered in. Some people assumed that he belonged there, and since he looked longingly at their cocktail wienies, they fed him some. The dog decided he liked this place a good deal, with its friendly people and lots of good food. About 3:30 p.m., he found himself getting drowsy and curled up under Bill's desk and took a long nap.

When the day's activities came to an end, he was still there. When Bill left, the dog followed him out of the office and all the way home, pausing repeatedly to leave his mark, but never getting very far behind.

Bill would have denied him access to the house, not knowing the beast or his origin, but the girls were now playing in the front yard and they included the dog in their hopscotch game. He wasn't very good at it, but when they came in, so did he.

He felt very at home in Bill's house, and though repeatedly invited to leave, he decided to stay. He was sitting on the porch the next morning, looking sad and hungry. He was allowed back in and fed, and that was it. He lived there.

Not an attractive animal in any way and of no recognizable breed or breeds, he nonetheless worked his way into their hearts in short fashion. He was roughly the size of a boxer, but looked not at all like a member of that breed, or any other. Ugly might be too strong, but not too far off the mark.

The girls came up with cutesy names for him, but Bill didn't think this big brute with rough origins was likely to answer to those. He settled on Rex, so Rex it was.

Rex turned out to be not just the perfect watchdog for the home, but a business asset as well. For the home, he was there at night after the office was closed. He was a minimal barker, but when he did bark, it was formidable. The single *roarff* that thundered from his throat could be felt through the soles of the feet. No trespasser would be found within a hundred yards of the house after Rex let one loose.

At the agency, he spent the majority of the day curled up at Bill's feet under his desk, when Bill was in the office. If Bill was out, so was Rex, and no one seemed to know where he went. But when he was in, clients immediately warmed to him and were obliged to pet him and scratch his ears, while talking with Bill, and in that mood, they were more likely to conclude a deal. The dog was making the agency money.

The girls often stopped in at the office after school and used the back room to do their homework and use the agency computer. When they left, they usually took Rex home with them, and he patiently participated in their play. No one would have dared mess with those girls when Rex was around.

One of Rex's big fans was Gary Springer, the lawyer with an office next door to the agency. Gary's name wasn't really Springer; it was Sprungstad. After law school, when he showed a proclivity for trial law and managed to spring a few miscreants from the county lockup, people started calling him Springer, and he liked it. It was good for business. Then the Gary was changed to Perry, as in Perry Mason, and after another infamous television show became well known, he became Jerry Springer. Some still called him Perry. A few remembered that his name was actually Gary. But, he answered to all of them.

Springer had met Rex at the open house and, like most everyone, assumed, a few hours prematurely, that he now belonged to Bill. Gary fed Rex about a dozen cocktail wienies during the three hours that he spent at the function, having no particular business that day demanding his attention.

Springer's law practice was something to admire. He wasn't a particularly good lawyer and, in fact, hated the biggest part of his business: deeds and trusts. Those required him to read the tiny print very carefully, looking for traps that would turn out to be unfavorable for his clients.

Gary wasn't a detail man, and he had a tendency to find himself head down on his desk and drooling less than halfway through a deed. So, he had hired a paralegal, although the only qualifications for the title that Carla Patch possessed were the three hours Gary had spent explaining how to read a deed and what to look for. Now Carla did all that reading, for which Gary paid her $7.50 an hour, and she left him notes to explain to his clients. Since Gary usually charged $150 for a settlement and had to pay Carla about $15 for her time, he made out pretty well on the deal.

Gary's true love was courtroom law. He was actually good at it, but there wasn't a lot to go around. Fortunately, there were actually no other lawyers in town who specialized in trials, and none that had his drive to find cases to try.

Every day, at least once, he visited the county lockup to see who might be in a cell. Sheriff McBean didn't mind, and he could stroll in freely at any time. If he found someone locked up there, he would introduce himself, if necessary, and inquire as to the guilt or innocence of the accused in the accused's opinion. Not surprisingly, nearly all had the opinion that they were innocent as newborn lambs.

That being the situation, many were eager for "Jerry Springer" to spring them, and the price was right. Gary would take on a simple case for as little as sixty bucks and let the accused pay him in four fifteen-dollar installments. Gary just wanted to get into court and do his thing.

He was fairly successful at getting most of his clients at least released on bail or time served, so his reputation as a springer was preserved and enhanced.

Sometimes he borrowed Rex during the discovery period more for appearances than for actual investigation. Rex did have a keen nose, and more than once, he found some lost object or clue that helped Gary win freedom for a client.

Once Rex ended up on the other side of the aisle, however. One day, a tousled and slightly drunk man crashed into the agency brandishing a shotgun and demanding money, or at least that's what everyone thought he was demanding. Myrtle Blumquist, Bill's secretary, was typing away, when the guy banged in through the door. She heard him loudly demand something, but before he could get a phrase out of his mouth, Rex hit him full force in the chest. How the dog could have gotten up that much speed in the few feet of runup he had, no one could explain. The man was sent sprawling, and the shotgun went in another direction. The guy fled from the office, leaving the gun behind, with Rex hot on his heels.

The sheriff found him up in a tree with Rex sitting patiently under him, preventing his escape. McBean joked that Rex was his star witness. Gary joked that he would put Rex on the stand and discredit him as a witness. On the day of the trial, Rex sat patiently next to Sheriff McBean. The perp pled guilty, so the greatly anticipated circus never happened. The eighty or so members of the public who had gathered in court that day went home sadly disappointed, and Gary was too.

Rex stayed with Bill and the agency for six and a half years. Since he had appeared seemingly out of thin air, no one had much of a notion as to how old he might be, but after about six years, he started losing it. He became progressively deafer and nearly blind. One day, he went out and never returned, repaying his hosts for room and board by not lingering on in misery or dying in their house.

Once it was clear that Rex was gone for good, Gary felt a great loss, as did everyone at the agency. But it was Gary who produced a portrait of Rex that he had framed and inscribed: *Rex Just, Junior Partner.* It still hangs in the agency front office.

A few days later, Myrtle was vacuuming the office and got up the last of the kibbles from under Bill's desk.

CHAPTER 21

Joe Fritzling

"Back in the sixties, the town had a notorious young prankster who was causing a good deal of concern to the town leaders..."

— *The Blackjack Press*

SUMMER SATURDAY NIGHT IN Blackjack was a busy one for the sheriff. First, there was almost always a concert in the park, and a crowd gathered for that. Not that one would expect trouble from the citizens of this nice, little town at a concert, but it was the way they gathered for it. Despite the fact that there were benches set up all around the band shell, people preferred to sit on blankets on the ground, and even to sit in their cars with the windows rolled down, or sometimes in the back of their pickups. There were often some little fender benders as people jostled for good parking places around the park, and sometimes someone forgot that their kids were sitting on lawn chairs in the bed of the pickup and drove off with them flying around back there.

Then there were the teenagers. Those not playing in the concert had to find something exciting to do. After all, it was Saturday night!

Sheriff McBean was pretty smug about the other aspects of his job. Except for those pesky murders, he had a tight hold on crime in the area.

There was some minor crime, but he almost always solved it in short order and was considered a top-notch law enforcement officer by the town voters and his peers.

What his peers didn't know about was McBean's constant problem with teenagers. Or maybe they did, but since everyone had those and dealt with them without much success, they didn't hold that against their compadre.

It seemed to McBean that there was always one kid who gave him a bunch of trouble, and that kid was a hero to the others who sought to emulate him. It was always a male.

For several years now, his problem had been with Joe Fritzling, the son of the highly esteemed editor of *The Press*. No one seemed to be able to rein in the boy, who was an inventive miscreant and whose exploits were told and retold nearly every week all over town, making him just the sort of role model that McBean didn't want in town.

Joe had one of those personalities that kept him the center of attention wherever he was, but that wasn't good enough for him. If somehow the attention shifted away from him for more than a minute, he had to do something to regain center stage. This made life interesting for his parents and his teachers and, once he was old enough to drive and be out on his own, for Sheriff McBean, as well.

Joe didn't invent the Halloween farm equipment scramble; it had probably gone on since horse and buggy days. However, he did perfect it. Since almost all of his schoolmates were happy to assist on any crazy scheme of his, all he needed to create mayhem was organizational skill and personality. At least he had the personality.

When he got too old to trick or treat, he organized a town-wide theft of farm equipment. The boys, and some of the admiring girls, were given farms to raid. Most of the kids knew how to start up and drive the tractors and harvesters on the surrounding farms. In fact, most of the kids in school lived on those farms.

The kids would go to their assigned farms, sometimes their own, and would get up at one in the morning. They would drive a large piece of farm equipment downtown, right onto Main Street, and park it in such a way as to obstruct traffic. The most obstructed traffic was going to be the farm equipment reclaimed by the farmers in the morning. They would spend hours untangling the mess. And then they'd do it again the next year.

Every year, tongues would cluck, and folks would say, "Why don't they guard it that night so they don't have to go through this?" But many suspected the answer was that the farmers got as big a kick out of it as the boys, and they had probably done it themselves when they were that age. They had a good time seeing everyone else's gear, plus socializing with their neighbors at the obstruction. Some even managed to spend a few hours in El Toro, while waiting to get their rigs headed back to the farm. Everyone knew Joe was the miscreant, and he got into a lot of trouble, but he didn't mind that.

One Saturday, he went to a new extreme. This new escalation bothered the Sheriff McBean, who now felt he absolutely had to act decisively on this one, but realistically, what could he do? Every time he tried to punish Joe, it just seemed to spur him on. In another year or two, Joe would be off to college, and he would be someone else's problem. Maybe he should just let it ride and wait until Joe moved on.

But, that Saturday, it went beyond the limit of what McBean could tolerate. After directing a little traffic at the park, the sheriff parked his patrol car on Main Street to keep an eye on the teen drivers who would be cruising up and down, looking for something to do and showing off by squealing their tires and speeding through town.

It was a warm night, and he had the windows down. That helped both with the temperature in the car and with his ability to hear approaching trouble. In his rear view mirror, he saw the big, red Cadillac approaching slowly and wondered what Joe was up to. He wasn't tearing through town in his usual fashion; in fact, he was going too slowly. Something must be up.

The Caddy was the most distinctive car in town. It was the only Cadillac in the county. Not just the sheriff, but every person in town, knew it when they saw it and knew whose it was. Joe continually pulled pranks from that car and seemed to want everyone to know that he was the culprit. People said he wanted to get caught, and he always was, so maybe they were right.

McBean had no desire to do something drastic, such as charge him with a crime, though he could have done so on many occasions. The boy had a bright future, and a criminal record could end that before it began. But that meant that adults had to invent punishments with the goal of deterring future such behaviors, and so far, he hadn't found one that was effective. So, as he watched the Caddy approaching ever so slowly, he had a sense of foreboding.

Joe pulled up beside him and stopped for a brief second. Joe lit the fuse on a cherry bomb, tossed it into McBean's lap, and then sped off laughing. The other boys in the car were practically wetting themselves as the big car exited the small town and continued up the highway.

McBean acted instinctively, grabbing the firecracker and hurling it toward the far window. It didn't make it. His hurried toss was a little high, and the bomb bounced back, landing on the passenger seat, where it went off almost deafening the sheriff and tearing up the seat.

McBean already had the siren on and was in pursuit. He caught Joe and the hysterical boys within 5 miles. Not that it mattered much, he knew who they were and where they lived.

He called Irma Fritzling from his car phone. "Irma, I'm bringing Joe and his buddies back into town in my patrol car. Your car is out at the intersection with County Road 1146 about 5 miles east of town. You can get your car anytime you want, but I suggest you do it now."

Later, he pleaded with Mrs. Fritz to get her son under control, but she just raised her hands in mock surrender. "I'll have a serious talk with him, ground him for two weeks, and make him pay for the repairs to the damaged seat," she told him.

The sheriff held out little hope that there wouldn't be similar exploits in the future. He could only pray that Joe would be sent off to military school or would get early admission to college and, in any case, leave town.

That couldn't come soon enough.

The sheriff knew deep down in his bones that it was Joe who had bombed his house last summer, but he couldn't prove it and Joe had an alibi. Alibi or not, it had to be Joe along with his buddies. No one else was as determined to embarrass the lawman or as clever in getting away with it, at least for a little while, until the need for notoriety caused Joe to make his participation known.

Sheriff McBean and the missus had been enjoying a quiet weekday evening at home, when they heard a loud explosion, followed in short order by nine more. They weren't actually counting, but both agreed when they thought about it later that they had heard ten explosions.

Not one to run headlong into an artillery barrage, Sheriff McBean told his wife to get into the bathroom and lock the door while he investigated. He strapped on his pistol belt, chambered a round in his drawn revolver, and went cautiously out the back door. Finding no one, he then moved carefully around the house. No one was there, but he could smell the burned powder from the explosions. He went back into the house at the front door and turned on the porch light. He could see ten large, burned spots in his front lawn and knew they had to be the result of the explosions, whatever those had been.

He treated the lawn as a crime scene, examining it carefully with his strong police flashlight. He could find almost nothing from the explosions, except a few fragments of paper from the outside of firecrackers, big ones, probably M-80s. Joe Fritzling! It had to be.

So he drove quickly to the Fritzling house a half-mile away. The Caddy was in the carport, hood over the engine warm, but not hot. Perhaps Joe wasn't back home yet. He rang the bell, and Mrs. Fritz came to the door.

"Evening, Irma," he said. "Is Joe home by any chance?"

"Yes, he is, Jackie. Do you want to talk to him?"

"Maybe, but if you don't mind, let me ask you, has he been here long?"

"I think he came in about three quarters of an hour ago, maybe longer. We've been watching Lawrence Welk, and he came in right after the show went on."

"Well, then, never mind, Irma. The fella I'm looking for would have been at my house twenty minutes ago. Sorry to have bothered you."

Mrs. Fritz smelled a news story, but McBean wasn't passing out any information.

He never did find out how Joe had done what he was sure Joe had done. In fact, he prayed that it was Joe, because if it wasn't, there was now a copycat Joe in town, and he didn't need any more Joes.

The next Monday it was the talk of the school. Joe enjoyed the hero worship, but he didn't want to spread the word while the sheriff was still angry. His problem was that he had an accomplice, his buddy Buck. If Sheriff McBean had stepped into the living room, he would have found Joe and Buck pretending to enjoy the Lawrence Welk show. Buck was enjoying the notoriety more than Joe, but he wouldn't have gotten any credit for his part in it if he hadn't told a few of the guys what he and Joe had done and how they had done it.

Joe and Buck had grown tired of simply throwing M-80s into people's garbage cans or chicken houses, although that was always good for a laugh. You almost always got caught when you did that, and Joe was sort of on parole from both his mother and the sheriff right now. He had to avoid getting caught while the heat was on. So the two of them began experimenting with delay fuses, and they hit upon a perfect solution: cigarettes. They found out that if you lit a cigarette and then stuck the M-80 fuse into the other end, it would take about ten minutes or more for the fire to reach the fuse. Their experiments also showed that the M-80s blew away almost all of the evidence. No traces of cigarettes could be found, unless you got stupid and bought filtered cigs.

On the night in question, they simply lit and then placed the delay-fused crackers, went to Joe's, and sat with his mom, until the sheriff came by and decided he couldn't pin it on them.

By the time school was out, every kid in school knew about it. No one told the sheriff.

CHAPTER 22

Grandpa Larsen

A FEW MONTHS AFTER Bill had come to Blackjack, an older man came to town one day asking about him. He had taken the precaution of bringing a picture of the boy he was searching for, although it had been taken four years earlier.

Oly Larsen had been in Blackjack a few times in the past, but hardly knew where to start. He decided to try the high school, since he knew that Bill wanted to continue his education. The school secretary looked at the picture and said, "No, don't know him, and we don't have any William Larsen in school here."

Oly asked, "Are you sure?"

That was a bad question to ask Dolly Mason. She took enormous pride in knowing every kid in the school. She took a long look at the old, weather-beaten, skinny-as-a-rail farmer and asserted her authority.

"Mr. Larsen, if you think the boy is in town, your best bet will be to ask the kids after school. You'll find them at either the library or The Ideal Dairy Bar," she said officiously.

Some of the kids at The Ideal weren't eager to rat out their new buddy, but others who hadn't yet become friends with Bill willingly told the man that he was in town, but that his name was supposed to be Bill Just. No one had any idea where he might be at that time of day, but they told the man, who said he was Bill's grandfather, where he was living.

When Bill returned from working at the Stringer farm that evening, he saw his grandfather's old car parked in front of his house. He wasn't sure how to proceed from there. Obviously, his grandfather now knew where he was, and he wasn't prepared to keep running unless he really had to. He thought that it was unlikely that Granddad would take him home forcibly, so he went up to the car and tapped on the window. Granddad woke up from his nap and grinned broadly.

"Billy!" he shouted, although from inside the closed car, only a muffled sound escaped to Bill's ears. Mr. Larsen flung open the car door and jumped out, still spry at the age of 72. He wanted to give Bill a big hug, maybe even a kiss, but his Scandinavian habits kept him from doing that. Instead, he slapped Bill on the back and jabbed him in the ribs. Bill laughed.

They walked to the house and sat down in Bill's living room. Bill fetched a Coke from the refrigerator and asked, "Would you like some supper?"

"Well, we have to eat something. Maybe we should go out." It hurt Granddad to even suggest eating out. He hadn't eaten in a restaurant more than ten times in his life.

Bill knew that his grandfather didn't have spare money for meals out, or if he did, he would think it a frivolous expense. He said, "No, I've got some TV dinners in the freezer. Let me heat them up for us."

While they were waiting for the dinners to warm up, his grandfather told him, "Billy, your dad is dead."

Bill was stunned. He wouldn't miss the old tyrant, but he hadn't expected this. "What will my mom do?" he asked.

"She's not well herself," Granddad explained. "She could go into a home at her age. You remember your grandma, of course."

Bill nodded.

"A few years ago, the doctor put her into one of those homes, for old folks, you know, in Fremont. She didn't stay long."

"I can't go back, Granddad," Bill said.

"I know," was all his grandfather replied.

They talked about all the things farmers talk about: the weather, the crops, the price of corn and wheat, news of the neighbors, etc. Granddad lived over 20 miles away from Bill's home farm, but he knew some things about the neighboring farms anyway.

"Billy, if you ever need a place to go, you come to me, hear?"

"Sure, Granddad, and thanks."

After he finished his beef slices with mashed potatoes and mixed vegetables, Oly Larsen drove away into the darkness. Bill felt more alone than ever. But he also felt as if he had abandoned his family. He had always wanted a family, a real family, where the people loved each other. If his parents loved him, he had no way of knowing it. He thought that he probably did love them once, but after years of mistreatment by his father and no defense by his mother, he just lived with them and longed for the day he could get away.

Now that he had gotten away, he wasn't going back.

CHAPTER 23

Cecille Tries Again

W HEN I ENTERED THE house by my backdoor route, I found a note taped to the glass in the door. It told me to call Cecille Gadd. I was a little surprised, since our first meeting had ended on such a bad note. I used the new cell phone I had talked my publisher into buying for me to call Cecille.

She started off with an apology. "I shouldn't have gotten so angry with you," she said. "I know you had to ask those things, but it always gets my goat. If you would like, we can talk some more. In fact, if you want, you can come over to the house for an hour or so. I really want to tell you the real Bill Just story."

"Can you give me some idea of what we'll talk about?" I asked.

Cecille said, "I remembered something today that I thought was so typical of Bill that I wanted to tell it to you."

"I'm listening," I said.

"We had a bird trapped in the house one time. It was a tiny little bird. Bill knew what kind it was, but I didn't. It was too scared to fly out any of the windows we opened for it. It got very weak after a time. Bill walked up to it, talking softly, and he gently picked it up, took it to an open window, and let it go. The amazing thing, and I'm still not sure I believe it, even though I saw it myself, was that after that, whenever Bill was out in the yard, that little bird would come sit on a branch near him and sing and sing. I think he knew that Bill was the one who had saved him."

"Wow," I said, also not knowing whether to believe it. I was no longer sure I wanted to talk with Cecille. It was clear that she wanted to influence my article, and I didn't feel good about that. I decided that, for the time being, I would try to get by with what she had given me so far. The rest of the story that I wanted was the one she wouldn't give me, and that was the one that would sell papers and set tongues to clucking all over the county, regardless of what it turned out to be.

Then she apparently had a new inspiration. She said suddenly, "There's another story I would like you to hear."

"Go ahead," I said, a little reluctantly.

"I think this will give you some more insight into Bill. You know how all kids decide they don't like certain foods? Well, most kids, anyway. My kids weren't fussy eaters most of the time, but every now and then they would decide they didn't like something—sometimes something they had liked just fine before. That happened one day when I made a dish out of hamburger and added some mushrooms to it. They had always eaten mushrooms before, but that day, Tiffany, the older girl, pushed her plate away and declared that mushrooms were "gross and icky." Of course, her younger sister immediately joined the mushroom boycott, and they had peanut butter toast for supper that night.

"The next morning, as I was leaving for work at the Piggly, Bill said, 'Please pick up a couple of pig ears from the meat department tonight.' I did, having no idea what he wanted to do with them. I certainly didn't know how to cook them or eat them, but I brought two pig ears home and Bill put them in the freezer. A few nights later, I got a good deal on some ground lamb, something we had never had before. I made some patties out of the meat and served it with mint jelly. It was really quite good. The girls revolted again and said it tasted like wool. Bill said, 'That's quite all right, ladies. We have a substitute for you any time you don't like what you've been served,' and with that, he put the pig ears on their plates.

"They sat there looking at those pig ears, not knowing what to do. Bill said, 'Take your choice, the nice lamb patties your mother has cooked, and I think they're really good, or the pig ears.'

"The girls decided to try to lamb, and after a few bites, they realized it wasn't so bad after all. We kept those ears in the freezer and brought them out whenever the girls didn't want to eat what I had fixed. I don't think we used them more than four or five times, and when we did, the girls almost always ended up eating my dinner.

"That's an example of how clever Bill was at dealing with problems. No fuss, no crying, no shouting."

I told her, "I need some time to go over what I have now and see what more I need. Can I call you back tomorrow?"

"Yes, of course," Cecille replied. "Let me give you my number at work so you can reach me during the day."

I suspected that Cecille had been thinking through a lot of things she wanted to tell me. She had probably been making a list of people she remembered had been helped by Bill over time and it was while she was doing that, that she realized she wanted to talk to the young reporter some more to make sure he would do a good job of making Bill out to be the hero she believed him to be.

Cecille's reminiscences had surely made her intensely sentimental, and she was missing Bill again and dreading a future without him. She may also have come to realize that her opinion of Bill was so colored by her own personal relationship with him, her love for him, she couldn't deny, that it was hardly unbiased. Still, if she could convince this young reporter that, no matter what he might uncover or suspect, Bill Just was a wonderful person, she would be happy.

I later learned that it had all begun thirty-some years before. Her rotten husband had beaten her for the umpteenth time, but he had also hit the children this time, so she took the children and left. She had no idea where to turn. They stayed in the little fleabag motel outside of town, until her checks started bouncing and they were thrown out. Then they had gone into town, looking for a place to stay, at least for a few days until she could get a job. By nighttime, she was faced with spending the night on a bench in the Court House Square.

Bill had walked by and asked her what she was doing out there at that time of night. She told him her story, and he took them home with him.

Bill's rancher, that had replaced the old house, had four bedrooms, and he had beds in three of them, not because he needed them, but because they were there when he bought the house. Cecille and her two children were able to make comfortable sleeping arrangements for the night without difficulty. Bill went to The Ideal and brought home the famous broasted chicken, fries, and slaw. While he was out he stopped at the Piggly Wiggly and bought children's cereals and Pop Tarts.

The next morning, he fed them breakfast and sat down with Cecille to try to solve her problem. What could she do? How would she take care of the kids if she was working? There were no good answers.

Bill had gotten Cecille a job at the Piggly as a checkout clerk. It didn't pay much, but with no working experience outside the home, Cecille had little to offer an employer. The grocery store manager wouldn't have hired her if Bill hadn't pleaded with him. She suspected that he must have owed Bill for something or he never would have taken her.

She was a good worker and surprisingly good at whatever job she was given. She managed the bakery section for nearly ten years. Meanwhile, her daughters grew up and became more independent.

Bill recognized that Cecille was smart, just not well educated. She had married while still in high school, and was not allowed by her school to continue after she got pregnant, so she had no high school diploma. This was an obstacle, but it was one that Bill had faced himself. Of course, joining the Army wasn't really a viable choice for a young mother with two children, so she and Bill had to come with a better alternative. Bill insisted that she needed to pursue her education. She couldn't afford it, but he was happy to help.

All this time, she had been staying with him. After a year or so, she was making enough money to go out on her own. She could not have lived well on her grocery store pay, but there were cheap places available in town. Bill was against it, though. He felt that the most important thing was becoming educated, and he convinced her to use her money to get an associate's degree. She pursued an accounting degree, because Bill knew that the one accountant in town had more business than he could handle. Gilbert Geiger, known to everyone in town as Geiger the Counter, was the accountant for the insurance agency. He was always late with his reports, and they were often full of careless errors. The town needed a competent accountant, and she was pulling straight A's in her accounting classes.

Geiger hired her, but she didn't stay with him for long. With Bill's encouragement, and with the security of having a place to live (his), she started her own bookkeeping service. Soon, she took many of Geiger's unhappy customers. Within a couple of years, it was profitable, and she no longer needed to sponge off Bill.

Many times, she offered to move out of Bill's house and live on her own, and every time, Bill talked her out of it. They both knew that the whole town was gossiping about that, and they had quit caring.

She often thought about Bill's life and how starved for affection he must have been. He got none at home apparently, and then he moved to a town where he didn't know anyone. He was lucky to meet Kenny right away, who became a lifelong friend, but Kenny had a life of his own. He went off for college and employment, not returning to his hometown for many years.

Bill had told her once, in an unusually open mood, about his first encounter with a girl his own age. He never told her the name, since that girl, now grown, was still in town. Cecille watched Bill's interactions with the town females of his vintage and had not been able to determine which one it was.

Bill said he was still new in town, but he was already living in the house he later bought. He had been flirted with by a nice girl that he would not name. One night, she showed up at the house with a bottle of vodka and some cranberry juice. She made the two of them some cocktails, and they drank them like water. They had no experience with alcohol and didn't realize how drunk they were getting.

It appeared to Bill that she had every intention of spending the night with him, since her parents were out of town. He didn't know what to do, but he thought that it might be a lot of fun. However, they both got drunk fast. Bill got sick to his stomach and spent about ten minutes bending over the toilet emptying his stomach. He was lucky that he got as much out as he did, and he was still very drunk. The girl staggered to his bed while he was barfing, and she passed out. Eventually Bill also passed out on the bed, so technically they slept together, but they actually had almost no physical contact except when one of them rolled next to the other.

When he told Kenny about it a couple of days later, Kenny asked about "protection," mostly from pregnancy. Bill hadn't thought of that, but Kenny had been cautioned by his father about girls who might want to get pregnant to force a marriage. Kenny was definitely a good catch. Bill, maybe not so much at that time, but still…

The thought of getting so sick turned Bill into a non-drinker for life. Just a whiff of booze would make him feel woozy. The thought of a pregnant girlfriend made him extremely leery of all friendly girls, which, of course, made him a wonderful challenge for the girls. But, he wasn't playing that game, no matter how much he craved it. Too bad he didn't stick to that.

Although this was all great insight into the man, Bill Just, it wasn't going to be written or published.

I thought, *Now Bill is dead, and everyone wants to know the answer to that old mystery. Why had they lived together all that time without marrying?* I guessed that Cecille had wondered that a million times herself. Maybe some of the explanation was in stories that no one would ever read in *The Press*.

CHAPTER 24

Cecille's Diary, July 16

Two days ago, Bill died. I have been in a state of confusion and concern ever since. Of course, now the question of our relationship is on everyone's mind, and even the new reporter for *The Press* is asking me about it. I have never really told the story to anyone, perhaps not even to myself. I hope that writing about it will help me, and maybe, just maybe, I'll tell others. Probably not.

The questions on everyone's mind are why did we live together for all those years and not marry? Did we love each other? Were we "intimate?"

The last one is easy. Of course, we were. We would have to have been dead or sick or something not to be.

Did we love each other? I think so. I loved Bill. I would have married him if he had asked me, which, obviously, he didn't. Why didn't he ask me?

That was something I lived with for many years without a true understanding, but I think I can explain it now. After so many years and so much thought about it, I have come to realize that it was my fault as much as his. He would never ask, but I could have and maybe he would have married me if I had pursued it. And maybe not. That was the fear I had that kept me from asking. If I did and he declined, then what?

But why didn't he ask me? I think he loved me, as I said. I don't know that for sure, because he never said so, and his acts of love toward me were not so different from his acts of kindness to many others in our little community.

Of course, I had known about his past and that he considered himself already married, but he lived with me! Some people thought that Bill was a cold fish. They thought he might be incapable of expressing emotion of any kind and that included love. They were very wrong about that. But, women want affection from their lovers, and Bill came up pretty short in that department. He enjoyed the intimate acts, I know that, but he never said so and he never said so much as that he liked me. He never brought me candy or flowers or a Valentine's Day card or anything like that. He never bought me jewelry. His idea of a great present was a new iron or a cake mix. Who would love a man like that besides me?

I think I know where that came from. He grew up with a father who treated him badly and expressed no affection for him. His mother was apparently so cowed by the man that she did little to make Bill feel loved at home. Their farm was remote enough that he had little interaction with others except at school. When his father pulled him out of school at 16, he saw his world collapsing and ran away. He never made contact with his mother again, and his father died shortly after he left. In other words, he grew up in a world without love, and it hardened his heart. No, that's not right; he had a big heart. He learned not to get too close to people, because his home experiences had taught him that it only led to disappointment.

Some men would have overcome that and become loving adults, but something kept Bill from doing that. He did become a wonderful member of the community, and it was in helping others that he expressed his love. As I said, I got that from him too, but it was just the same as total strangers got.

Interestingly, there was only one person in town, or really anywhere, that Bill seemed to be genuinely fond of, Ken Jackson. Ken left for college just a few years after Bill arrived, but Bill has never forgotten the friendship that Ken showed him when he came to town. He has sought ways to repay him for that ever since.

So, even if Bill never verbally expressed a love for me, I was certain that he loved me, and I got by with that.

The first test, I guess, was our first intimacy. Usually he spent evenings in the library while I got the kids to bed, but one night he stayed home after supper. He had noticed that I was depressed from a bad day at work. I had just started working in the office of the town's only CPA, and he had raked me over the coals that afternoon for a minor error. He made mistakes daily that I corrected for him, but I made one little mistake and he inferred that I was stupid and incompetent.

After supper, Bill told me to just relax, while he did the dishes and got the kids ready for bed. After they were in bed, I felt better, and I went over to him and kissed him. He was obviously aroused, so I kept kissing him and then led him to my bedroom. I woke up around 2 a.m., and he was back in his own bed. That was the pattern our lovemaking followed from then on. I initiated it, and he left my bed during the night.

Bill put me on my feet—something I am eternally grateful for. I don't know what would have become of me if he hadn't. After I got some education and turned it into a good job, and later into my profession, he still supported me in many ways. We worked out an arrangement for sharing expenses in the house, but if I had never paid a penny, I doubt that he would have said anything. My share was little enough that I was able to save some money. Bill paid most of the expenses of educating my kids, and since that was what I had been saving for, my savings remained intact. I used them to start my own accounting firm, even though I am not a CPA. I am doing well with that. I'm not rich, but I have money in the bank and can afford whatever I need.

There, I do feel better now that I've written all of this. For over thirty years, I haven't been able to talk to anyone about it and haven't even written in my diary about it.

No one has mentioned it to me, and I haven't even thought of it until right this minute, but what will happen to Bill's house now? Did he have a will? I don't know. Perhaps I am about to be homeless. Of course, I can afford to buy a house in this town. Real estate here is cheap. Maybe I should take this opportunity to leave for a bigger town or city. We'll see what happens with Bill's estate. I'll take that as a sign for what I ought to do. He has always guided me in the right direction, and I believe he will now too.

CHAPTER 25

Cecille's Diary, July 17

CHARLIE GLITTENBERG CALLED ME at work today and asked me to drop by his office when I could, but he made it clear that he wanted it to be today. I went by during lunch, but he was out, so I went back during the afternoon. He said he was Bill's attorney, which was something I didn't know. He also said that he was named as executor for Bill's will. I didn't even know he had one. He told me that Bill had left the house and an amount of money to me. He couldn't tell me how much money it would be, because there would be expenses that have to be deducted, but the way he talked about it, he made it sound like it was a lot.

I'm a little surprised by all of this, but not surprised that Bill had money. He was so smart and worked so hard. He was also very generous, and I guess I had assumed that he had given much of his money away, or would do it in his will. He probably hadn't thought he would die so young and would have more time to decide where his money should go. If it turns out to be a lot of money, it will certainly make my life interesting. For one thing, I will have to live a life that I think Bill would want for me, but I don't really know what that would be. It seems that Bill is still challenging me.

P.S. Jul 29th

Today, I found a sealed envelope attached to a copy of Bill's will. He had left the will with me a few years ago, and I had almost forgotten it. When I thought of it today, I remembered where I had put it and decided to look at it to see if it agreed with the one Charlie was using. It did, so there was no news there, but this was attached:

My dear Cecille,

I'm sorry that I was so bad about expressing my love for you. You know that I was raised in a loveless house, and it remains difficult for me to express my emotions. I've tried to compensate for that by helping people, such as yourself, but I'm sure it's not the same thing. I've let you down.

Of course, we never meant to be "lovers," though obviously we were. At first, it may have been convenience more than love, but it grew into something else and I could never say it to you. I'm sorry, I'm sorry, I'm sorry.

Now that I'm dead, since you probably won't see this until then, I can say it. I think that's odd too, as I'm sure you do, but after all these years together, you know me as well as I know myself.

Let me say how proud I am of you and your girls. Our girls. But, especially of you. You came from nowhere to become a successful and admired businesswoman. I was happy to play a small part in that, and as I write this, I'm immensely proud of you. Since I am probably gone now, you will be on your own, and you can more than handle that. Congratulations. You're smart and hard-working and beautiful too. You're dynamite! And I love you.

You have blessed my life for many years. Thank you.

Bill

After a good cry and then another, I called that young reporter from the paper. I told him to get a six pack and a pizza and come over, we could talk. He was there so fast he must have already ordered the pizza for himself.

We ate the pizza and drank the beer, and with a full stomach and a couple of beers, I felt ready to talk. Ralph asked me what I would do now.

"I don't know exactly," I said. "I will own the house without a mortgage, so my expenses will be minimal. Bill left me money, so no problems there. There will be some expenses I didn't have before, such as utilities, but that's not a big deal. I'm making good money at my business, but don't put that in the paper, you hear me?"

"Yes, ma'am," he said.

"What's with the 'ma'am' all of a sudden?" I asked.

"I don't know. It seems that you're mature. Don't get me wrong, that's a good thing, while I'm not. You're a success in your business, and I'm not anything yet. I guess I think I owe you respect."

"Well, thank you, Ralph, but let's keep it the way it was. You call me Cecille, and I'll call you Ralph, Okay?" I said.

Of course, he agreed. But then he got to the more personal questions I guess I had just given permission to ask. Did I think I would marry someone else? Would I stay in Blackjack now that Bill was gone?

For the first time, I felt the loneliness of being alone. And it took this kid to make me feel it. How did he know just what buttons to push? My girls are grown up and will have families of their own. Will I be alone for the rest of my life? Nice going, Ralph.

I poured out my guts to him. I sure hope he doesn't put all of that in the paper for the whole town to read.

CHAPTER 26

Bill's Funeral

SATURDAY MORNING STARTED OUT damp, dark, and gloomy. When I awoke and looked out, it reminded me of some of the things I had just learned about the weather on the plains. Warm, damp air from the Gulf of Mexico collided with cold air from Canada to create, at best, soaking rains, and at worst, tornados. Today was looking like a good one for the farmers, although from listening to the weather and farm reports on TV, it seemed that no weather situation was viewed as good by the farmers. It was always too dry or too wet, too cold or too hot.

While eating breakfast, I glanced at my pocket calendar and was surprised to see that Bill's funeral was that day. I had almost forgotten what day it was.

I pieced a number of things about that day together later. This is how it went:

Cecille looked out at the threatening rain and wondered if anyone would come to Bill's funeral. *Maybe to the church,* she thought, *but to the cemetery?* Then she wondered what she could do with her hair in this dampness. She had spent considerable time planning her wardrobe for the day. She knew, of course, that it was customary to wear black to funerals as a show of mourning, but she had nothing appropriate in black. Instead, she had set out a navy suit she often wore to work, with a white silky blouse and a set of faux pearls.

Pastor Jansen at the Lutheran Church went over his remarks about Bill again. This was an easy one, since Bill had many friends and a resume full of good works. He thought he should ask if others would like to say something, but that was when he would lose control of the service. He hated losing control of services almost as much as he hated dead space, or "white space," as he called it. Something had to be happening at all times or the service seemed to lag, losing forward momentum. But people standing up, sometimes going up to the pulpit, to speak randomly? That was almost more than he could stomach in his church. He also wondered if the hay-bale church would be able to hold all of those who would want to attend.

Irma Fritzling picked out another bright red dress for the funeral and some blazing red fingernail polish to touch up her nails. She put on a chartreuse warmup suit for now, since she needed to go into *The Press* to check the wire services before she got dressed up. She looked like a Granny Smith apple in her green suit.

At the new fire station, Doug Jones, the long-time chief, formed up an honor guard of volunteer fire-fighters to serve as pallbearers and color guard. He found that some of the men didn't have complete uniforms, and he would have to make some calls to try to find missing pieces. That's the way it was with volunteers, he was thinking. In fact, he hadn't had a uniform himself until he was elected Chief. He hadn't wanted to be Chief and had nominated Bill Just, but Bill said he didn't have the time it would take and that he really was one of the least trained and experienced men in the department. Bill was like that. He was always modest and willing to serve as an Indian when he could have served as a chief. Doug knew just what he would say if given a chance to speak at the funeral.

At The Ideal, Johnny Jackson was busy with the breakfast crowd and trying to find time to write out instructions for the staff to follow while he was at the funeral. He was anxiously awaiting Ken's arrival from the community college, where he was a director/producer at the public television station. Johnny hoped the weather would hold off long enough for Ken and his family to get to Blackjack.

Joe Fritzling slept fitfully though the morning. He needed his rest for a big Saturday night ahead. The night before he had driven in from Kansas and brought a big box of fireworks. He was dreaming about something on the order of the 4th of July, 1976, something he had only seen replayed on TV.

At 10 a.m., Sheriff McBean arrived at the church in a new cruiser with the huge light bar. This was not Jackie McBean, who had retired at the age of 68; this was his daughter, also named Jackie McBean. She had married a guy named Smith, but he was gone and she was McBean again. She suspected that parking was going to be a major hassle and that a lot of people would park along the street, causing all kinds of congestion. No one in town was used to having to wait for traffic except for when a semi or farm truck would back up to the feed store blocking Second Street. Then they just had to drive around the block to avoid it. There probably wasn't anything McBean could do about the impending traffic mess, but being there, looking official next to the cruiser with the lights flashing, was both expected and good for her reputation.

The first arrivals, other than the sheriff, were those who had driven in from long distances and had allowed more time than necessary just to be sure. There were people driving up that McBean didn't recognize

The fire department honor guard showed up on the fire truck. They had to be ready to go if an alarm should sound. They looked great in their now-complete uniforms, despite some fitting problems, especially around the waists.

Parking the fire truck so that it could get out, if called, turned into a project. Doug drove the truck into the parking lot, but he could see that it was probably going to fill up and worried about maintaining an unobstructed route out.

"Jackie!" he called out to the sheriff. "Can you keep a clear path outta here for us, in case we get called out?"

"I can't promise that, Doug," the sheriff replied. "Why don't you take it down the street a ways and put some cones out in front to keep some space for getting out?"

After some negotiations, that was what Doug did. The firemen who were to serve as pallbearers lined up in front of the door awaiting the arrival of the hearse. The color guard continued to practice off to one side. The manual of arms that they once knew no longer worked very well, since they had to move their rifles around protruding bellies that hadn't been there years before.

A light drizzle began to fall. People arriving scurried into the church, squeezing by the firemen who now crowded the entryway. The town folk poured in and took all the room in the pews. People were standing along the walls on the sides and back of the sanctuary. Luckily, the entire fire department was involved in the service, so no fire marshal was available to invoke a maximum occupation rule.

As expected, lots of people wanted to talk about Bill, and the service went 40 minutes overtime. Then everyone went out to the cemetery, despite the rain, which the earlier drizzle had become. The graveside service went better than Doug could have hoped, and everyone was impressed. Then, it was back to the church for a reception.

The ladies of the church had prepared all the usual delicacies, including cheese balls, spreads for Ritz Crackers, and any number of casseroles made from mushroom soup and chicken or hamburger. Everyone had a wonderful time telling stories about Bill and all the things he had done in town, and it didn't cost any of the ladies more than ten dollars for the things they had prepared. Nearly every woman in the church had baked a cake, so most of them had to take half a cake home with them. There was so much food going back to houses that Johnny Jackson thought he might as well close The Ideal the next day.

I took so many notes that I knew I could write a great article with what I had. I was tempted to start writing, but some things I had heard made me think there was a story here that I hadn't found yet. I went back to the library, the place where the spirit of Bill Just seemed to dwell, for inspiration.

One name had come up several times during the reception, and when

I got to the library, I tried to remember it. Unfortunately, I hadn't taken a note on it. What I remembered was that this fella was one who did whatever he did to extremes all the time. I asked Mary, and she knew immediately whom I was thinking of: Karl Lintzen. She went to the phone book and gave me his phone number. The next day, I called him, and after three or four tries, I finally did connect with him at home. It was fairly late in the evening, and I guess he had finally come home from whatever he had been doing before. We agreed to meet the next day, a slow day for him, I guess, at The Ideal for broasted chicken.

Karl was a truly German "Aryan" specimen, with light-colored hair, some blond/some grey, pale skin, tall, and slender. Well, the slender part was untypical.

I asked, "How do you keep in such good shape, Karl?" Again, I was taking liberties by using his first name, but he didn't object.

"I used to play a lot of sports, but now injuries have wiped most of that out. What was common to them all was running. They've got that "Rails to Trails" trail out there where the railroad tracks were. It's not finished yet, so it's kind of rough in places, but I can navigate on it if I'm careful. I go out there on my lunch hour, four days a week, and run. I just run until I can't run anymore, and then I have to run back, so it's a pretty good workout."

"I guess I'm taking you off the track today, then?" I asked.

"No, today's my day off from running. Tomorrow, I'm joining the guys in Bison for a club run, and so I'm resting today."

"How do you stack up against the Bison guys?" I asked.

"Oh, I beat them most of the time, although I'm older than most of them. So I'm going to try out for the Senior Olympics to find more competition."

"This is great stuff, Karl," I said. "What else do you do that's interesting?"

"Listen," he said, "I actually didn't realize you were a reporter when I agreed to this… interview, I guess. I don't like publicity; in fact, I hate it. Please don't write about this. Okay?"

I had to agree. It wasn't worth antagonizing him just for the story, and

I had a feeling that he would turn this and other things into bigger stories if I could just wait. But I kept the conversation going just to see what else there might be that I could use.

Somehow, the subject of beer came up.

"My sons gave me a beer-making kit for Christmas, and I made my first batch of beer that night," he said. I had some experience with beer making myself, since the guys I lived with while in college made beer and I joined in with them. It beat buying it. The first thing I learned was to let the beer age for at least two weeks, sometimes longer, before drinking it. I mentioned this to Karl.

"Oh, yeah, that's what everyone tells me," he said. "But I can't wait that long. In fact, no batch of beer has lasted me long enough for me to find out if it gets better."

"You mean a batch of beer, that's five gallons, I assume, is completely gone before two weeks are up?" I asked incredulously.

"Yep," he said. "It's like everything with me. Once I start, I can't seem to stop."

"Karl," I said, "maybe you need a different hobby."

The next week, I heard that Karl had qualified for the Nationals in track. Again, he didn't want any publicity, but I had to report that. He didn't seem to hold it against me when it came out in the paper. Then a couple of months later, he won his age group in two races. He was the national champion. I wrote the article.

I was beginning to suspect that his proclamation of disinterest in publicity wasn't entirely genuine. It seemed that he always managed to tell me about his deeds, only to then tell me he didn't want to read about it.

Having become the national champion, he immediately quit running.

Karl isn't an easy guy to figure out. I kept trying, though, and one day, he told me an even stranger story. I had come across an article about his family name, Lintzen, written by someone of that name. I showed it to Karl.

"Oh, yeah, he's my cousin," he said. "He's a real pain in the butt. He's always bugging me for stuff for the family tree. I give him a bunch of bogus stuff, and he doesn't know any better."

"But Karl," I objected. "First of all, this article he wrote is fascinating. Did you know all this about the origin of your name?"

"Don't care," he responded.

And that's the way he was. If he cared, he cared to the max, and if he didn't care, he didn't in the least. Someday genealogists will be mystified by the bogus Karl Lintzen family information in the family tree.

It's funny how things go in the news business. I got to write a long description of Bill Just's funeral, but I also picked up on Lintzen and I got about five more articles out of knowing him.

Maybe I should attend more funerals.

CHAPTER 27

Zephyrs

My first editorial in *The Press:*

In the 1930s, a sleek new train was put into service called the Zephyr, and much of its early service was between Lincoln and Omaha. Many plains folk weren't familiar with that exotic name and had to ask what it meant. The answer, "a pleasant breeze," only increased the mystery.

The stainless steel train looked like it would go a hundred miles an hour with ease and, in fact, averaged around seventy mph. Even in Nebraska, a seventy mph wind isn't considered pleasant, so what was the origin of that name, and what was the relevance to a train traveling across Nebraska where winds, often quite strong winds, were a constant condition? (AMTRAK still operates a train called the California Zephyr.)

The answer could be found in advertising literature, which likened the ride on this beautiful conveyance to a pleasant breeze, something rarely experienced on the Great Plains. If World War II hadn't intervened and prevented non-critical travel, many Nebraskans would have purchased expensive tickets on that train just to find out what a pleasant breeze is like.

Later, many of them traveled to Chicago where they could see the famous train in the Museum of Science and Industry, where the original resides today.

Wind is a fact of life on the plains. Without exaggeration, it's possible to stand on a hilltop around here and look westward into the prevailing wind, and not see a single tree out to the horizon. We don't know, so far as I can determine, whether trees actually slow the wind down, but it seems logical that they would. It takes some energy for the wind to make its way through a forest, and it may not make it to the other side of the forest at all. The wind that you find on the other side has traveled over or around the forest, not passed through it.

A friend of mine is a crop duster. He owns a million dollar plane with the latest technology for everything from spraying to precision location, so he finds it expedient to be dusting crops at every possible opportunity in order to pay his bills. That means he is flying over Nebraska from sunrise to sunset every available dusting day. Thus he has had plenty of opportunity to observe the absence of trees. He reports that the most interesting part of that is the present ability to see where farmhouses stood hundreds of years ago by the trees that the farmers once planted around the long-since-disappeared houses. Nearly every quarter section has a little grove, but most of the old houses are gone. If it weren't for those little groves, there might not be any trees out there at all.

History tells us that when the pioneers got to the plains, they found only grass, no trees. That is, of course, the reason they had to build their houses out of sod. No wood. As soon as they could, they planted trees for shade, wind protection, and future wood.

Today there are still not many trees on the plains. Some places such as in towns and cities, there are trees and just like the old farmhouse groves, all of them were planted by settlers. Of course, by now we're seeing the offspring of those original trees, but Nebraska trees came there by being planted there by people.

Now wind farms are sprouting like corn stalks around the plains states, Nebraska included, and the question must be, what effect will that have on the wind? If the wind is stopped by the trees in a forest, and if it is less windy in places where forests are common (along with mountains and tall buildings), because of the effect of those impediments to the wind, what will those huge windmills do to the wind?

Energy isn't free. The wind must impart some of its energy to the windmill in order for the windmill to perform its task.

Two things come to mind. First, as just mentioned, we don't yet know how this will affect the wind. Will it slow it down? If it does, what will be the accompanying effects? How will they change our weather? We depend on copious rainfall for our crops. Will we lose that?

North Dakota is actually advertising that it has "available wind", as if that is an asset. What it is saying is that wind generation is becoming a major industry there because it's so windy. And, since it's windy in Nebraska, we have "available wind" too. All over the Great Plains wind farms are sprouting into the air, and those windmills are securely anchored to the earth.

The wind passes through the windmill vanes and causes them to turn, and it also transfers force to the entire structure and thus to the ground. Our earth is constantly rotating, dragging us through our atmosphere. The force applied through the windmill structure to the surface of the earth is, due to the wind, most often to the east, or counter to the earth's rotation. When the plains are covered with those huge windmills, will they slow down the earth's rotation? If it were even by a thousandth of a second a day, over a few decades, time would have to be kept differently.

People don't like change, and we have gone through enormous changes in just a few years. It's nearly impossible to stay current with information and communication technology, for example. Imagine the effect of a change in the length of our days.

CHAPTER 28

Jailbird Bill

"Bill's membership in the fire company led to not only cases of leadership and heroism, but to some humorous incidents as well. One time he was actually sentenced to jail for…"

— *Blackjack Press, by Ralph Anderson*

THE THING I HAD heard that made me curious enough to postpone writing his article was "Jailbird." One of the firemen had referred to Bill by that as if it were a nickname, and none of the other firefighters had shown any surprise at hearing it. It appeared that they all might have called him that.

Mindful that I was not about to write an exposé of the local hero, I still felt I had to find out where that moniker came from. I knew of no better place to start than the firehouse.

Sunday afternoon, when I could have been watching a strongest man competition on my fuzzy TV, I sauntered over to the firehouse and found the bays wide open and the guys washing the trucks. I walked around introducing myself to them and explaining that I was new at *The Press* and was trying to become more familiar with the town. I spent 20 minutes or so in small talk while my prey worked on their equipment. I was hoping the subject of Bill Just would come up, without my having to raise it.

Then Doug Jones, the chief, came out of the office to see what the new reporter might be up to.

"Say, youngster, I'm the chief here. Can I help you with something?"

"Not really," I lied, "I'm just getting acquainted."

"Sure, that's great," said Doug, his suspicions unabated. "We're always looking for young blood here. When you're done, I'll give you an application. By the way, I saw you at the funeral yesterday, didn't I?"

"Sure did," I replied, sensing an opening. "I learned that Jailbird was a member of the fire department. Maybe that's what piqued my interest, I'm not sure."

Doug was taken aback by my use of the name "Jailbird." It was common around the firehouse, but no one used it in public, so far as he knew.

"You mean Bill Just?" he asked.

"Yeah," I said, "I've heard him referred to as Jailbird, and I thought that was what you guys called him. Am I wrong?"

The firemen nearby hooted in laughter at that, and one of them said, "He was a real criminal all right. The guy ran a poker game, and some hanging judge gave him a day in jail for it when he got caught. So, of course, we all called him Jailbird. He was about the straightest arrow in town, so it was kind of funny. He was a great guy, so we probably won't call him that anymore."

I made a note of who the firemen were who kidded about the name and decided to look them up later when the chief wasn't around.

Later that night, I called Karl Swenson, the one who had spilled the beans, so to speak, at the firehouse. Karl had been counseled by Doug after he had told me about the poker game, and at first, Karl was hesitant to say any more.

I advised him, "I'm not going to put anything like that in the paper, I promise. It's just that I have to learn as much as I can about Bill before I write another article about him, and the poker game is an insight into him that would help me to understand him better. If I write anything about it, and I don't think I will, I'll let you read it and veto it if you want. Is that fair?"

Karl was dying to tell the story anyway, so my promise was all he needed. He told me the story of the poker game.

"There had been a poker game in the firehouse every Wednesday night for years before Bill joined us. The game was, frankly, a mess. No one was in charge. The cards were all bent up in ways that everyone recognized them without having to see their fronts. Half the chips had gotten lost. Guys got up and left to get beer and snacks, and arguments over who should pay for those got some guys upset."

"Did Bill play poker with you?" I asked.

"Nope, he never did. He would stand around watching sometimes, but we couldn't get him to play. Then one night he asked us if we would like him to run the game. He said he would take one chip from each pot, and with that, he'd buy the snacks and beer, new cards, and chips and clean up afterwards. We thought it was a heck of a deal.

"I don't know if Bill made or lost money doing that, but the game sure got better. He'd bring not just chips and dips, but sandwiches too. It's hard to imagine that he wasn't losing money on the deal.

"Then one night the state fire marshal came in for a surprise inspection and found the game. He called in the sheriff and had him arrest everyone. The only one who got charged with anything was Bill, and like I told you earlier, some stupid judge put him in jail for a day. The sheriff let him out after a few hours, but he was Jailbird from then on."

I thought a minute. "Do you think everyone in town knows about that?"

Karl laughed. "Maybe not everyone, but just about. I mean, the fire department is half the men in town."

I thanked Karl and said this was such a good story, and didn't reflect badly on Bill, that I might try to write it sometime. If I did, I would get Karl's permission before it ran in *The Press*.

CHAPTER 29

Ralph the Reporter

A CURIOUS TRANSFORMATION HAD occurred while I was researching Bill Just's life and legacy: I had become a reporter. Now my nose for news was tuned up and active, and I was actively looking for stories. What do you know?

Seriously, what do you know? Tell me about it.

It wasn't easy to turn up real news in Blackjack, as I had found out. But I had also found that there were plenty of smart folks in town who had information. While perhaps it was not hot breaking news stories, nonetheless, it was of some interest.

I knew, for example, that I could go back to my landlord at any time and learn a great deal about agriculture, the heart and soul of this community, and the surrounding countryside. As the former county agent, Mr. Lindstrom knew plenty about the problems facing the farmers and some of the solutions. He was also a link to the current county agent, if there was one. I hadn't discovered that yet, but I would soon.

I had learned that I could pick up interesting tidbits from the firehouse, where calls came in every day for some sort of assistance. These usually didn't involve big deals. However, a fire in a hayloft is a big deal to the farmer who is losing not just his hay, but probably his barn in the bargain. Since the farmer is probably known to many people in town, they will be interested in the story—not just that the fire occurred, but how much was lost and how it happened. Who fought the fire and how successful they were also seemed to be of potential interest. I would try a few such stories out on Mrs. Fritz to see what she thought.

It had just occurred to me that I needed to establish a closer relationship with Sheriff Jackie McBean. I had watched her expertly directing traffic at Bill's funeral and had observed that she knew her business, at least the traffic part of it. I suspected she had a lot of insights into events going on in town that passed under the radar of the newspaper, at least until now. So I paid her a visit.

It took several tries to find Sheriff McBean, since she was out on patrol much of the time, but on my third attempt, I found her in her office writing a report.

She looked up as I entered. "Can I help you, sir?" she asked.

"Sheriff, I'm Ralph Anderson the new reporter for *The Press*," I started.

"I know who you are, Ralph. That's part of my job. Anyone new comes into town, I know it. How can I help you?" she offered.

"Maybe you can't right now, but I'm hoping we can get to know each other and that you can help me with news stories since if anyone knows what's going on in town, you do."

Jackie laughed, and I sensed this was going pretty well. "The old police beat, huh? Not much exciting happens around here, and if it does, Irma is right on top of it."

"Yeah, I bet she is," I said, "but there must be some stuff going on that she doesn't pick up on, and that's what I'm looking for. Even the little stuff can be interesting to the readers if we handle it right. I'd like to give that a try if you're willing to help me."

"Sure," she said, "it's public record. If you want to dig into it, you're welcome. I can always use a detective on my staff so long as I don't have to pay him. So, let me show you the log."

She opened a large account book that was sitting on her desk. She turned it so I could read it and pointed to the date on the top of the page.

It was Sunday of this week, so the page had all the calls for the week up till now. I read:

5/15/05, 1940hrs – Complaint by Hester Lindgren that a vehicle is parked on the wrong side of the ball field. Ticketed same.

5/16/05, 1055hrs – Complaint by Alma Petersen that two goats are in her yard and eating her flowers. She alleged that the goats belong to her neighbor, but she would not name same.

Found goats in yard and chased them home. Talked to Mrs. Czaplewski about securing goats or fencing yard.

5/16/05, 1543hrs – Complaint by Lars Larson that a badger is digging in his yard. Informed him that he is responsible for wildlife in his yard.

Visited property and found large groundhog. Assisted Larson in chasing animal from yard.

5/20/05, 1112hrs – Complaint by anonymous caller that Earl Farris is in town with a huge pistol sticking in his waistband. Found Harris eating apples from the barrel at the roadside vegetable stand. Appeared calm and under control.

5/20/05, 2324hrs – Call that a vehicle is off the road on Rte 119.

Found abandoned Chevy Caprice in ditch. Smell of alcohol. Traced car to Jimbo Durran. Found Durran home in bed, drunk. Charged him with DUI. Called tow to remove vehicle from ditch and store until Durran trial.

I was intrigued by the report of a man with a "huge pistol stuck in his waistband." I asked Jackie about that and why she did nothing about it.

"Earl is a loony and he's an armed loony, but he has a permit for that hogleg. He wasn't carrying concealed, so there was nothing I could do about it at the time. Maybe someday I'll get him committed or at least get his permit revoked, but for now, he doesn't hurt anyone and he says he has his guns to protect his goats. He's afraid they'll be killed by coyotes, he says. You might get a story there, but be careful if you go to see him."

"So," I thought out loud, "he has more than one gun."

"Yep, he's got that pistol for up close and a rifle for longer ranges. I don't recall anyone ever reporting that he's fired either one, though."

I found out from Jackie where Earl lived and went out there later in the afternoon. I checked first to see if I could call ahead, but Earl had no listing in the phonebook. As I approached the place Jackie had told me about on a scruffy dirt road outside of town, I saw the shack with about a dozen goats munching grass. The goats all looked up at my approaching car with quizzical looks on their handsome faces. Then I was greeted by the smell, which nearly overwhelmed me at first.

I stopped the car and stepped gingerly out, ready to dive for cover if shooting started. The only sound or movement was from the goats. I decided a bold move was in order, so I called out, "Anyone here?"

A disembodied voice responded, "Who the hell are you, and what do you want?"

"I'm from the paper, and I'd like to talk to you about your goats," I answered.

"What about my goats?" the voice said.

I scanned the area looking for anyone who wasn't covered with fur and sporting horns, but I saw no one.

"I hear that you are very careful with your goats and protect them from coyotes. That's part of it," I said.

Out of a shadow, near the house, stepped someone or something. Earl was looking bad, as usual, apparently. He hadn't shaved in weeks, or bathed, probably, or changed his clothes. His hair was matted and full of twigs and assorted debris. A limerick flashed through my mind, something about an old man with a beard full of larks, wrens, owls, and hens.

Earl was holding a pistol in one hand, but otherwise, he didn't appear angry or irrational. He walked out into the open yard and said, "Well, come on in," just as if he had visitors calling every day.

This was the part I dreaded. I wasn't wrong to dread it. The house, or shack, really, seemed to be one room, and it was obvious that the goats lived there with Earl. Little goat pellets were strewn around the floor. It smelled like the monkey house in August. I hoped Earl wouldn't ask me to sit on anything in that place, but he did. I chose an old crate and placed my notebook on it to shield my khakis from goat detritus.

I got my first look at Earl up close. His skin looked like pine bark, dark and flaky. I guessed he spent all day out in the sun with no protection. He smelled bad, but I noticed that his teeth were a bright white. I wanted to ask about that, but I decided it would have to wait until I had built some sort of friendly relationship with him.

I stuck out my hand for a shake and was surprised at the bony hand I got hold of. When I shook it, I could feel bones clanking against each other further up the arm. I dropped his hand as if it had suddenly caught fire. He didn't seem to notice.

Earl asked, "How did you hear about me?"

I lied, "I don't remember, really. People talk, and I listen."

"When they talk about me, what do they say?" he asked.

"They say you are protective of your goats." I realized I needed to get control of the Q and A right away, so I went on, "Do you really have coyotes around here?"

"Do they say I'm crazy?"

I paused. "They say you are fond of your goats, and protective. Do you have other guns?"

Earl brightened. "Sure do. Got me a Remington thirty-aught-six. I can hit a beer can at fifty feet. If I see a coyote, I'll nail 'im."

I asked again, "But have you ever seen one?"

"Nope, but I hear 'em howling at night, so I know they're around."

I almost didn't ask, but my curiosity was getting the best of me. "So, you've never seen one, but you have a rifle and a revolver to shoot them if you do."

"I hear them. If you hear them, they're there. Are you goin' to write about me in the paper?"

"Maybe so," I said. "What should I say about you if I do?"

Earl sat and stared at the ceiling for nearly two minutes before answering. "Come on outside, and I'll show you something."

I was happy to get out of that shack, though the yard wasn't much of a relief.

Earl said, "See that brown nanny? Her name's Jezebel. Watch this." He put his hands up to his mouth to focus the sound, the way people often do when they call to someone, and yelled, "Jezebel!"

The goat he had pointed out looked up at him and bleated a reply.

Earl put his hands up to his mouth again and yelled, "Jezebel, come here."

The brown nanny goat trotted over to Earl and nuzzled his hand.

Earl scratched her behind the ears and told her she was a good girl. She seemed to understand that her session was over and walked slowly away. Earl yelled, "Blackie!"

A large black billy answered just as Jezebel had. "Blackie, come here!" Earl yelled. Again, the goat trotted over and received an ear scratching.

"You can write that goats are better than people any day," Earl said, and with that, he walked back into his shack, letting the screen door, missing most of its screen, bang behind him. I sensed that the interview was over.

On the way back into town, I thought of several different angles I could take. Gun control was obvious, but if I called Earl crazy in the paper, I might regret it. "Goats raised like dogs" was another angle. The role of government or law enforcement concerning unusual lifestyles was another, but perhaps too deep for a newspaper article. I had a lot to think about.

Back in Blackjack, I went looking for the current county agent. I decided to start in the courthouse, and if that were wrong, I could ask where to go. As it turned out, when I parked my car in front of the courthouse, it was right in front of a door to the lower floor with a sign over it saying:

WEED CONTROL

EXTENSION AGENT

I figured extension agent and county agent might be the same person, so I went in that door and found two offices, one on each side of the hallway. I found the one that said Extension Agent and went in.

Seated at the lone desk in the room was a heavy man with a concerned look on his face. He was eating his lunch, or so it appeared from the items spread over his desktop. I stopped in the doorway and looked at the items on the desk. I saw a pile of papers in one corner, apparently a manual of some sort that had been taken out of its binder. Next to the papers, I saw a can of Coke, an orange, and an ashtray full of cigarette butts and ashes.

The agent, I assumed, was reading something in the papers, and it must have been what was worrying him. He didn't look up for a minute or so, and when he did, he accidentally nudged the pile of papers with the side of his hand. The papers gave the orange a push, and it started to roll off the desk. The man lunged for the orange and knocked the papers, the Coke, and the ashtray off the desk.

I stood and watched a comic scene. The papers fluttered to the floor, landing in a puddle of Coke and butts, while the ashes floated toward the floor in a gray cloud before settling onto the Coke-soaked papers. It was one of the worst messes I had ever seen, and I doubted that the papers would ever be useful again.

"Oh my gosh! I'm sorry," I said. "I must have startled you."

"Oh, no, my fault," the man said. "Happens all the time."

"Would you like me to come back?" I asked.

"No, no, just give me a few minutes. I have to save that manual. It's the third one I've gotten, and I don't think I can ask them for another."

I pondered the situation as I watched the agent attempt to clean up the mess, shaking Coke off the pages, but not succeeding in making them more useful. Finally, in great frustration, the agent scooped up the whole soggy mess and dumped it into the wastebasket.

"I guess I'll have to ask for another," he said. At least his sandwich was still on top of the desk. He picked it up and took a bite. "Now, son, what can I do for you?"

After introducing myself, I told him, "I'm new at this newspaper gig, and I'm also not too well versed on agriculture. I thought you might have some leads on stories, maybe not today, but either now or in the future. And you could probably explain a lot to me to make me a better reporter in this farming community."

"Now that sounds like an opportunity for me," the agent declared. "My name is Doc Sevin, spelled with an "in" at the end, not "en." Originally pronounced some other way, Bohemian you know. What are you doing the rest of the afternoon?"

As a matter of fact, I had no plans, so when Doc invited me to accompany him to Bison, I agreed.

The agent looked like he was 40 or 50 years old, old enough to be my father in any case, yet I had a recurring urge to talk to him about things, such as the next can of Coke, purchased from a machine down the hallway from the extension office.

As we got into the car, Doc set the can on the dashboard while he started the ignition. Then, as he backed out of his parking place, I reached up and caught the open can as it slid off the sloping dash.

I wanted to ask, "Why did you put it there?" but didn't.

What I did ask was, "Why did you have all those pages from the manual loose on your desk?"

Doc, driving with the remainder of his sandwich in one hand, noticed that the Coke was no longer on the dash and looked over at me, so I handed it to him. "I just don't like things in binders, you know. They catch on the rings when you turn the pages and drive me nuts, so I take them out."

"What happened to the first two manuals?" I asked.

"Pretty much the same thing," Doc said, without any acknowledgement that he might be the cause.

As Doc drove, I noticed that whenever he approached another car, he raised the index finger of his right hand, and that the approaching driver did the same. "What's the finger thing all about?" I asked.

"It's the Nebraska one-finger salute," Doc answered. "I'm surprised you don't know that. But anyway, since almost everyone knows me, I have to assume they do, and I have to be sure to wave at them."

In Bison, Doc managed to copy some pages from a borrowed manual that would have to do until he could requisition a new one. He had been talking to me ever since we left Blackjack. I was learning a lot, so I was happy I had come along. I was also learning a lot about Doc Sevin.

When Doc opened his briefcase in Bison, I noticed a large black stain covering almost the entire inside. It looked and smelled a lot like shoe polish. I just had to ask about it.

"I always carry a bottle of liquid shoe polish with me," Sevin explained. "You don't want to show up for a meeting with scuffed shoes."

I mentally added, *Or shoe polish all over your papers and briefcase.*

"So…" I ventured, "…one day the top came off?"

"Exactly!" Doc said. "Why do these things happen to me?"

I desperately wanted to say, "They only happen to people who carry shoe polish in their briefcases," but I kept quiet.

Then, the next week, when I was having lunch with Doc at The Matador. Doc got a hamburger, fries, and a large Coke, but he wasn't happy with the fries. "I like them extra crisp," he told me, and took his plate in one hand and Coke in the other up to the bar to get the fries put back into the fryer. On his way back to the table he tripped, went down face first, and watched his plate of hamburger, fries and Coke go sliding and sloshing down the floor in front of him.

This time when he asked, "Why me?" I couldn't restrain himself. "Because you're the only person in town who would carry his plate through the lunch crowd at The Matador to get his fries refried."

"You might be right about that," Doc said, without any indication that he thought it might have been a bad idea.

CHAPTER 30

The Barbershop

My main source of town news and gossip that I planned to exploit at every opportunity, the town's only barbershop, was ripe for exploitation, so I dropped in again. I liked to go in more often than I needed just to listen, but it still resulted in my hair being cut better and shorter than ever before.

I walked by, checking out of my peripheral vision to see if it was crowded, as it usually was at this time of day. Hardly anyone was there when it opened at 7:30, but by 9, it was full every day. I had made sure I arrived at 5 after 9. My sideways check revealed that it was pretty full, but there was still one seat in the waiting area, so I went in.

"Morning, young fella," Clyde Ingman, the barber, said. "Back so soon?"

"Yeah," I answered. "I've got a little time to kill and thought I would see if I could get a haircut. If it's too long a wait, I'll just come back tomorrow."

I was proud of that subterfuge, thinking I had gotten away with it, but now I know that Clyde wasn't worried. He was glad this new reporter was using his shop for a source. He meant to keep me interested.

Clyde primed the pump. "I hear that Lillian Quillen raised hell about the town making a donation to the fire department at the last council

146

meeting and that they're going to bring back the old fire siren and put it up next to her house."

"That'd serve her right, " Axel Burbrage said. "She sent me a letter last week telling me to cut my hedge, and if I don't, she'll get someone to do it and send me the bill."

"Why did *she* send you the letter?" a man I didn't know asked.

Axel said, "She's on the town council, I guess. All's I know is she signed the letter."

"Why would she raise hell about that measly donation," another man asked.

I wished I knew all these men. I would soon, but didn't yet.

Not getting any answer, the man went on. "Her late husband, George Quillen, why, he was a member of the fire company for 40 years. He would be rolling over in his grave if she said anything against them."

Clyde wanted to keep it going long enough to think of another topic. "Have you ever been near that siren when it goes off? It'll peel the paint off your car if you're driving past it."

"I sure have," said unknown man number one. "I was up on the pole working on the phone line when it went off one day. I was deaf for a week."

"Why is there a phone line on that pole?" I asked.

Number One knew the answer. "Those fire alarms are run by the county. Someone at county dials a number, and the siren sounds off. It's four blasts for an ambulance and eight for a fire."

"That's too many, I think. One for the ambulance and 3 for the fire would be enough, don't you think?" Clyde put in. Here was some grist for the town gossip mill.

"You know, over in Bitburg, they've got a system with their siren that makes a lot of sense to me," Number Two said.

"Well," Clyde said, "are you going to tell us about it?"

"Sure. You see, they've got the town broke up in segments like north, east, and even northeast or northwest, and the number of short blasts on the siren tells the fire company where the fire is. It works so well that lots of times the volunteers arrive at the fire before the equipment. So, say you're on a job in the north, and you hear a signal for the northeast, you jump in your car, and you're there in a minute and a half. If it's a big enough fire, you'll see it right off."

Everyone thought that was a good idea, but some thought that cell phones would be better and wouldn't be making such a racket.

I got the picture, and I could easily check this out with the fire company. It might work for an article. I'd see. Meanwhile, I wanted to know more about Earl.

"Do any of you know Earl Farris?" I asked.

There was a general nodding of heads and grunts in response. No one seemed ready to volunteer much. Clyde again acted as the catalyst. "Some folks say he's crazy, or so I hear."

"SAY he's crazy?!" shouted Number Two. "He lives with GOATS!"

"Right in his house, or so I hear," Clyde added.

"And," I threw in, "he's armed and, I suspect, dangerous."

"Oh, I don't know about dangerous," Axel said. "Earl wouldn't hurt a fly. He's a sad case, but so long as he don't hurt no one, there's nothin' no one can do about him."

"Has he always been that way?" I asked, pondering the profusion of negatives in the last sentence.

"Oh, I guess you could say that," Axel answered. "I went to school with him, and he was just a little strange. He was usually dirty, and he didn't come to school all that often, but he's a nice enough fella."

I should have known that no one would say much bad about anyone in this public a place. But, ask about the highway system, federal taxes, or New York City? Now, that was another story.

A new customer had walked in, and everyone but me knew him. He was greeted by one and all, and I picked up that his name was Paul something or other that sounded like "airs." Now I know it's Ayres. Paul jumped in as soon as there was a break in the talking.

"You fellas all know about my monthly golf game up to Lincoln." It was a statement, not a question.

There was a general nodding of heads and grunts of agreement, but

Clyde said, "You'll have to fill this new reporter from *The Press* in on that, Paul."

I was introduced, and Paul said, "I have three university classmates in Lincoln, and when I worked there a few years ago, we started a golf game on the first Wednesday of every month. I never miss it, unless there's over a foot of snow on the course."

"He plays at some swanky country club up there," someone put in.

Paul went on, ignoring the interruption, "We were all on varsity teams at the U, but time has taken its toll. We don't play golf so well now. We call ourselves the Short Hitting Intervarsity Teammates; you can work out the acronym for yourself."

He continued, "We always meet at this sort of seedy restaurant for breakfast, because the breakfast special there costs a buck ninety-nine. It's two eggs, bacon, toast and a cup of coffee. Best deal in the city.

"Well, I was up there the other day, and I drove up to Wolfs, that's the name of the place, and went in. There they were chowing down on specials. I can't eat that stuff. My doctor would have a fit, so I had eaten a banana and a couple of granola bars on the way up. I ordered a cup of coffee and that cost a buck. The S.H.I.T.s all gave me a hard time about that, and that's a good sign if they are feisty enough to start the harassment at breakfast."

"Man, are you going to talk about breakfast or golf?" one of the customers asked.

"Just be patient," Paul said, "I'm filling in background for this kid. He's new in town."

"Lucky him," said another guy. "It's probably the first time he's heard the story." Everyone laughed.

Paul resumed, "Well, after they finished their specials, they wiped all the grease off of their chins, went to the men's room (laughter), and went out to Mike's big Hummer. It's the only car big enough to carry all the stuff, four bags, and the robot."

That got my attention. "Robot?" I asked.

"Yeah, see this one guy, Bill, we call him Regular Bill, you'll see why in a minute, has got this mechanized golf cart with a remote control. He tells it how far to go after he hits his ball, and it goes there, sometimes. One time, he thought he told it to go a hundred yards, and it disappeared over the horizon. We think he put in 1000 by mistake. So, anyway, we stow all the bags and Robo in the trunk and drive out to Eastwood."

"It's called Eastwood, because the only thing east of it is corn," Clyde put in.

"And they've planted a few trees on the course, I guess," another added.

"It's out there at 105th Street, hain't it?" someone asked.

"Something like that," Paul said.

"What is it with all the street numbers out there?" Clyde asked. "I think the numbers go all the way to Omaha. My nephew has a farm, used to be on a county road 1127, but now it's 198th Street."

"Oh, that's for the day Lincoln and Omaha grow together," Axel joked, and everyone laughed again. The general consensus was that they would meet within the next decade.

Paul broke in to continue his story, "So we get out to the course early, and I've got this new Callaway Big Head club I've never used before. I want to take some practice drives off the tee, but they say, 'No way.' Mike hits his drive, and it dribbles off the tee and goes about 50 feet. We all congratulate him, because he's on the fairway, and we mean it. It's my turn to hit, so I take a few swings, and it feels really different. They tell me to hurry up and hit or this women's foursome will go ahead of us, so I 'address the ball' as golfers say, swing at the ball, look hopefully down the fairway, and I can't see it anyplace. I think that maybe I hit it out of sight, but then I hear them laughing. I look over, and there's Big Bill doubled over, holding his crotch, and my ball is lying at his feet. I go over and pick it up. Bill tries to say something, but he can't talk."

"He was the football player," Clyde told me. "Paul here's lucky Bill didn't kill him."

"But here's the story," Paul went on. "We don't see each other much except for golf. I'm all the way out here, and the other guys are sort of in different social circles. But not long ago, Regular Bill's wife decided to invite all the S.H.I.T.s to a party at their house to welcome home their son, who was visiting from Hawaii, where he runs a store and surfs, mostly the latter. She knew everyone's name, except for Mike's girlfriend's last name. We all call her Sue, but Sue 'what' we don't know.

"It seems that Regular Bill sent an email to Mike asking, 'What's Sue's last name?' But Mike, who is an investment advisor, doesn't answer non-business email, so Mrs. Bill went ahead and sent Mike an invite saying Mike and Sue, no last names. Later that week, Bill gets an email from Mike saying 'Reynolds'."

"So there we are, out on the course, and Bill says, 'Hey, Mike, thanks for the tip.' Mike doesn't give away free advice, most of the time, but sometimes he kind of hints. If you pay attention, you can make some easy money. But Mike says, 'What tip?' Bill says, 'Reynolds.' Mike says, 'You chowderhead, that's Sue's last name!'

"Bill says, 'I don't care if it's Osama's last name, I bought a thousand shares, and it went up 4 bucks a share'!"

When the laughter died down, I decided I had enough material to last until I actually needed a haircut. "I'll be back, Clyde," I said.

On my way out, I shook hands with Number One and Number Two and got their names. By an odd coincidence, one was Dusty Rhodes and the other was Sandy Beach. It got me thinking about a story I could write on names and nicknames like those. My all-time favorite, of course, is Ima Hogg... but that's for another day.

CHAPTER 31

The Dominatrix Crew

I WENT BACK TO my rooming house to compose my thoughts and, I hoped, some articles for the paper. When I entered through the back door, I was surprised to find the living room full of chatting women clustered, it appeared, around a table.

Mrs. Lindstrom, my surrogate grandmother, called to me from her seat at the table. "Ralph, come into the living room, I want you to meet the Dominatrix Crew."

I thought I knew what a dominatrix was. *Something to do with unusual sex practices and involving torture,* I thought, so the mere presence of such a crew in Blackjack was shocking, but in Mrs. Lindstrom's living room! That was beyond comprehension.

I tentatively entered the living room and saw that the members of this "crew" were all about Mrs. Lindstrom's age or older, and were playing Dominos.

Seeing the look of apprehension on my face, one of the ladies announced, "We all play Dominos together every Wednesday, so we call ourselves The Dominatrix Crew." They all laughed. I blushed. That made them laugh even harder.

Mrs. Lindstrom introduced each of the ladies by their first names: Inez, Polly, Marianne, Lizbet, and Karen, pronounced Kah-ren.

"Would you like to join the game?" Mrs. Lindstrom asked.

"I don't remember how to play Dominos," I said, although I was pretty sure I did remember. I had no desire to spend the afternoon playing with these older ladies.

"You probably don't want to listen to us gossip all afternoon," Inez said.

Ah, but I do, I thought. *This could be better than the barbershop, even!*

"Well," I said out loud instead, "I have some work to do, but I could sit in for a game or two."

"We'll have to teach you our rules. By the way, we play for money. Do you have some with you?" asked Lizbet.

"Are we talking dollars?" I asked. I probably only had about ten dollars in my wallet.

"A nickel a point," Mrs. L. explained. "But I have to warn you, Ralph, it's a cut-throat game."

The first money I needed was a penny. Their game allowed you to shut off branches to other players, but you needed to mark each closed branch with a penny. It only took about 10 minutes for me to lose a dollar thirty five. After 20 minutes, I was down almost three dollars. All that while, gossip was flowing around the table, and I was paying too much attention to that to pay much attention to learning the game.

As expected, the Bill/Cecille relationship came up pretty fast. I figured that the old girls were dying to know what I had found out. I tried to string them along without telling them anything.

I said, "I met with Cecille, and I really liked her."

Karen replied, "Of course you did, honey, everyone likes her. But that just makes the situation even more interesting, doesn't it?"

So they bantered about it, watching me for reactions the whole time. I tried not to give anything away, but I wanted to know what the town thought. What the town thought was that they were as married as anyone else in town—in fact, more so than many. They just didn't bother to make it legal.

Other topics ranged from the clothes worn by teenagers, which in this case meant grandchildren, to who got drunk on the communion wine after serving on the Altar Guild at the Presbyterian Church.

When I had lost eight of the ten dollars I had on me to those Domino sharks, I made my excuses and went up to my room to write down some notes. Luckily, I was able to take two pieces of cake, a slice of pie, and three brownies up with me. I left the celery and carrot sticks on the table.

CHAPTER 32

Nebraska Triptales

Local Businessmen Working Far Afield

"Two local businessmen, Bill Just and Pete Thorson, are finding opportunities in the surrounding communities…"
                                    — *The Blackjack Press, November 5, 1969*

BILL TOOK LITTLE TIME in expanding his territory fairly far from Blackjack. He found plenty of potential customers for his mutual funds in the small towns all around Blackjack. He never went into bigger towns, such as Bison, since they were the territory of established insurance firms and stockbrokers. But, small towns were not, and the residents were happy to have someone come to them, instead of having to drive into the big towns.

Pete Thorson had started him down this path, taking him along on some of his sales trips and introducing him to the small town folk he already knew. He also introduced him to the small town cafes that Bill came to love.

As in many things in life, the trip was often more interesting than the destination. Bill often commented on this to Pete as they drove along.

Depending on the season, Bill would say something like: "In the summer, Nebraska disappears behind the corn."

It was true. When the corn stalks reached six or seven feet high, they were all you saw. The only break in the walls of green you drove by came when the occasional soybean field offered a lower profile and a view of more than 20 feet.

In the fall, Bill would say, "This is the beginning of ugly season." And that was true too. The corn turned yellow and brown and stood dying and drying in the fields. As fall progressed, it got uglier and uglier. The saving grace was that it was then football season, which is the big time in Nebraska.

In the winter, Bill longed for snow to cover the black dirt, then lying naked and exposed to view, especially in the feedlots. There's little on this earth uglier or stinkier than a feedlot full of cattle. Well, I hear pigs are worse, but most of them seem to be in Iowa.

Finally spring would change it all. Bill would glory in the spring, saying, "This is what we've been waiting for, and it was worth the wait... Eh, Pete?" The winter wheat would be up and soon would be living up to its reputation as "amber fields of grain." Corn plants, and beans would be just sticking their heads out through the soil and reminding everyone of the new crops on their way. There are still not many trees in Nebraska on the whole, but the few that are there are leafing out and some are blooming in brilliant colors.

One of Bill's favorite scenes was a pasture full of Clydesdales. He didn't know why that farmer raised Clydesdales, but he loved to look at them as they drove by. He never asked Pete the "why" question, because he preferred not to know. That way he could dream up his own scenarios. They were the ones you saw on the Budweiser ads, or they marched in the Rose Bowl Parade. Well, at least they did in his imagination.

Pete seldom commented on the aesthetics of his native land, or any aesthetics at all. He was plotting his sales activities and ignoring Bill's banter. He was also fighting to keep the car on the road in the plains wind.

A constant on the Great Plains is the wind. The more aerodynamic cars don't have too much trouble with it, but anything large or boxy does. It is common to see vehicles swerve off the road when hit by a sudden gust, and the sight of semis lying on their sides beside the highway is not uncommon. Sideswipes were a common accident before the highways were widened, as cars got blown into each other. Pete usually drives too fast and erratically to handle the wind well.

Somehow, the two salesmen always ended up someplace where they had to revert back to business. Sometimes that worked out and sometimes it was just an adventure.

On one such trip, Bill asked Pete, "You know what I love about this?"

"Just being with me," Pete snarled in his usual festive mood.

"Oh, sure," Bill said, "but what I meant was: meeting so many interesting people. Except for you, Nebraska is full of happy and friendly people, and we're getting to know them, one at a time."

"Peachy," grumped Pete.

"Remember that guy I sold the mutual fund to in St. James last week?"

"The guy with the odd name?"

"That's the story I've been thinking of," Bill replied. "His name was Ephwardt, remember?"

"Yeah, sounds like "F-word.""

"It does," said Bill. "I had to call him back yesterday, and his wife answered. Want to guess what her name is?"

"No," Pete said.

"I'm going to tell you anyway," said Bill. "Get this: Her name is Gaye."

"Gay F-word?" Pete actually laughed.

"I wonder if she works. She might be a teacher, a high school teacher, with classes of 30 or 40 adolescents. Can you imagine what they would call her?"

They spent the rest of the trip guessing what high school students would call Mrs. Ephwardt.

Pete had a habit of trying to control the temperature in his car manually, despite the fact that the car's temperature control system was totally automatic. You told it what temp you wanted in the car, and it made it that. You didn't have to do anything. But, Pete, like so many people of his age, wasn't satisfied having the temperature just what he had set. As soon as he got in the car, he started fussing with the controls. Since the only control he had was the temperature setting, he would set it at 55 to make the ac come on, or at 90 to make the heat come on. Then, once the ac was working or the radiator was hot, the car would become uncomfortable, and he would have to fuss with the setting again. Bill tried to talk him out of this, but he was too far gone to listen. He'd been doing that all of his life.

Similarly, he insisted on closing the intake for outside air. The result of that was fogged up windows in the winter, which led Pete to open the windows a crack. Even though that didn't work very well, Pete thought it was the only solution. Sometimes Bill could divert his attention and change the vent to allow outside air to circulate. The windows would instantly clear, and Pete was sure that he had done that by opening the windows.

One other problem for Pete and his car was his irrational fear of bridges. He was certain that he would drive through the guardrail and fall into the river or whatever chasm the bridge spanned. In Nebraska, those "chasms" are maybe four feet deep. Bill would try to reason with him that he had no fear of driving off the road, otherwise he wouldn't careen around corners the way he did. Therefore he shouldn't expect to drive off the same width of roadway on a bridge. That fell on deaf ears. If they ever crossed a long bridge, Pete would stop and get out and make Bill drive across.

You could imagine how much fun these driving trips were for Bill, especially if he made no sales. For example, they drove to Piltzn one day, and Bill found no one interested in his products. By noon, he was out of ideas.

He had lunch in a place called Elsie's. The waitress pointed him to a table at the back next to the restrooms, but Bill said he would prefer to sit at the only other empty table in the place at the front. She wrinkled her brow and seemed about to say something, but instead just let him sit there.

The menu was an interesting mixture of Middle American "cuisine," burgers and BLTs, and Czech dishes, such as liver dumpling soup. He ordered a taco salad, opting for neither of the two predominant menu choices. He was sitting there, sipping his ice tea and awaiting his salad, when the biggest person he had ever seen came through the front door and sat right down at his table. Bill was surprised and a little bewildered. Sure Nebraskans are aggressively friendly, but they would still ask before they sat down at your table.

The big guy took off the enormous ten-gallon Stetson he had on when he came in, and promptly replaced it with a baseball cap that was sporting a John Deere logo. Bill wondered at the act of putting a cap on one's head at the dinner table, but he wisely held his tongue.

"Hi," said the big guy, "how are you?"

""Fine, thanks," Bill said. "My name's Bill."

"So's mine," roared the big one. "Bill Heinz."

"Nice to meet you, Bill. I'm Bill Just, or just Bill, take your choice."

"Visiting our fair city?" Heinz boomed.

"Yes, I am. I sell no-load mutual funds, mostly to farmers who've just sold their farms. Provides them with a safe income. Not much business today, though."

"Did anyone tell you this was my table?" Heinz asked more quietly and with no show of emotion.

"No, but the waitress looked at me funny when I said I wanted to sit here."

"Well, I'm glad to have you. From now on, though, only sit at this table at lunch time if I invite you."

"All right, if you say so. I don't imagine I would like to tangle with you over it," Bill said, thinking it might be funny.

Heinz snorted and said, "Guys come to this town all the time just to tangle with me. I don't really mind. It's the only exercise I get these days, but I do get the occasional bruise or broken bone."

"Are you serious?" Bill asked. "They really come here just to fight you?"

"Not so much as they used to. I'm almost eighty now, and I guess it's not such a big deal to beat up an old man. Oh, but when I was younger, say 65, it was a fight a week."

"You can't be serious!" Bill said.

"Oh, yeah, I am."

"Don't the police stop the fights?" Bill asked.

"Nah, they watch them. I worked on the railroad most of my life, and I still know everyone at the yards. They clean out a boxcar for us, and a crowd gathers on each side. We go at it until I knock the jerk out, which doesn't usually take too long. I weigh over 300 pounds, so the first time I land a solid punch I break something in their bodies. Then everyone buys me drinks, until I'm too drunk to stand up. It's my way of drinking free."

"And they still fight you in your late 70s?"

"Yep, they do. It's like the Wild West, where a fast-draw gunslinger has to fight every wannabe gunslinger in the territory. They all want to say they fought Bill Heinz and lived. They come from Wyoming and Colorado, for God's sake!"

"Well, Bill, I don't want to fight you, so you can eat in peace. Here's the waitress now."

She plopped down the taco salad and looked at Heinz for his order. He snorted at having to even make an order; the waitress was apparently supposed to know. He ordered a steak, rare, with fries, and black coffee.

Another customer came over to the table. He was tall and sort of skinny, except for the little bulge above his big silver belt buckle. He was dressed in Western clothes, as many people are out there, and had a cowboy hat slanted back on his head.

Ignoring Bill Just, he spoke to Heinz: "Hey, Bill, where's your boy Jerry these days?"

Heinz squinted at the man and seemed to recognize him after a few seconds. "He's out in California, the land of fruits and nuts."

The new guy laughed, too loudly, and went on, "I remember one time I had Sunday dinner at your house, and Jerry shot a rat right in the dining room. Remember that?"

Heinz said, "Not particularly. He done that a number of times."

"Yeah!" the guy exclaimed. "I guess that's why your wife said what she said. Do you remember what she said?"

"Nope," Heinz said, obviously not much interested in this conversation.

The other guy ignored that and went on, "She said, 'How many times do I got to tell you, don't shoot in the dining room.'" He laughed too loudly again. "How many times, don't shoot in the dining room…" He walked away repeating it over and over, laughing.

Heinz said, "I wish he'd want to fight me. I'd break his jaw, and he'd have to shut up for a month."

"So," Bill surmised, "you have a rat problem?"

"Nah," Heinz said, "I'd catch one down at the yard and let 'im out right before Sunday dinner, so's Jerry would shoot 'im and my wife would have a fit. Never failed. Hard on the wallboard, though."

Bill Heinz took a great liking to Bill Just over the course of their lunch and told him, "Next time you're coming to town, you call me ahead of time. I know everyone here, and I can line up some customers for you. We got guys here with money under their mattresses or buried under their chicken coops. You could be a big help to some of them, and then they could finally pay me the money they owe me."

Bill Just called over the waitress. He handed her a credit card and said, "Both lunches are on me."

Heinz smiled.

The next trip was to Clovis. It was the oddest town he had been to, and he suspected that Pete Thorson had brought him there just to see his reaction.

Pete took him to the school where he sold cleaning supplies and introduced him to the principal and a few of the staff. It wasn't long before he heard several of the staff speaking what sounded like Russian. He had a few minutes before he went looking for business, so he asked Pete what was going on with the foreign language. Pete told him to find out for himself, not out of meanness, but because it would be a better story that way.

When I was there much later, I had the same reaction to people speaking what sounded like Russian, I asked and was told that it was

Russian. "Okay," I said, "I'll bite. Is this town ethnically Russian?" I hadn't heard any Russian-sounding names, so I was just fishing for information.

"Nope," Gertie Holmstrom answered. "We're a bunch of Swedes and Germans, mostly Germans, actually. It all happened because of Flo."

"Who's Flo?" I asked.

"Flo Schumacher got real worried after we went into Bosnia, and then Ukraine, that we would end up in a war with the Russians. She was an English teacher here in the high school and didn't know a word of Roosky, but she decided not only to learn it, but to teach it. She enrolled in classes at the university, and after two years, she began teaching it here in the school. She taught high school students during the day and adults at night.

"Lots of folk signed up for classes, because she went around to churches and clubs telling everyone we had better learn to speak Russian, because the Russians would probably win the inevitable war and things would go better for those people who could speak their language.

"I'm not sure how many people believed that we were going to lose a war to Russia at first, but after a while, it kind of became the thing to do. It was sort of a clubby thing, you know? The more-educated people in town learned Russian. And while they were learning it from Flo, she was preaching that the war was coming. That's why we've got all these bomb shelters in town."

"You don't really have bomb shelters here, do you?" I asked.

"We sure do," Gertie said. "Just look around town, and you'll see them in folks' back yards. They do come in handy for tornado shelters, war or no war."

And that's why Clovis, Nebraska is the bomb shelter capital of the Midwest.

Bill did manage to get one appointment with a retired farmer after lunch. It turned out it was a good thing he didn't have more, because at the rate Karl Ogren operated, it took the rest of the afternoon.

As always, the meeting began with a handshake. Just a few months off the farm, Karl had the big, swollen hands of a farmer. Bill was never sure why farmers' hands were so big, but he assumed it was due to working in the cold, since his hands tended to swell in really cold conditions. The skin on those fellows' hands was as tough as leather, but the swelling made it like shaking hands with Herbie Husker, the Nebraska mascot.

Herbie is an inflated costume with a person inside, and actually his hands are not covered with inflated ones. If they were they would be a lot more realistic. Bill thought of Herbie's inflated hands, if he had them, and thought that was what Karl's were like.

Of course, you had to be a big, tough, hardy person to make it as a Nebraska farmer, so maybe the hands just go along with the rest of the body. Bill didn't think so. His own hands had been slightly swollen when he was on the farm, but he left before it became a chronic condition. A lifetime of working outdoors will change your physique.

When Bill could extract his hand from Karl's grasp, they sat down, and Bill began his pitch. He always attempted to make it clear to a prospective buyer that he wasn't really selling anything for his own profit, only for the welfare of the buyer. This was always a tough proposition, since no one else ever approached the buyers with a deal like that. Oh sure, various salesmen tried to make it sound like it was only for the benefit of the buyer, but those old farmers were too cagey to believe it. That was what Bill had to overcome: their natural disbelief.

Karl smiled from the moment he came to the door, and it made Bill wonder what that meant. He never found out. Karl was unceasingly nice and polite.

Bill had just finished explaining how a no-load mutual fund worked, and Karl asked, "So, how does that work then?"

Bill tried again, pausing to make sure Karl understood everything he was saying, and then he asked, "Do you understand, Karl?"

Karl said, "Oh, sure. Now tell me again how that works."

In this way, the afternoon passed, and Bill began to think Karl was using him as entertainment.

Finally, when it was nearly time for Bill to meet Pete Thorson for the ride back home, Karl said, "I guess I'll try this out, then."

He signed the application and wrote out a check for $20,000. Some months later he added another $80,000 to it. Bill wondered how much more he had if this was trying it out. He told Karl to be sure and tell his fellow retired farmers about Bill and said he'd call him in a couple of weeks to see if there was more interest. He made a mental note not to let Karl sit in on his meetings with others.

Calling it a successful day, at least for Karl, Bill left to meet up with Pete for the return trip. Pete told Bill to drive, because he wanted to use a mobile phone he had purchased on trial to see if it worked. Pete called a number, and within one minute, he was arguing fiercely with someone.

As soon as he hung up, he called another number, and the same thing happened—a fierce argument over the phone. When he hung up that time, the mobile phone started ringing. He answered, and the first argument broke out again. Then, the second guy called back, and that argument revived as well.

Pete stomped back to the car and said, "Why do these things always happen to me?"

Bill decided not to answer that. He reached over and opened the air vent to circulate outside air. Pete closed it again and opened a window a crack.

CHAPTER 33

Even Smaller Towns

I THOUGHT THAT BLACKJACK was a really small town when I got here, but upon further reflection, a skill I am just starting to develop, I realized that out here in the nation's heartland, it's actually relatively large.

There was a time when the small towns served a need, but that time was past and many of those towns have just died. Maybe some people still live there, driving a few dozen miles to work someplace else, and a very few hang on, operating small stores or cafes, hoping for a passing tourist out searching for ghost towns. However, many of these old towns were, for all practical purposes, dead.

I had seen one of these once when I was a scout. My father had accompanied the troop on a trip up to the Niobrara, camping and canoeing. I knew the old boy was not inclined to sleep on the ground and that he would be bugging out to a motel at the first opportunity, but that first night there he was pitching a tent and unrolling his sleeping bag.

I asked him why, and he said, "Town's dead."

He had taken this trip specifically because he had a cousin who owned a ranch in the Sandhills and his mailing address was Cody. He was always entranced with the name of Cody, Buffalo Bill's name, and the one for whom the town was named.

So, when it got to be late afternoon, he drove over to Cody with two expectations. First, he hoped to contact his cousin and to be invited to spend the night with him. Several phone calls to the ranch reached only an answering machine, and he got no calls back.

As a precaution, he had been looking for a motel to stay in. That was as fruitless as the calls to the ranch. He found two motels on the highway that ran through Cody, but both had been closed for, it appeared, years. He drove around Cody to see what he could find, and what he found was old, dilapidated buildings, unlikely to be occupied now or ever again. There was a small post office, but the sign on the door said, *Delivering Mail.* A barn-like garage had a few old pickups outside that might have been under repair, but most likely, they were just sitting there rusting to death along with everything else.

On the way back home, Dad took me through Cody to show me. He still had not made contact with his cousin, the rancher, and never did, so far as I know. I hoped the cousin was just busy and not dead. If he were dead, would anyone know?

It isn't hard to find such places in Nebraska. If you take the back roads, roads with numbers like County Road 1035, you will find not just abandoned farmhouses and barns, but even little ghost towns.

I also remember going to look for a town that was somehow important to my mother's past. It was called Malmo, and that is the name of the port in Sweden, out of which most Swedish immigrants sailed. Some distant relatives had lived there at one time and that was interesting enough to my Mom that she wanted to see if they or their descendants were living there still. We looked and looked for that town, driving back up the road on which it was supposed to lay, according to the map, but all we found was a couple of farmhouses and a church. I suppose that the church was all that constituted the "town" of Malmo, Nebraska.

One town had been named after one of our great-great-uncles, and we drove out there one Sunday, only to find a few houses and three bars. Quite a heritage!

It's amazingly sad to see these places. You think about the people who originally settled there, struggled through years of backbreaking toil to clear a patch of land, made a go of it if they were lucky, built the house you can still see and were immensely proud of it, raised a family and sent their children off to college or good jobs, and then watched the entire enterprise collapse. Maybe they didn't live long enough for that, if they were lucky.

But, that's the dynamic nature of the United States. It's not Europe, even though most of its people came from there. In Europe, buildings stand for entire millennia, knocked down in time of war and rebuilt exactly as they were before. There are houses in Europe that were built by the Romans! Here we build with wood and steel. The wood decays and the steel rusts, but often not as fast as the people move on and leaving them behind.

True to this tradition, Bill Just had just picked up and left his old life behind at an early age. Somehow, I need to impart this insight to his many friends.

Someday, I'll write an article about some of the ghostly towns near Blackjack. I'll have to be sensitive to the memories of some who have moved here from them, who have the fears of others living here, and who were concerned about the future of this little town.

I have a lot I want to do, and I sure wish I knew how to do it.

CHAPTER 34

The Convention

Just to Attend Conference in Missouri

"Bill Just, insurance and mutual funds broker, will attend a national sales conference in Branson, Missouri…"
– The Blackjack Press, June 22, 2001

ONE THING ABOUT THE insurance business, or the mutual fund business for that matter, is that the company management thinks there is a crying need to juice up the sales force with inspiring talks from high achievers. Bill had no interest in hearing about how much money those guys were making. He was making enough to live the way he wanted, and his main motivation now was the protection and security he was providing for his customers. But, it went with the territory, so to speak, and Hank had insisted he go to a convention in Branson, Missouri.

Since Bill's old pickup couldn't have made it from the middle of Nebraska to Branson, he had to borrow Cecille's old Cavalier to make the trip. The Cavalier wasn't in much better shape than the "Chivy" pickup, but at least there might still be parts for it, if needed.

As luck would have it, the Cav broke down in a little town in Missouri named Nose Mountain. He had never heard of it before, but he found that it was a nice little town with a state park, also named Nose Mountain, not far away.

He would never have been in this town, except for his fervent wish to drive on the back roads, avoiding interstates at all costs. He knew it would add almost a day to the trip to do this, but at least he was able to limp into the town when the Cav quit. What would have happened to him if it had quit on I-70?

He pulled into a gas station with the last gasp of the engine. It was nearly five in the afternoon, and he feared no one would even look at the car until the next morning. He strode into the office to see if he could get it repaired.

A very round man with a bright red face and a thick head of white hair was sitting at the desk wearing a green work shirt and pants, with the name "Sam" embroidered over the shirt pocket. He was in the middle of an intense conversation on the phone. After a few minutes, he cupped his hand over the handset and asked, "Somethin' I can do for you, buddy?"

"I'm afraid my Cavalier has pulled up lame," Bill said, smiling and hoping his little joke would break the ice.

"Got a flat?" the round man asked.

"No, I was just kidding. Actually, the engine is barely running. I hope you can take a look at it."

"Sure," Round Man said. "Be there in a minute."

When he came out of the office, some 15 minutes later, the round person introduced himself as Sam of Sam's Service, while pointing to the name painted on the front of the station. He got one of the boys working there to help him push the old car into the garage, raised the hood, and disappeared under it for another half hour.

When he emerged, he had a solution, although he suggested, "Time for a new car, fella. This one is 'bout wore out."

Sam said he would need another hour at least. Bill asked if there was some place he could get something to eat, and Sam pointed him down the street to a place called The Tepee.

Bill had noticed something odd about Sam. He didn't figure it out at first, but after some extended face-to-face contact, he realized that Sam had one brown eye and one blue eye. He had seen that in a dog once, but never in a human.

When he got to The Tepee, the woman who greeted him and showed him to a booth also had one eye of each color. That was quite a leap for a guy who had never seen even such a thing on a human before. Then the waitress came with a glass of water and a menu, and she had one brown eye and one blue eye too. Bill was beginning to think he was the victim of a weird prank.

Sam worked feverishly over the Cav until nearly 10, at which time he declared he needed to go home for his supper. He offered to drive Bill to the motel on the edge of town.

When Bill went into the office of the little motel, he was greeted by the smell of Thai food cooking somewhere nearby. Then a man came out who obviously went with the Thai food, followed by two little Thai children. Bill marveled at the amazing ubiquity of Asians over this huge country, and he wondered how long it would be before a family of Laotians or Cambodians showed up in Blackjack.

The motel was very basic and threadbare, but it kept him under a roof and between clean sheets for the night. Plus, it was cheap. There was nothing to watch on the little TV that barely got a picture, but Bill never watched television anyway. He decided to read a book he had checked out of the Blackjack library in case of such an emergency.

When he paid his bill in the morning, he found himself looking intently into the eyes of the Thais, but they were uniformly dark brown. He thought no more about it until he picked up the car from Sam and drove up to the gas pump to fill up. The boy who came out to see how he was doing also had one brown and one blue eye.

The car still would not run right. Bill turned back into Sam's after a fruitless attempt to leave town. Sam clucked his tongue and looked at Bill as if to say, "This has to be your fault; I fixed it." He offered to loan Bill his Camaro for a few hours and suggested that he visit Nose Mountain State Park.

This wasn't the first time Bill had borrowed a car from a mechanic, so he wasn't too surprised to find wrenches and screwdrivers on the floor under foot. When he reached down to pick them up he noticed that he could see the road surface through a large hole in the floorboards. He made a mental note to be careful not to let his foot go through to the road.

Bill drove the four miles from town to the park, where he found a talkative ranger and no other visitors. The ranger, a tall, wiry man of around 30, with thinning brown hair, was obviously delighted to have someone to tell about his park.

Ranger Shea told him, "The mountain got its name from the early settlers who thought that it looked like a man's nose. This is one case where the name didn't come from the Indians, whose noses didn't look anything like the mountain."

"Yep," Bill agreed. "Looks pretty Caucasian to me."

"That's what I think," Shea said.

Then he went on: One winter, a particularly heavy snow fell on the mountain, followed by rain and below-freezing weather. The mountain turned into a mound of ice. In the spring, when the temps warmed up, a strange yellowish stream oozed out of the "nostrils." This confirmed that it was a "nose" and led to an odd tradition. We celebrate Phlegm Phest here every spring when the snow begins to melt."

Bill asked, "Do you mean that this happens every year, this discharge?"

Shea laughed. "Well, it does happen once in a while, but not more often than once every ten or twenty years. So the Phlegm Phest Committee has to recreate it with food dye and warm water. It's the biggest celebration they have in Nose Mountain all year."

Bill had been kidding when he said the nose looked Caucasian. He hadn't actually seen any resemblance to a nose. Now he tried to see a nose in the mountain, but Shea told him that it had to be seen from just the right angle at the right light, and Bill thought it might be more important to get going to Branson.

When Bill got back to Sam's, the car was purring, and Sam said he needed 60 bucks for his six hours of labor. Bill gave him $100 and considered it a heck of a deal.

Bill drove on to Branson, not knowing if those blue and brown eyes really were different colors or if the folks in Nose Mountain had pulled an elaborate prank on him. He considered the possibility that Phlegm Phest might be a tall tale to tell strangers too. He never found out for sure, but it made a great story for years to come and not a few of his friends went out of their way to visit Nose Mountain. All reported that many of the residents did, indeed, have one eye of each color. None of them stayed for Phlegm Phest.

Bill missed the first day of the pep talks because of the car trouble, but he really didn't care about that. When he got to his hotel in Branson, he had a message waiting for him. He took it up to his room and called another room in the hotel. A woman answered, and after a short conversation, Bill went down to the hotel restaurant where he was invited to join her for lunch.

Anyone observing this might have mistaken her for his aunt or a friend of his mother's. She looked bad: overweight, bad bleach job, too much makeup, shoddy clothes. She smoked at least five cigarettes during lunch. Her lunch consisted of three cups of coffee and a couple of bites out of a burger and fries. The conversation was intense and apparently strained. She left the booth crying softly. Bill paid the lunch bill and stopped by the front desk to pay her hotel bill, as well. It would be the last time Bill ever saw her.

CHAPTER 35

Graduation Address

Bill Just To Give Graduation Address

"Local businessman and community stalwart Bill Just has agreed to
give the graduation address at Blackjack High School next week…"
— *The Blackjack Press, June 13, 1978*

WHEN MRS. STEARN, THE principal of Blackjack High School, asked Bill
to be the graduation speaker, he was astonished and a little reluctant. He
had never graduated from high school himself, for one thing, and had
minimal academic credentials. He didn't understand why she asked him.

Over the next few days it became known that the planned speaker had
cancelled and there wasn't a lot of time to get someone else. Cecille's older
daughter, Tiffany, was the senior class president, and she recommended
Bill who was, for all intents, her stepfather. Bill's reputation around town
was such that Mrs. Stearn was delighted with the suggestion, as was the
school board.

Bill worked hard on his speech, not writing it so much as thinking
about what he could say to the graduates that made sense and wasn't just

boring. He had the impression that graduation speeches, unless made by Bill Cosby, are usually less than interesting.

His speech was preceded by that of the class valedictorian, Amy Amondson. She used all the usual magic phrases, such as "change the world." Bill listened with interest, marveling at the innocence and optimism of youth. He wondered if four years from now she would be making another valedictory at her college, and if so, what would she say then? He suspected she might take a different tack. "Capitalist imperialism, burn your bra, down with the bosses," whoever those would be.

Then it was his turn.

When he was introduced, he stepped up to the front of the stage, ignoring the rostrum with the microphones, and stood with his toes over the edge, as close to his audience as he could get. He had a mic clipped to his lapel. He spoke without notes.

"This is a rare honor for me, a farm kid who quit school in tenth grade. Look at this robe they made me wear! I don't even know what this thing around my neck means. Do you?"

There was a smattering of laughter as a few of the seniors and some of the parents were actually listening and got the little joke. While he waited for silence to return, he looked at the seniors, arrayed in two rows in front of the rest of the crowd. Some of the boys had pulled their robes up over their knees, showing off the fact that they were wearing swim trunks under their robes.

He went on, "Actually, I've never heard a graduation speaker before. I never had a graduation." A murmur went through the crowd as they recognized the irony of that.

"So, when they asked me to speak to you, I had to think really hard to come up with something that I hope will be useful to you in the rest of your lives. I think I have, but you'll be the judge of that. I'm going to give you three pieces of advice. I had to learn these things the hard way, so maybe I can save you the trouble of having to learn them by trial and error.

"By now you have learned all that you need to know, right?"

The senior class seemed to be split just about fifty/fifty on that, judging by the nodding and shaking heads.

Bill sided with the shaking ones. "No? That's a good attitude, because it's fairly common for 18-year-olds to think they know it all. One of the special days of your life is when you realize your mom and dad are pretty smart after all.

"So, despite the fact that you have already spent most of your lives in school, you are about to embark on the greatest learning adventure of your lives, whether you go to college or not. Those of you who go to college will find out there's so much you don't know that it will blow your minds. Over the next four years, you'll have to learn a lot of it so that you can graduate again, and even then, the main thing you will have learned is how much you still don't know."

At that moment, a large beach ball came bouncing up from the students seated behind the seniors. Bill ignored it.

"Those of you going straight to work will have a similar experience. You're not finished learning either.

"Learning is a wonderful thing. It gets in your blood, and you want to learn more and more. With luck, you'll never stop learning, because it's fun and it's pretty useful too."

Marv, the school janitor, had been lurking in the back of the gym, something he did frequently, but this time, he was there because Mrs. Stearn had put him on duty for just this beach ball occasion. He walked in a direct path to intercept the ball on its downward trajectory, scattering students and chairs as he stepped through them. He caught the ball and pulled a screwdriver, from the tool belt he always wore, and plunged it into the ball. The big ball deflated with a whoosh. Bill waited until Marv trudged away, carrying the former ball like an old rag.

"Thank you, Marv."

He waited for the applause for Marv to die down and then continued, "Now, my first piece of advice is to stay on the fairway. I'll have to explain that a little. I don't play golf, and I doubt that many of you do either, but you probably know what a golf course looks like. The designers put what they call 'hazards' all over the place and leave a thin strip of beautiful grass in the middle, called the fairway. On the sides are 'roughs,' and sprinkled around are sand traps and water holes that eat golf balls. Stay on the fairway, and the next shot is easy. Go off the fairway, and you're in trouble. In many ways, life is like that. There are traps and roughs all around, and to do well, you need to avoid those traps.

"I want to illustrate that with one example: alcohol."

A muted cheer for alcohol was heard coming from the second row.

"Alcohol is a trap, and worse yet, it's a death trap. Those of you who'll be on a college campus for the next four years will find that alcohol is easy to get, and you're almost expected to abuse it, even if you're not old enough to drink legally."

((Another little cheer.))

"I look at it this way. I wish I was smarter than I am, stronger than I am, and better coordinated than I am. So why would I want to put something in my blood that makes me stupid, weak, and clumsy? That's what happens when you drink alcohol. You can tell already that I'm suggesting that you refrain from getting stinko, even if your parents can't see you doing it and everyone else seems to be doing it. This won't be easy, but you can learn to drink moderately or not at all.

"When I was not much older than you, a friend suggested this to me. He said, 'The next time you go to a party, try this: Don't drink all night and watch what happens to your friends.' I tried it, and it was really educational. I watched as my friends got stupid and ridiculous, and I wondered why I would want to do that.

"So the first advice is, stay on the fairway and out of the traps."

Now the students seemed to have settled down and were listening to what he was saying.

"One day, I was doing a school assignment. I forget now just what it was I had to do, but it involved this sentence: 'He who seeks happiness shall find it.' The reason I remember that so well is that my first reaction was, *That's not right.* Seeking happiness doesn't lead to happiness. No matter how hard you try to find it, you can't. Why is that?

"I think the answer is that happiness comes from within, not from the outside. So the piece of advice number two is this: Be a happy person.

Wait a minute, you're thinking, *isn't that circular? You're saying be happy in order to be happy.* And my answer is, you're right, but so am I.

"It works like this: If you are a happy person—you know the kind of person I mean, someone who is always upbeat and never the prophet of doom and gloom—you will attract lots of friends, and they'll be happier for knowing you. Having friends, especially happy friends, leads to happiness. By being a happy person, you will find happiness. It's the only way I know to find it—not by seeking it, but by being it.

"Philosophers have pondered the meaning of life for centuries, and there are as many opinions about the answer to that as there are philosophers. You can't do much better than being a happy person, making those around you happy, and making yourself happy as a result.

"But you know something? I think I have discovered through careful observation the true meaning of human life. Now I could spoil it for all of you future philosophy majors if I tell you now, but think about it, have you ever seen a want ad for a philosopher?"

((Laughter.))

"So I will tell you. Why were humans put on this earth? To feed the ants?"

((Laughter.))

"Yes, there are ants in my house, in my garbage, in my garden, at my picnics, everywhere I go, and they are all eating my food. I think the answer is clear.

"So, to review, stay on the fairway, and be a happy person. Are you with me so far?"

From the nodding of heads, it seemed they were still following.

"I told you I was going to give you three pieces of advice and there's just one left, so we're almost done already. There will be an exam; did I tell you that?"

((Laughter.))

"Number three is: Take care of your body. Americans have the best opportunity of any people on earth to be healthy, and we're not. We do it to ourselves. We overeat; we eat the wrong stuff; we drink; we smoke; and we don't get enough exercise. All of that comes from being wealthy, which in this country, we are. Having money is a good thing, but to use that opportunity wisely we need to be disciplined, and we're not.

"Overeating and the resulting obesity is one obvious example. And how about smoking? We all know that smoking causes many diseases and often results in premature death, so why do we do it? I sincerely hope that you don't smoke, but if you do, you really, seriously, should quit while you have the chance. It just gets harder.

"Sure, I know that at your age you really don't care if you die at 55 or 60. That seems so far away that you don't care. But think about this. If you abuse your body with food, drink, drugs, tobacco, or lack of exercise, your last 10 or 15 years of life will probably be as a semi-invalid. You'll essentially be handicapped. No one wants that, do they? But they go on doing themselves harm anyway. My advice is: Don't.

"Eat good food. The last time I checked, pizza was not a food group. Colleges have given up on feeding their students healthy meals, so those of you going off to college will find it a challenge to even find healthy food. College food courts are dominated by hamburgers, pizza, and pop. You can do better if you pay attention.

"Colleges also seem to have stopped educating their students about their bodies. I've heard of colleges where you don't even get credit for taking PE. I think that's outrageous. Teaching you to live healthy is one of the most important things they should do. So it's up to you to get the food and exercise you need. There are gyms on all college campuses and in most towns and cities. Use them and add some life sports to your repertoire so that you can keep it up. You need to exercise all your life if you want to be healthy later on.

"Now it's time for the final exam. It's called life. If you will stay on the fairway, be a happy person, and take care of your body, you'll get an A. The exam starts now. Get out there, and do great things!"

The students, faculty, and parents applauded earnestly. The Superintendent of Education presented Bill with another high school diploma. He was proud to have it.

Bill really had given that short speech a great deal of thought, and it pretty well summed up his personal philosophy. He had long ago decided that he grew up in the rough, and his leaving home was his first attempt to get onto the fairway of life. It took some time to get there, but when he did, he worked hard to stay on it.

He reckoned that it was his two years in the Army that put him on the fairway for good. The Army doesn't care where you came from or who your father is. The only thing those sergeants cared about was how you did your job. For the first time in his life, someone appreciated his talents. He found out that he did have a talent in finance, and that had served him well ever since.

Another thing he learned about himself was that if he could read something and understand it, he owned it from then on. He could read a book on bowling and then bowl a credible game, for example. He actually did that once.

He had not been a cheerful or a happy person as a youth. His life was hard and unpleasant, and it showed in his attitude. But when his life changed, he decided that he didn't like being a grouch, and he willed himself to show his happiness, even if he didn't exactly feel like it. He was surprised at how well that worked out. Suddenly, everyone around him seemed to be happier too.

And, as for his body, that came later. He had worked hard on the farm everyday so he didn't need to exercise, but after settling into a desk job, he grew soft and a little chubby. He saw a roll of fat around his middle when passing a mirror in his house, and determined at that instant, to get rid of it. He went out and walked hard for an hour. In the library, he read articles on weight control and learned that the body burns mostly carbohydrates at first but transitions to burning fat over time. It was that fat he wanted to burn. He made sure that he walked or rode his bike hard for an hour, burning fat for the last half of that time. Six weeks later, he had to go out and buy new pants and belts. Then, a few months later he was down another size. He vowed to himself that he would never put that weight back on.

Bill was passing his own exam.

CHAPTER 36

The Prom

Prom Decoration Damages Gym Floor

"Extensive damages occurred to the gymnasium floor at the high school
as a result of prom decorations..."

— *The Blackjack Press, April 8, 1984*

BLACKJACK WAS JUST TOO small a stage for a star of Joe Fritzling's magni-
tude. He shined all over town without having to do anything and that
was getting boring. When he acted up, which was most of the time, he
attracted too much attention: from the sheriff, the principal, the pastor,
his mother. Well, maybe not too much from his mother. Joe missed his
dad, although he had hardly known him. What he missed was *having* a
dad. He was able to get a lot of adult male attention, but it was seldom
the positive attention that he craved.

In a little school like Blackjack High, a brick building erected in 1893,
everyone got plenty of attention, because there were just so few students.
In big city schools, a teacher can see you down the hallway and have
no idea who you are. Even in many rural schools that is the case, since

students are bussed in from miles around to form huge student bodies where most students remain basically anonymous. Not so in Blackjack. So it was not lack of facial recognition that ate at him; it was mortality he chafed against.

When Joe was a freshman, he would stand in front of the old trophy case in the center hallway staring at the trophies from 1907, for example, when the basketball team won some championship trophy. He didn't know what the abbreviations meant, so he had no idea whether they had to beat one or a hundred teams to get it. He supposed that one talented player could make a great basketball team. Suppose, for example, that someone like a Michael Jordan happened to grow up in Blackjack. Well, it wouldn't be anyone really like Michael since no black people lived in town, and how likely was it that a white guy could play like Michael? But, it was something to wonder about. Fame. How did you get it?

There were old footballs in the case commemorating victories over teams that didn't even exist anymore, like Hilltop, for example. He had never heard of any place like that, and he didn't know where the nearest hill was. Hills are scarce in central Nebraska.

This is what bothered Joe. If he turned out to be a big athlete and trophies commemorating his prowess pushed aside the dusty old cups and game balls from years past, would anyone in the future even care? Wasn't he the only one who ever stood staring at the trophies? No one cared now, and no one would care in the future.

Joe would have loved to be a great football player, but he wasn't really big enough and he didn't really have the stomach for it. He played on the team, but so did every other boy in school with two legs and arms. In fact, he had heard that a few years earlier the team had a player with only one arm. If they were going to field a team, they needed every boy in school.

Joe quickly learned that playing football wasn't all fun and games. It was widely believed by the linemen that if they smelled bad enough, their opposite player would try to avoid physical contact with them, so they never washed their uniforms or the underwear they wore under them. Jockstraps turned green with sweat, as did armpits of t-shirts. Just opening your locker and taking out your clothes gagged you.

Needless to say, fungi proliferated. Most of the boys had raging cases of "jock itch" which the coach treated unsuccessfully with some liquid that, if it touched the wrong tissue, sent you flying into the rafters howling in pain.

And then there was Tuffskin. Apply it to your feet, and they wouldn't blister, they said. Changing socks and getting the right size of shoe would have worked better, but both were out of the question for most of the boys. Shoes were expensive and no one remembered to take his sweat socks home to be washed.

Maybe Joe didn't have the "stuff" to be a great football player, but he did shine as a reporter and then editor of the school paper. He was expected to, of course, coming from a newspaper family, but he wasn't happy doing it and got no pleasure from being named editor when he was still a junior. He got enough of that stuff outside of school, and he knew how much work was involved with putting out a paper, something the faculty advisor didn't seem to appreciate.

Joe noted that there were no trophies on display for editors, even though his paper won awards each of the two years he was editor. He asked the principal about that and was told that the trophy case was for athletics. If he wanted people to know about the paper's awards, he should put it in the paper. He did, but it seemed to be too much like bragging, something that teenage boys do NOT do if they want to keep their friends.

Joe spent a lot of time in detention, and there he made friends with the school janitor. Some boys in school idolized Marv, the janitor, who jangled all around the school with his huge key rings hanging from his belt. While other boys sought to mimic Marv by acquiring key rings of their own, Joe recognized Marv's lowly place in society and spent most of his idle time playing tricks on him while staying on his good side. That took talent.

Some things were just too easy. One day, Joe had been sent, as punishment, to assist Marv, who was painting a reserved spot for himself and his big pickup on the parking lot next to a side door. Marv asked Joe how to spell "Loading" and Joe spelled if for him: "Loding." Marv looked at him a little funny, but he knew better than to try to spell it himself, so he painted LODING ZONE on the asphalt, except that he forgot what letter he was painting at the end and actually painted LODINO ZONE. It stayed there for years and was, in an odd way, the trophy that Joe had always craved. Everyone in town saw it and kidded Marv about it. Before long, someone figured out how it had gotten that way, and Joe was even more famous, if that was possible.

Proms were always the province of the girls, who were usually the only ones who danced anyway, but Joe's senior year, his girlfriend of the moment, one Judy Colgins, asked him to head up the decorations. Joe listened impatiently to the suggestions: Purple Grotto, Paris in the Spring, The Isle of Capri, and so on. He wanted something exciting but manageable with local, meaning free, resources. He got a few of his buds together and attacked the problem from the "supply side." What was readily available that you have never seen in the gym before?

Someone had seen a picture of the Royal Hawaiian Hotel fountain and suggested that they could make one like it out of a stock tank, *papier mache* and some sod. That sounded pretty easy to Joe, who had no idea what it looked like, and his guys had access to the materials. Sod turned out to be too expensive, but the son of the local mortician said they had plenty of artificial stuff at the funeral home. The boys stole toilet paper from the school bathrooms for weeks to use as *papier mache*. All the other boys had to bring their own TP to school in case they might need to use it.

The week before the prom, Joe and his team hauled in a stock tank, rigged up a fountain powered by a small electric pump, laid the fake sod around it, and added some *papier mache* touches, plus a few ad hoc items that came from farms in the surrounding countryside, such as a very nice pig trough filled with straw and a couple of nesting hens.

The Prom Committee (in other words, the girls) was not well pleased. It was too late to do much of anything else at that point, but the hens were sent back home to roost and the straw was replaced with red and white balloons. The two eggs that had been laid were given to the cooks in the cafeteria.

At the prom, the fountain was a big hit with the boys who found many ways of splashing each other from the stock tank, now full of water. Not that the fountain didn't already splash considerably. When they tested it, the tank was only half full and the splashing was confined to the inside of the tank, but when the tank was full, the splashes reached out a good six feet.

On Prom night, Marv, hanging out in a dark corner and salivating over the girls in low-cut gowns, was the first to realize that the gym floor was getting a real soaking. He thought hard about it for at least three minutes before going out to the baseball diamond and dragging in a heavy tarp that was covering the pitcher's mound. He didn't have time to clean it off, so the clay from the tarp mixed readily with the inch or so of water sitting on the gym floor and turned to a greasy mud. A few couples oblivious to their surroundings in their blissful clutches, danced onto the mess, lost their footing, and slid on their backsides through the mud. Two lovely prom dresses were ruined, and the two couples ran tearfully to their pickups and didn't return. Marv really enjoyed watching the girls run in their dresses.

After the last "Mexican Hat Dance," and "Good Night Ladies," played by "Donny Jordan, DJ the DJ," from scratchy LPs, all who remained unsoiled concluded that it was a great prom, and Joe got lots of pats on the back and a few kisses on the cheek—one with such ardor that he forgot to take Judy home.

Joe's crew was supposed to take the decorations down on Sunday, but Irma Fritzling had other ideas. She had a paper to get out, a sick reporter, and pictures of the prom to process. Joe spent the day working on *The Press*.

Joe slept in on Monday and didn't get to school until 9:30. When he walked into English class, the teacher promptly handed him a note to go to the principal's office.

Mrs. Stearn wanted to know why the prom decorations had not been removed. Joe tried to explain. Mrs. Stearn reminded Joe that gym class was held in that place now occupied by a stock tank full, well, half full, of water, soggy artificial sod and papier mache, and a large muddy expanse. Fortunately, she said, it was a warm day, and the coach had taken the kids out to the track for a few laps and some stretching.

"Tomorrow," she declared, "we will have our gymnasium back, do you understand, Mr. Fritzling?"

Joe and some of his crew met in the gym after classes. Joe said, "Buck, you drain the tank..."

"How?" asked Dick Buckmeister.

"How the hell do I know?" Joe replied. "Just do it."

Joe now turned his attention to the "fountain."

"You guys," Joe said, pointing to Harv and Melly, "get that pump out of here. And, you two," he pointed at William and a freshman whose name he had forgotten, "get that stupid paper mah-crap and grass to the dumpster."

The sod was totally soaked and was hauled out to the dumpster along with armfuls of dripping wads of *papier mache*, leaving a wet trail across the floor. The pump was another story. Harv suddenly turned white and dropped to the floor, twitching and holding an electric wire to the pump. Melly was jumping up and down in little bunny hops and whimpering. Joe grabbed the only wooden thing he could find nearby, a broom that Marv had been leaning on, and used it to disconnect Harv from the circuit. Harv couldn't uncross his eyes for two days, but he was otherwise not permanently damaged so far as the other boys could tell.

So far, so good, but the tank still had water in it. Buck was standing and staring with no idea how to get the water out.

Joe was not a detail man, and he preferred to leave these petty details to his crew. He issued his last orders of the day, "Get it out of here today!" and headed for the Ideal Dairy Bar for a chance to see Judy and explain why he had left her at the dance while he was out in the truck getting more familiar with Angie Norgren's mouth.

On Tuesday morning, Joe was summoned to the principal's office again. Mrs. Stearn said, "I believe I was quite clear in my instructions yesterday, was I not? I told you to return the gymnasium to service by today, do you remember that?"

Joe did, and he was surprised that this nagging little nit was still biting him. Hadn't he told Buck to take care of it?

When he found Buck third period, Buck told him, "I couldn't figure out how to get the water out, so I left it there until you could explain it to me."

Joe hauled Buck and a couple of other guys he found standing around in the hallway down to the gym. When they arrived, they found that Marv had hooked a long hose to the tank and was attempting to siphon the water out. They concluded that their work was done. Joe told Buck, "Get that tank out of here this afternoon."

Wednesday morning, Joe arrived to find Mrs. Stearn standing at the door of his first period class. "Please come with me to the gymnasium, Mr. Fritzling," she snarled. When they walked through the doors of the gym, there it was, the stock tank sitting in the middle of the gym floor with about a foot of water in it. Marv was sucking on the hose, but the tank was now at just about the level of the ground outside and the siphon wouldn't work for more than a few gallons at a time.

Mrs. Stearn handed Joe a bucket and told him to start bailing, adding, "And you are not to stop until that tank is off of my gym floor!"

Joe bailed for over an hour but finally got to the bottom of the tank. He found some members of his crew, including Harv, who had to be led by another since his eyes were still crossed, and they hauled the tank out to the parking lot. Now the gym floor was fully exposed for the first time in a long time. The tank had leaked steadily from the first time they put water into it, then the water had splashed out and been aided in its escape by some boys. The water and clay from the tarp had thoroughly soaked the old hardwood floor, and the boards had expanded and buckled. Where the tank had stood, a new indoor, hardwood pitcher's mound now stuck up from the previously flat basketball court. It was a good thing that basketball season was over or all remaining home games would have had to be cancelled. Gym class remained problematic.

An emergency budget revision was necessary to replace the entire floor that summer. The new floor was much better than the old one, and the new seniors started calling it the Joe Fritzling Memorial Floor.

Ah, Joe mused when he heard about it, *enduring fame at last.*

CHAPTER 37

Grandad Larsen, Later

AFTER GRANDAD LARSEN HAD come to Blackjack looking for him, other kids privately relayed the information to Bill. One of them had a note written by the old man with a phone number. Now Bill wondered about his mom. Grandad had told him she had been put into a home. Maybe he ought to at least know where she was. He thought about it for a few days before calling.

Grandad had never been mean the way Bill's dad had been, but he could be very critical and his idea of affection was teasing. Bill didn't like being teased, no matter how much it seemed to entertain adults.

When he thought of his grandad, he thought of phrases like, "Put a little elbow grease into it." Sure, it was easy for that 200-pounder with farmer's hands the size of cantaloupes to put pressure on a saw or a scrub brush or whatever was the tool in question, but quite another for a six-year-old boy. So Bill wasn't really sure what his relationship was to the elder Larsen, who was his father's father. Wouldn't he logically be closer to his son than his grandson?

Finally, Bill decided that his granddad was someone who had proved trustworthy and, perhaps even loving, on his first visit to Blackjack, and he called him.

His grandfather's ring was one short and two longs. They still had party lines on the farm, and actually anyone could listen in, but the rings told them whom the call was actually for. Bill knew he had to call after dark because that was the only time he could be sure his grandfather would be back in the house.

He immediately recognized the voice that answered, and all his fears vanished. He could almost hear the love in the old man's voice.

"Billy, it's so good that you called. Where are you?"

"I can't come back. Do you understand what I'm saying?"

"Sure I do, Billy, but there's something you need to know. Your mom is gone, Billy. She's dead."

Bill stood silent. He was shocked by this news and realized a great loss, though he didn't know why. Finally he said, "I didn't know."

"Of course you didn't. How could you? If you want the farm, I guess it's yours. It hain't worth nothing, I guess. Probably just pay the bills if you sell it. Why don't you come see me and let's talk about all this?"

"Sure, Grandad," Bill said.

And he did.

The lawyers agreed that the best thing would be to let the farm go for taxes and other debts. Bill was allowed to go back into the house and take his personal stuff. He took some winter clothes that still fit him, and his shortwave radio. When he drove away, he didn't even look back.

His grandad died too, the next year. That part of his life was gone for good.

How could someone as caring as Bill turn his back on his parents that way? That was the question he asked himself a thousand times. The only thing he could figure out was that they had hurt him too much. They had driven the love for them right out of him. He had to acknowledge that he had hated them for that.

CHAPTER 38

The Matador

As AN ADULT WITH a college degree and years in television, Kenny Jackson bought The Matador, the town bar, but he was too busy out of town with his real job, a producer/director of Nebraska Public Television, to actually run it. When he could fit it into his schedule, he even taught Television Production at the community college.

Ken's wife kept the books, and they hired an old friend, someone they could absolutely trust, to manage it on a daily basis. Ken had known Butch Kreutzer since fourth grade, and Butch had worked for years in The Ideal for Johnny, Ken's dad. Between the three of them, Ken, Beth, and Butch, they had many years of experience in the business, only without the booze.

Having someone like Butch in the place every day paid off in a myriad ways. For example, when Jim Shimak borrowed a draft card from a college buddy and tried to buy a vodka tonic at The Matador, Butch peered at the card and said, "I've known Charlie Cutter since the day he was born, and you're not him." Jim spent the next few hours being fingerprinted and mugshot, and he didn't try to buy another drink in The Matador until he was nearly 23.

Ken and Butch had always been in the food trade, not the booze business, and they both entered into it with some trepidation. But the thing about booze was the profit margin. At the Ideal, the item that made the money was pop. A glass of Coca Cola cost them about a cent and a half and sold for 30 cents. That was pretty amazing, but most people only needed one pop. Sell a man a highball with a similar markup, and he'll probably want two more, at least. Ken had actually learned this in college, but not in classes. He said it was "through research."

Eric Fedje was a classic town drunk. He was usually standing at the door when it opened at 10 a.m. or, as most of the denizens of The Matador called it, "10 a.m. in the morning." Eric's only friends were the other guys who came in at something a.m. in the morning and stayed all day. In fact, you pretty much had to be drunk just to be near Eric. Since he usually arose shortly before 10, he just managed to put on the same clothes he had worn the day before. Any other personal toilet would be postponed until later, which often meant some other day.

Butch liked to maintain high standards in The Matador, although that was a losing battle. If he could prevent the glasses from being broken, he could count it a good day. Eric didn't measure up to Butch's standards, partially formed during his five years in the Marine Corps reserve.

Butch would say to Eric, "Before you come out in public, Eric, perhaps you should consider bathing, shaving, and dental hygiene."

Eric would respond, "Before you start tellin' yer customers how to live, you might wanna consider that we could go sumplace else for breakfast." Then he'd laugh until he coughed up a big wad that he spat on the floor. It was kind of funny, since there was no other bar in town, anyway, so all of his friends would laugh too. Butch would seethe as he got out the mop and wiped up the floor around Eric and his buddies.

Eric was actually a talented carpenter, and he was usually in the middle of two or three jobs—jobs that he had promised to finish weeks or months before. Sometimes his customers figured out where he was every morning, and they would come in to try to get him back on the job. Eric was too smart for that.

For example, Peter Stearn, the high school principal's husband, was not accustomed to paying people money and then having to make the worker actually work. He had been a manager for the phone company most of his life, and when he told someone at Ma Bell to do something, it got done.

Peter came into The Matador one Tuesday morning at about 10:20 (a.m. in the morning) and found Eric, who was supposed to be re-roofing his garage, already well into his second Canadian and Seven. Peter took Eric by the arm and led him to a booth. "Sit down, Eric. I want to talk, and I don't want to embarrass you."

"Hell, you cain't embarrass me, Pete (no one called Peter Stearn "Pete"). These guys are my friends."

"Yes, that is no doubt true, but you are my employee and I need you on the job today, tomorrow, and every day until my roof is finished." Peter, though well-educated and somewhat persnickety, pronounced "roof" in Nebraskan, meaning it rhymed with "hoof."

"Yeah, well, there's no place I'd rather be, Pete, but there's nothing I can do until them roofing nails I ordered from Lindstrom's comes in. Maybe today. Hell, I'll be right on it soon's I get them nails."

There was no order for roofing nails, of course. In fact, you could get as many as you could carry from Lindstrom's right then, but Peter didn't know that.

Peter spent a few more minutes trying to impress on Eric the necessity for getting on with the job before it rained or snowed or whatever might be likely. Eric considered countering with, "Mights well wait until after the next twister, 'cause it'll just get tored off again," but that didn't seem like a very good marketing pitch somehow. Eric tossed down the rest of his second drink and waved for a third. Peter knew the rest of the day was lost, for sure, and he went home to consider a Plan B.

Most towns seem to have a town drunk. One has to wonder about the even distribution of drunks among towns. Do they dislike competition? That would seem to be the opposite of reality. They didn't just like each other; they were pretty much their only society. But it seemed that one always stood out. The guy who would get so bombed that he would stagger out onto the sidewalk and fall down in a stupor. Someone would call the sheriff, and he, Eric in this case, would get carted off to jail to sleep it off. For some reason, the other guys knew about when to quit.

The financial considerations of drunks should be an interesting study for bar owners. Despite the obvious need for it, there is no course on this at the university, or even the community college. To be sure, any business management course would teach you that you ought to maximize the use of your fixed assets and labor. In other words, having customers at your bar at 10 a.m. "in the morning" and 11 p.m. "at night" was a good use of your real estate and your bartenders. But, how much money do you really make from the drunks? Oh, sure, they spend money recklessly, but they also break things, make messes, and annoy other customers. How much business do you lose because a drunk is sitting at the bar mumbling incoherently, or worse, passed out on the sidewalk next to the entrance?

Butch made a semi-scientific study of this and concluded that the trick is to move the slobbering drunks out before noon and again before 5 p.m. No one was likely to come in for a drink before, say, 11:30 a.m., except the usual hard core. Then, only a few farmers, in town "on business," would come through the doors during the afternoon. Those guys were willing to put up with Eric and his friends if they had to.

Five o'clock was another matter. The guys from the dog food plant would come streaming in for a quick one before going home. Even Pastor Lesher stopped by a couple of days a week, sometimes joined by the "Evangelist" from the Church of the Almighty Redeemer. It was best that they found a congenial atmosphere. So Butch would cut Eric off at 11 and again at 4. Eric usually left at those times, and if he was still walking, he went to the old-fashioned mom-and-pop grocery where he could bum a stale bun and a slice of bologna. *There was order in his life, after all,* he would think, as he sat on the grocery doorstep, eating his sandwich.

Eric could take pride in the orderly life he led, because he chose to compare himself with only those who were even worse off. For Eric, that only left one man in the entire county.

Everyone in Blackjack agreed that Earl Farris had something loose in his head. He lived in a shack with a herd of goats, but he managed to smell worse than the goats and stayed dirtier than they were. You didn't see much of Earl in town, but he came in for groceries once or twice a week. He would ask for rotten apples from the very bottom of the barrel and would eat them whole.

Some days, when Earl shuffled out of the grocery store with brown apple mush on his chin, he would have to step past Eric slumped over in a semi stupor. Earl would think, "There's a sorry case." And Eric would look up to see who had bumped by him and think, "There goes a sorry case." It was a sublime moment for both of them.

CHAPTER 39

A Crafty Attorney

I HAD JUST MET Barry Scoggs, a name I had heard and a face I had seen, but whom I had never actually met. He was a short man, but his torso seemed to be normal size; it was just his legs that were short. I wondered where he could buy pants that short and still large enough to go around his ample waist. His sandy hair was unruly, and he had a day-old growth of stubble on his cheeks. I didn't expect to learn anything from him, but since I had been in town, I seemed to have learned something from just about everyone. From what I had heard, Barry was retired on a disability for a railroad accident. I didn't see anything wrong with him, though, and I hoped to learn something about his railroad days.

Barry said, "Hey, I know who you are. You're the guy who writes for the paper. There's actually someone in town for a few days who you oughta interview. Ever heard of John Rush, the lawyer?"

I hadn't.

"Well, he's a famous Texas prosecutor, and he was born and raised right here in Blackjack. Boy, does he have some stories to tell. I think I can tell you where to find him."

He did.

Rush was staying with a nephew who lived in town and said I could come right over, but he was leaving in the morning so it had to be today.

The famous prosecutor said, "Listen, Ralph, did you say your name was? You don't want to hear the ramblings of an old, retired attorney. I can't imagine anything more boring than that."

I said, "No, sir, I do want to hear about what everyone is telling me is a fascinating career in law. I'm just afraid, as ignorant of legal matters as I am, that I won't be able to write it well. I'm even hoping that I can get you to write it. Maybe a short memoir."

"Nope, I won't do that, but if you insist, I'll talk to you a while. I see you've brought a tape recorder so you won't even have to take notes. Pretty clever."

"Sir, I…"

"Oh, for God's sake, don't call me 'sir.' Makes me realize how old I must look to you."

"Okay, but what should I call you?"

"You know what? Call me Tex."

"Okay, Tex, where should we start?"

"I suppose we should start with how I came to be Tex, which no one calls me but you. Coming from Nebraska, you wouldn't think I'd have such a name, but I fell in love with western stories and read them almost non-stop all of my youth. All I ever wanted to be was a cowboy. But my folks had different ideas and insisted that I had to go to college. Of course, they thought I should go to a college around here, but I said that, if I had to go to college, it had to be in Texas."

"And they went along with that?"

"Not at first, but by the time fall came around, I was enrolled at the University of Texas in Austin. While I was there, I learned enough about cowboys and lawyers that I decided it was better to be a lawyer and buy a horse if I wanted one, but go out and make my money in the practice of law. Besides that, I wanted to get married and my wife-to-be wasn't about to marry a cowboy."

"And that worked out great, I assume."

"No, surprisingly, two years after getting my law degree, I seriously considered buying a horse and becoming a cowboy, but I couldn't afford a horse."

"So, what happened?"

"I had graduated right into the Great Depression. No one was hiring anybody for anything, but especially not brand new lawyers. My brother had graduated the year before in Lincoln, and he hadn't gotten a job yet either. He started taking pro bono cases just for the experience, and the Attorney General was taking some interest in him. He suggested that I do the same, so I did."

"But that meant you weren't earning anything."

"That's right, most of the time. Sometimes, I'd get someone off who actually had a few bucks in his wallet, and he'd be so grateful he'd pay me something. You know, in a way, it was easy money. The prosecutors thought that those pro bonos weren't likely to get any effective defense, so they didn't bother to really prepare for trial. It was easy enough for me to win, because they wouldn't actually prove their cases, and I would point that out to the judge. It was a great experience. I was winning cases that I shouldn't have won, and people took notice. Especially the Attorney General took notice that this kid was getting bad guys off, and he had to do somethin' 'bout that."

"So he...?"

"So he hired me. And he didn't just hire me; he made me his special assistant. I don't think he meant for that to be the big deal it was; he just didn't have any openings. As it turned out, it became a good career. You see, a lot of the counties didn't have district attorneys with much trial experience. Hell, most attorneys never see the inside of a courtroom. You'd think... well, don't let me get off track.

"Since I had a lot of courtroom experience and some of it for some serious crimes, he started sending me to assist DAs who were in over their heads. I never ran out of those, so it was a whole career."

"Sounds like you spent a lot of time on the road."

"Yep, that's so, and remember getting around wasn't all that easy. Lots of places I could get there on the train, but if there wasn't any train, I had to drive, and there weren't a lot of good roads back then.

"I learned some tricks, even before I had that job. I found out that juries like people who they think are just like them. When I was a kid, right out of college, poor as a church mouse, juries liked me. Meanwhile, I was up against the big bad DA. I got a lot of sympathy from the juries and used that to my advantage. Now the shoe was on the other foot. I was now the big bad DA, so I had to win their sympathy. I had a whole routine worked out to do just that."

"I hope you are about to tell me about that."

"Sure, I'll never try another case, so I can tell you anything you want to know. For starters, people like other people who talk like they do. I didn't naturally do that, being from Nebraska, but while at UT, I had learned a few Texas accents: East Texas, South Texas, Panhandle, and so on. As soon as I came into the town the trial was going to be in and the jury was going to come from, I spent as much time as I could talking with the people and mimicking their accents until I had it down pat. That meant I had to show up early for the trial, but I had to do that anyway because the local DA would have done most of the pre-trial work. I knew where to go to talk to the locals: grocery stores, cafes, car dealerships, feed stores, and so forth. I would also try to learn as much about the town and what was going on there, and what they thought about the case, if anything. I did a lot of work before the trial even began.

"I would get aholta, that's Texan son, an old car from some car dealer, usually a Ford or a Chivy, because that's what the townies had mostly, and would make sure that everyone saw me driving it around town. I bought my clothes at either the western store or J. C. Penney, just like they did. No fancy clothes, no fancy cars, no fancy nothin'. I even had an old pocket watch that didn't run, and I always kept it on me during the trial. From time to time, I'd pretend to look at it, and at the time I judged to be best I would take it out of my pocket, look at it, bang it on the table a couple of times, look at it again, and then turn to the defense attorney and ask if he had the time. Since he was probably a high-priced defender from Dallas, he would put out his arm to look at his gold wristwatch, and I knew I owned that jury.

"And all that time, what you wanted was to overcome their natural prejudice against an out-of-towner from the gummint."

"Exactly. Well, here's a lesson in law, son. Prosecution is a matter of proving your case. If you know you can't, you shouldn't even go to trial, and lots of times I looked at the evidence and told the DA not to go to court. Sometimes we'd work out a plea deal, and other times, we'd just drop it. Saved the state a bunch of money. But when we had the proof, all we had to do was show it to the jury in a way they could understand. If we did that right, it didn't matter much how the defense tried to confuse the jury. If they believed the defendant was guilty, there wasn't much the defense attorney could do. The point is, I almost always won the case. And as long as I was doing that, I had a good job. I did it for over forty years and retired to a life of ease. Now I come back here to Nebraska to visit old friends, but there aren't many left. About all I do now is look around the town, go by Lincoln to see nephews and nieces, and go to the Capitol Building. I always go to the Capitol Building and go into the State Supreme Court and marvel at that beautiful room. Have you seen it?"

"Nope, Tex, I shor hain't," I drawled.

"Say, there's a career for you in law, young fella."

CHAPTER 40

The Escapee

I had been checking out a story at a farm just outside of town and was on my way back home when I passed an elderly lady carrying a suitcase and walking along the road toward town. I stopped just past her and waited until she caught up. I asked through the open window if she needed a ride.

"I don't ride in cars with strangers," she said.

"Well, in that case, allow me to introduce myself. Maybe you've heard of me, because I'm Ralph Anderson of *The Press,*" I said.

"I don't read that rag," she replied.

"That's okay, I'll give you a ride anyway."

"Why would you do that?" she asked.

"Because you look like you could use a ride and I'm going your way. May I help you with that suitcase? Let's just put it on the backseat."

"Well, all right, but listen, young man, you can't write about this in the paper."

"Fine, but why?"

"Because I just escaped from jail."

I didn't believe that.

"I won't write about it, but you have to tell me about it. This is too good to ignore."

"Oh, it's no big deal, sonny. I just made a rope ladder out of my sheets and climbed out the window, that's all," she said without emotion.

"That doesn't sound like a very secure jail," I said.

"They haven't made a jail that will hold me," she snorted.

"It wasn't really a jail, was it?"

"They don't call it that, but it's the same thing. They hauled me out of my house and dragged me there in an ambulance and said I couldn't leave."

"Might you be talking about the rest home?" I guessed.

"I don't care what you call it; it's a jail."

"How many stories up was this window you used the rope ladder from?"

"Just one, but I wanted to be safe," she said. "After all, I'm eighty-eight."

I knew the place she had escaped from. It had happened before, and in fact, she was probably the one who had escaped before. That time, she just walked out the front door and hitched a ride back home.

The Whileaway House was a lovely place. I had written an article about it when it opened. The owners, Les and Sue Hagen, had gotten into the business by an indirect route. Les was principal of the elementary school, and he was having trouble recruiting teachers. The school didn't pay teachers much, and even with real estate prices running pretty low in Blackjack, teachers couldn't afford to buy. Les started by buying a house that had been for sale for some time for a bargain price and renovating it. He then hired a new teacher and rented it to her for a price she could afford.

That was followed by a second house, and then a third. Les and his wife, Sue, weren't making much money from that, if any, but Les was getting good teachers and that's all he wanted.

Then, the only rest home in the area was closed by state inspectors. No one had complained about the place. It was nice and inexpensive, but new, severe regulations had come down from Washington and it could no longer pass inspections. Les was between house renovations, so he bought it and fixed it up. He worked closely with the state inspectors to be sure it would pass, and it did. He knew he couldn't charge enough to make a profit, but his mother needed a place to go and had been living with him ever since the old place had been closed. He almost didn't care how much money he lost as long as she was happy living out of his home. Anyway, he had more of his labor than his money invested in it.

We had reached her house, and I didn't even know her name, so I asked.

"Mrs. Theo," she said.

No first name.

"Well, Mrs. Theo, let me help you with the suitcase if you won't tell anyone I aided and abetted your escape."

"You're an accomplice now, sonny!" She laughed.

"Would you tell me what was so bad about the Whileaway?" I asked.

"Not that anything was wrong with it. You just don't understand. I don't need to be in there. I can live just fine by myself. I have for the last 45 years."

"If you were doing so well, why did they come for you in an ambulance?"

"Because I fell down and couldn't get up. And they found out that I couldn't eat because I can't open cans anymore."

"Did you fall down from hunger?"

"Yeah, maybe I did, so what?"

"Then, how are you going to eat tonight, for example?"

"I don't know yet," she said.

"I do," I said, "because I'm taking you to dinner. After that, I'm buying you an electric can opener, and we're going to practice opening cans with it."

"Who died and made you God?" she asked.

"You almost died and I found you, so now I'm God for the rest of today. Come on, let's get some supper."

Of course, I took her to the Ideal for broasted chicken. It was wonderful, as always, but she complained. She insulted the waitress and complained about everything. I was beginning to understand that God doesn't have it easy.

Between insults and complaints, she did tell me her beef with the Whileaway.

"It's the people in there. You know, Czechs, Swedes, Germans, Irish Catholics, those people."

"And what are you, then, if you're not one of those?'

"I'm American," she said.

I took her home and checked her kitchen cabinets. She had forty-four cans of Dinty Moore Beef Stew, a few showing marks from the can opener where she had tried to open them. We tried out the new electric can opener I had bought her. She finally got it, but it took all of her strength to do it.

She claimed she didn't have any relatives, so I had a research project to work on. I left her safe at home, called Sue Hagen, told her where her inmate was, and went to bed feeling very proud of myself for once.

CHAPTER 41

Big Brother

Sheriff Jackie McBean assigned Bill Just to the position of Big Brother to Joe Fritzling, son of the publisher, last night in a meeting with the mayor and the town council. Fritzling has long been a thorn in the sheriff's side, along with many other town and school leaders, but an incident involving skunk hunting yesterday prompted....

The Blackjack Press, May 3, 1984

The whole town seemed to get fed up with Joe Fritzling on the same day. It was the first warm day of summer that just about ends the school year, no matter if it occurs in June or April. From then on, the kids may be present in school, but their minds are at the swimming pool.

In Joe's senior year, that day occurred on May 4th. The day started off normally, but the weather forecast was for highs in the 70s, so naturally, the kids all came to school in shorts, apparently thinking that it was going to be too hot to wear real clothes all day. Never mind that when they were waiting for the school bus, it was 52 and windy. By 11 a.m., it was up to 74, and the school year ended with a huge thump. You couldn't hear it, but the teachers all recognized the sound. Heads hit desks, notebooks were closed, the school year was dead and gone.

Joe and his buddies were the first to be affected, as usual. All were dressed in shorts and sleeveless Ts, just right for the 95-degree day they must have been anticipating, and their minds were in the pool, in the woods, in their trucks… anywhere but in the classroom.

Joe had been waiting for this day. He had gotten money for Christmas, and he hadn't spent it until a few days ago when he bought a hunting rifle. Joe had never actually been hunting, since he didn't have a father to take him, and no one else's father wanted to be anywhere near him when he was armed. Joe could hardly wait to go hunting, and he was sure this day was sent to him by God for just that purpose.

"What are we going to hunt?" Harv asked. Harv was an experienced hunter. He had been hunting with his grandfather since he was 7. His grandfather told him that when he was a kid, no one thought twice about a boy with a gun. He, grandpa, walked over a mile to school every day and he carried his shotgun with him, hunting for supper, both going and coming. He brought home rabbits, pheasants, and quail, and, rarely, a deer. Later, he drove into town for high school, and hunted from the window of the car.

Harv went on, "You can't just go hunting anytime you want anymore. You need a license, and you have to hunt in season. I don't know of anything that's in season in May."

"Aw, you're such a jerk, Harv," Joe countered. "Can't you think for once? What *don't* you need a license to hunt? There must be something."

Harv wasn't sure, but he suspected there were some things you could hunt without a license. He mentioned the only one he could think of offhandedly: "Skunk."

"Sure, skunk! There'd never be any reason to have a skunk season, would there? You can hunt them anytime you want," opined Joe, with authority born of ignorance.

So, that's how it happened that Joe, Harv, and Buck cut classes all afternoon to hunt skunks. They had to sneak home to get their rifles, which was no problem for Joe, but more of a challenge for the other two. Finally, armed for bear but going for skunks, they lit out for a patch of woods out back of Harv's house, where he was fairly sure a bunch of skunks lived—at least that's where Harv's old dog seemed to find plenty of them.

It was a scene from Laurel and Hardy at first. Joe had no idea what he was doing, and the other boys had to constantly tell him not to carry his rifle loaded and cocked, not to let it point at them, and so on. Then, there was the problem of actually finding a skunk before one found you.

Joe came up with a brilliant idea. They would get on three sides of the woods and work their way in, thereby forcing the skunks to come out and run toward one of them. Unfortunately, it worked.

As the boys started into the woods from three directions, a skunk stuck his head up and assessed the situation. He had never been hunted before, but instincts developed in the genus of skunks over hundreds of thousands of years of evolution took over. He decided that offense was the best defense, and he headed off for the gap between Joe and Buck as fast as his little legs would carry him, which was pretty doggone fast. Joe instantly chambered a round and lifted his rifle. This act created more fear in Buck, who thought Joe was going to shoot right at him, than in the skunk.

Buck was yelling, "Don't shoot! Don't shoot!"

Joe had no idea how to shoot a rifle. He had never zeroed the sights, but that hardly mattered, because in the tradition of the countless westerns he had watched, he simply raised the rifle and, after waiting for the skunk to pass by, fired. The bullet struck a back window in Harv's house, as luck would have it, penetrated the kitchen window, and ripped through the refrigerator, lodging in the wallboard behind it.

The sound woke up Harv's sleeping old dog, Wheezer, who was chained behind the house. Wheezer's hunting days were behind him, but the sound of a rifle and the blur of running game coming in his direction, brought forth natural responses bred into his ilk for eons. He leapt up and easily snapped the chain that had supposedly held him for over three years. He bounded toward the running skunk barking furiously. Skunk decided the boys were less of a threat. He gave Wheezer a short shot of stinkum, saving the rest for the boys. He darted back the same way he had come out, and then paused briefly to lay an odiferous screen between himself and the boys.

The three manly hunters decided at this point to call it a day. They retreated to Harv's house hoping to find food, but when they opened the back door they found Harv's grandmother, awakened from her seemingly perpetual nap by a bullet going through the refrigerator.

Teetering on her walker, she yelled, "Get that dog out of this house! He's been sprayed by a skunk again!" They had inadvertently let Wheezer through the door, but Granny was only partly right. That skunk had gotten all of them.

Sheriff McBean, called by four neighbors who heard the shots and saw the boys toting their rifles, decided it was time to take strong measures with his main problem, Joe. He convened a meeting in the court that evening, attended by the boys and their parents, as well as Mrs. Stearn, the principal, the mayor, and Bill Just. Bill had no idea why he was invited. In fact, the "invitation" sounded more like a command.

The meeting got off to a bad start when the skunky boys came in. Three baths and a tomato juice treatment had barely made a dent in the smell. They ended up sitting in the jury box, and everyone else sat in the back of the room.

Opinions were offered, but no one seemed to have any good ideas of how to change Joe's behavior.

Finally, McBean said, "Bill, I want you to be this kid's big brother until he leaves for college. Will you do that?"

Bill was vaguely familiar with the Big Brother program, but he thought it was for inner city kids with no male role models. Well, this was similar; it just wasn't inner city, so he said, "I can give it a try, Sheriff. I can't make any promises as to success, though."

"That's all we can ask," McBean said. "Include his cohorts, too."

Bill had no idea what to do, but he remembered his basic training in the Army, where he had seen not a few kids about this age learn some discipline and, most of all, kept too busy to get into trouble.

He started with marching, called "close order drill" in the Army. When marching, soldiers have to obey every order instantly. Hesitate a second and a messy pileup occurs. For this, Bill recruited as many of Joe's buddies as he could get and drilled them two hours a day until they were exhausted. Then he had Joe, Harv, and Buck report back in the evening for two more hours of the manual of arms. When they finished at 10, Joe was too tired to do anything but go to bed.

Next, Bill taught them how to fire their rifles. He taught them sight alignment, sight picture, trigger squeezing, the various shooting positions, and most of all, care and maintenance of a rifle. After two hours of shooting at the Rod and Gun Club range, they spent another hour or two cleaning their firearms and passing inspection. Once again, they ended the day too tired and sore for any more activity.

Quiet returned to Blackjack. Several single mothers and even a couple of fathers asked Bill to take on their sons. Bill explained his program and suggested that they run one like it through scouts. A little later, he set up a similar program for the scout troop, but it took a special man to make the kids come and work at it.

Joe was a smart kid, too smart maybe, and he was accepted by every college he applied to. He decided to attend Kansas State, and when he departed for college in the fall, he was a different boy.

...until he joined a fraternity.

CHAPTER 42

The Family Historian

I WAS WORKING IN *The Press* one day, something I seldom did, since there was no room for me there, when a man came through the door and looked around as if not knowing what to do next.

"Can I help you, sir?" I asked. I wasn't so sure I would know any of the answers, but I wanted to appear helpful.

The man said, "Hi, I'm Orin McRae, and I'm looking for information on my ancestors. I was wondering if I might look through your files to see if I can find anything out about them in there."

"Gosh, I don't know about that," I said. "I'd like to help you, but I don't know the policy here. My boss isn't here right now. How long are you going to be around?"

"I just have two days and it's nearly noon today already, so I guess I have a day and a half."

"I would imagine that she'll be back before too long. I'll have to ask you to wait until I can talk to her."

"That's all right," Orin said. "I have to go by the courthouse anyway, so I'll do that now if you'll try to get an answer for me in the meantime."

"I shall," I said, proud that I had actually used the word "shall" in a sentence, correctly, I hoped.

When Mrs. Fritz returned, I told her what McRae wanted, and Mrs. Fritz told me that the answer was in the library. "Every issue of *The Press* ever published is on *fiche* in the library. Anyone who wants to see our files should go over there."

I was actually a little miffed that Mary hadn't told me that. Maybe I should have asked.

At 12:45, Orin returned. I told him where to find the files, and Orin was very grateful. "Let me take you to lunch. Maybe you'll help me just by telling more things about the town."

No one had ever offered me lunch, other than my mother and grandmother, so far as I could remember. And for some reason, I sort of liked this guy and thought lunch might be interesting.

We headed off to The Ideal.

As we sat and chewed, Orin launched into his story. It seemed as if he was sort of rehashing what he already knew in preparation for doing further research.

"My great grandfather, J. J. McRae, came to this town back in the 1890s. I don't know exactly when, and that's one of the things I aim to find out. Before he came here, he had gone to college, which was probably more like high school. I'm not really sure.

"After college, he had worked as a druggist for a couple of years, all of this taking place in Iowa, and then, for reasons I can't understand, he became a conductor on the railroad."

"Boy!" I interjected. "That's quite a comedown."

"Oh, no, it's not," McRae said. "Perhaps you don't know it, but it's the conductor who runs the train. Everyone else on the train works for him. In the early days of railroads, there were so many unexpected things to deal with that the conductor had a very important job. My guess is that he was well paid."

"I didn't know that," I said, reaching for my notebook.

"Yep. Well paid is my guess. He was married and had two children, when all of a sudden he jumps up and leaves that all behind and comes here. Why? That's what I want to know."

"I hear it was the age of romance and the west..."

"Sure, that's the easy answer. I was ready to believe that, but the next question was how did he start off right after he got here, by opening a bank? That takes money or investors or both. I hope to find the answer in the newspaper files."

"Sounds reasonable," I conjectured.

McRae went on. "A few years later, the other bank in town was on hard times, but his bank wasn't, so he bought out the other fella and then he had two banks in the same town. Today you would call that a monopoly."

"What did they call it then?"

McRae laughed. "If anyone cared, I guess he would have called it a monopoly or a big mistake, I'm not sure which. But over the next few years, he opened banks in all the little towns around here. I'd sure like to know how he did that."

"Yeah, so would I. I could stand to have a few banks of my own," I joked.

"It worked for him. He ended up with that big house in town. You know the one?"

"I have seen a pretty big house, I guess."

McRae explained, "Some people call that the McRae house still, although there hasn't been a McRae in Blackjack for 75 years. He probably foreclosed on some farmers because he also owned some ranches in the area and shipped a lot of cattle to Kansas City every year. I expect I'll learn more about that from the old papers."

We finished our broasted chicken, and McRae didn't seem to be springing for dessert, so we left a tip and went to the library. I introduced him to Mary and chided her for not telling me about the files. "Oh, that was coming, Ralph. One thing at a time," she said.

As we parted, I said, "Orin, when you find out more stuff about your family here in Blackjack, will you pass that on to me? I'd like to put it in the paper, if that's okay."

"Sure. Well, maybe. Let's see what I find first." McRae went over to the fiche machine, and Mary brought him boxes full of reels.

A few days later, I remembered Orin McRae and was surprised that I had heard nothing from him after he dug into the newspaper files. I went to the library with two missions in mind. First, I wanted to learn how to use that fiche machine. I had a lot of looking I needed to do, and I needed to do it fast. Second, I wondered what Orin had found out.

Mary had both answers for me. She showed me where the reels were kept, pointed out the reels that represented Bill's time in Blackjack, and told me the reason McRae left without talking to him again. It seemed that his grandfather, a man he had never met, was a real scoundrel.

"He sold stock in worthless companies, cheated on his wife with every prostitute in the county, had syphilis, which he passed on to his wife and may have resulted in his first son's death, and skipped town to avoid going to jail," Mary told me.

"Atta girl, Mary!" I said. "There is a story here after all."

CHAPTER 43

Lake Powell

Blackjacks Hit the Waters

"A new summer retreat is replacing the traditional trip to one of Minnesota's 10,000 lakes. Lake Powell located mostly in Utah…"

— The Blackjack Press

EVER SINCE THE JACKSONS had had enough money to do it, they had spent a couple of weeks at Lake Nokawewa in Minnesota every summer. The lake was about three feet deep and clogged with weeds now, but the "big lunkers" lurked among those weeds, and that seemed to be the *raison d'etre* of being there: to catch big lunkers. Either that or feed the mosquitoes.

Ken was making good money from The Matador now that he had quit working for Public Television, plus some on the side from his job at the community college. From the first day he worked there, he had saved all the college money for a cabin of his own.

A funny thing happened on the way to the northern lake, though. On a flight from the West Coast, they had flown over a huge lake, and from the plane it looked like the Grand Canyon with water in it. Reflections from boats led him to believe that it was dotted with hundreds of houseboats. He was intrigued.

When he got back home, he sat down with a map and tried to reconstruct where that lake might be. Luckily, the pilot had announced several landmarks as they flew over them, and he could draw lines between them. One line went right over Lake Powell in Utah.

A little research revealed that Lake Powell is indeed the Grand Canyon with water in it. It's just a little north of the canyon, so it's the same formation, and it is full of water due to the huge Glen Canyon Dam. He immediately made some calls, trying to find a way to get onto that lake on a houseboat. He finally hooked up with the National Park Service at the lake and was told that the houseboats are normally reserved far in advance, but there was one boat available in two weeks if he could make it then. He could.

Ken and Beth and their oldest son, Greg, spent four days on a beaten up old houseboat on Lake Powell and didn't want to leave, ever. Within a week, Ken had taken his college money and bought himself his own houseboat and placed it on Lake Powell. His days of going after lunkers in weed-choked lakes were over. Besides, there were no mosquitoes on Lake Powell.

Everyone knows the old expression that a boat is a hole in the water you pour money into. Ken found that to be all too true. And the corollary is that you don't buy one boat, you buy ten, one at a time. Each boat leads to a bigger, better boat. So, two years later, Ken bought a floating palace and started inviting friends to join him on the lake. Bill Just was one of the first to go.

Even though Ken had been telling him about the boat, Bill was unprepared by what he found. It had five bedrooms, if you counted the pull-out bed in the living room, three bathrooms, a hot tub, a diving board and a slide, a massive gas grill, and a wet bar. It looked like it was as big as a Mississippi riverboat, and might have been. What he didn't know was that it consumed about 80 gallons of gas a day when moving, which was the reason that Ken took it to one of his favorite spots and tied up there for days.

Bill was also surprised at the number of Nebraskans they met on the lake, easily recognized by the big red flags with the white Ns on them, signifying the football team. Judging by the size of the owners, he guessed that they might just be former football players who made a pile playing in the NFL or in Canada. Every evening, the smell of broiling slabs of Nebraska beef covered the huge lake.

Life on the boat was idyllic. Coffee, juice, and eggs on the top deck with the sun just peeping over the eastern hills. Swimming or tanning during the day. Cocktails and dinner on the top deck again and the sun setting over the western hills.

Since the canyon is all rock, there is really no beach to push up on, no soft bottom to anchor to, and no trees to tie up to either. They tied up to the shore every night and for most of one day. Finding a way to do that would have been a challenge, but Ken had invested in a rock drill that allowed him to place pegs in the rock for lines from the boat.

One day, they remained tied up until after lunch. The guys went exploring from the boat, and Bill was surprised to find fossils of clams and oysters, millions of years old, just lying on the ground. Ken reminded him to leave them there, since removing fossils is against the law. Still, they must have seen hundreds of them. They were in search of petroglyphs, which Bill imagined were carvings or writings on stone, probably made by Indians, hundreds or thousands of years ago. They didn't find any, but it led Bill to ask Ken about the origin of this canyon.

Ken said, "No one knows for sure, but there is one theory that it resulted from the breaking of a huge ice dam at the end of the ice age. A body of water about the size of Lake Michigan was probably trapped behind the ice dam, and when it broke, that whole thing ran out, probably taking thousands of years to completely drain. Trillions of tons of water flowed fast, cutting through the rock, until the deep crevasse was left behind.

"By the way, did you know that this was where *Planet of the Apes* was filmed? You're walking on the planet of the apes."

Bill saw no reason to ever leave, but his invitation was for three days, and at the end of that time, Ken dropped him off back in Page, Arizona where his car was parked. He went through Sedona on his way home and had to pry himself out of there to continue back home.

Bill could have afforded a boat on the lake too, if he wanted. But his money went mostly to others. He continued to live simply and never went back to the lake, no matter how much he wanted to. It was much too tempting. But if he wanted to find all those missing Nebraskans during the summer, he now had two places to look: Minnesota and Lake Powell.

CHAPTER 44

The Big Bucks

I WAS AMUSED TO find this in the files, although I still don't know what I'll do with it:

Girl Bags Huge Buck

"On the first day of hunting season, eleven-year old Amy Lynn Johanson bagged the biggest buck killed here in years…"

– *The Blackjack Press*

HUNTING IS A BIG sport in Nebraska. Different folks have their favorite hunting seasons. Dentists and farmers enjoy pheasant season. The dentists know they'll get a lot of business mending cracked and broken teeth from chomping down on shot pellets hidden in the succulent pheasant meat. Farmers enjoy renting out their fields and watching hunters spend a day vainly looking for birds in a completely clean field. Even the hunting dogs seem to be amused as they look back to their owners wondering, *Where do you think I'm going to find a bird out here?* There are plenty of pheasants in the state, but you have to know where to hunt for them.

The biggest holiday in most of rural America is the first day of deer season. Not only do all of the local good old boys, and young boys too, take the day off from whatever else they ought to be doing, but dudes come in phalanxes from the cites to try for their share of the local fauna. Every motel, B&B, and relative's home is stuffed to the gills with city folk bearing arms.

No shooting is allowed until dawn, but by the appointed hour, the hunters have been in place, hoping to have a deer in their sights so they can shoot it before someone else does. It sounds a little like the Battle of the Bulge for the first 10 or 15 minutes.

For those who actually know how to fire a rifle with accuracy, it's still a matter of luck. If there's a buck to shoot, they'll kill it. For the others, it's doubly a matter of luck. First they need a deer, and second, they need luck to hit it.

It's not a good idea to go out of the house until the shooting calms down. Bullets that don't embed themselves in deer flesh strike whatever else they come to before ending their flight. Aluminum siding makes a pretty loud sound when struck by a high-powered round. Vinyl isn't nearly as resonant. Some hunters say Chivys sound louder than Fords when hit, but most would prefer to hit Toyotas anyway, since they're made by "for'ners."

No one has figured out how the deer know when hunting season begins, but they do seem to know. They may have been eating your petunias the evening before, completely ignoring your presence and the barking of Ol' Blue, but on opening day, they are nowhere to be seen. This can lead to a lot of frustration, and seasoned hunters know that. They realize they could sit in a blind or on a platform for days without so much as seeing a deer, so they are careful to take enough beer or bourbon with them for morale maintenance. Drink enough and you may even forget how cold and wet you are.

So the woods are full of hunters with guns and bourbon. Wise Nebraskans stay indoors. Even semis driving down highways have been shot.

A famous hunting story from North Dakota, where it is truly cold during deer season, involves a hunter who shot a teenage boy passing by on a bright red snowmobile. The hunter said he thought it was a deer.

The hunter was charged with manslaughter, but the jury found him not guilty. They all knew what it's like to sit for three days on a deer platform in the snow, and just when the only buck you've seen the whole time is getting almost close enough to shoot, the roar of a snowmobile frightens it away. That's known as "justifiable homicide" in hunting country.

The ultimate deer-hunting story in Blackjack involves an 11-year-old girl hunting with her father on opening day. Within five minutes, she shot the biggest buck anyone had seen in 20 years. She and her dad had to bring it to the deer station to register their kill. The huge rack on the old buck's head was hanging over the side of the bed of the pickup as it sat outside the combination gas station, restaurant, motel, and deer station. All the other successful hunters were bringing in their deer too, and they were awed by the sight of those enormous antlers. They hurried in to ask who had shot it. Little Amy Lynn was sitting at a booth having breakfast with her dad.

All that testosterone stirred up by slaying unarmed animals, and that little girl had the best trophy of all.

"Hummpph!" each one said when they found out, "I bet she didn't carry it out."

CHAPTER 45

GTK

IN THE NEWSPAPER BUSINESS, you often need to fill out a column, and there is a source of very short articles known in the trade as GTKs, or Good-to-Knows. These are available from all over the country, but it's best if you have something local that your readers might actually be interested in. This appears to be a locally-produced GTK that exactly filled out a column.

Common Era Explained

Overheard in the library yesterday: Bill Just was helping a young lady with her homework, when she asked him why the former "AD," as in 2011AD, is now called "CE." Bill, who is not known for his mischievousness, answered this way:

> "AD" referred to a period starting with the birth of Christ and was eventually converted from Latin to English as Christian Era. That offended some religions, so they looked for another word starting with C so as not to have to change both CE and BCE, before the Christian Era. A historian from Wisconsin

suggested calling it the "Cheese Era." It would be called the Cheese Era today, except that the chairman of the panel was lactose intolerant, and he was offended by that. He called on the panel members to think of a "common word" starting with C, and then realized that "common" was such a word. So now it's called the "Common Era."

The young lady said, "Oh, Bill!"

CHAPTER 46

Town Meeting

THE SMALL-TOWN NEWSPAPER BUSINESS tends to revolve around town meetings. That's natural, of course, since whatever news of general interest there is in town is likely to be caused or discussed at the town meeting by the members of the council and, sometimes, by the public.

I was excused from writing up the first meeting after my arrival, because I was writing the Bill Just article, but I went with Mrs. Fritz anyway to get the feel for it and to meet some of the players.

My favorite right from the start was the feisty little town mayor, Gerry Merriweather, who was popularly known as Merry Mayor Gerry. Apparently the Merry, derived from his last name, had stuck with him since grade school.

I was surprised to find that there seemed to be two factions in town, and the two factions held strongly opposite opinions on most matters. Obviously, Merriweather's faction had the majority at this time, but it was a narrow one of three to two. Mrs. Fritz explained that the situation put a lot of pressure on council members to be present at meetings.

The center of the disagreement between the town's factions was over, needless to say, spending. The town had little money, and Mrs. Fritz explained that the minority was always trying to find ways to raise taxes to put enough money into the treasury to do things they considered important, mainly storm sewers, whereas the majority was having none of that, despite having spent every last penny of the town treasury on a new equipment building.

I already knew a few people in town and recognized some of the council members, such as Doug Jones, the fire chief. But it turned out that Doug was himself a source of contention. He had voted for the new equipment building in which the fire company stored some of its equipment. This was considered a conflict of interest by the opposition.

I couldn't sufficiently suppress a laugh when Merry Gerry actually stood up at his seat to answer criticism of Doug's vote. He reminded me of Jimmy Cagney strutting and hopping around like a bantam rooster, spitting out his phrases in a rapid staccato. It was effective, though, and the criticism ended, at least for the time being.

I made a few notes for the future. What were the sources of revenue for the town? Unlike a larger town or city, there were no parking meters, no hotel or restaurant taxes, no building permit fees, or at least not many. Were storm sewers really necessary? I might have to wait for the hundred-year flood to find out. It seemed to me that the river running by about a half-mile from the center of town was a much bigger threat. But what did I know? I was the new kid.

Another big issue that night was a request for a business license for an "Adult Entertainment Emporium." It would offer a wide range of "adult" products from videos to whips, apparently. This was met with the most vocal opposition by the public. Linda Walden said that "the devil would take over Blackjack" should this license be issued. It failed by a unanimous vote. I almost wished I could write the report on that item.

Then Mayor Gerry raised a seemingly trivial matter: "Last month, we received, as I'm sure you remember, a request for a building permit from Bill and Nancy Lyons. They bought a lot in Wonderland, the first sale there in probably twenty years, and want to build a house on it. But Don Tolgren told us that some years ago a *cul de sac* at that location had been moved so that it took up a good piece of that lot. We had to do some homework to find out if that was right, which it was. Now we have to decide what to do."

Tolgren raised his hand to speak, but the Mayor motioned for him to sit down. "Not now, Don. We have some things to discuss first. Bring us up to date please, Harry."

Mrs. Fritz leaned over toward me and whispered, "Harry is the town manager."

"This little place has a full-time town manager?" I asked, surprised.

"I wouldn't say 'full-time," she answered briefly, since several council members were looking at us disapprovingly for talking during their meeting.

Harry Loberg is a small man, maybe 5'5" and 110 pounds. He was dressed informally in wrinkled slacks and a faded short-sleeve shirt. I guessed he didn't make much as town manager. He opened a manila folder on his desk and read a few seconds before speaking.

""Don was right. For some reason, our town map didn't show it, but it was registered with the county. How that happened I don't know. The *cul de sac* now, instead of looking like a lollipop, looked like a letter "P" with the circle extending into the lot in question. I doubt that the Lyons can build the house they have in mind if they comply with our town setback requirements, which they will have to do."

Bill Lyons started to say something, and it didn't look as if it was going to be pleasant, since his face was nearly beet red.

"Hold it, Bill," the mayor cautioned. " Let us finish getting the information first."

I was thinking of going outside to wake up a little, afraid that if this went on for long I would fall asleep. But something told me this was going to get interesting, so I pinched my cheeks, a technique I had used many times in college, and blood flowed back to my head.

"Where do we go from here?" the mayor asked.

Loberg looked uncomfortable. He pulled on his left ear, tucked his shirt into his pants, for no reason, and looked like he was hoping someone would answer before he did, but no one did.

"Well," he said, drawing it out as long as he could. "We could disapprove the building permit on the grounds that it doesn't comply. But we could really use the taxes on the house these folks are going to build, so I don't suggest that we do that. The thing that worries me is that I think *cul de sacs* are required by the county at the end of dead-end streets so that fire trucks can turn around there."

Gerry looked at Doug Jones.

Jones said, "At the end of that little street? We can back out."

"So, you're saying you don't need a *cul de sac* there, Chief?"

"That's right," the fire chief answered.

"Well then, it's simple," said the mayor. "Let's just make it go away."

From the council table, there came a low rumble. Several council members were clearing their throats. Merry Gerry apparently recognized this as a sign of trouble.

"Does someone object to that?" he asked.

"Yeah, I do," said a woman I didn't recognize. I looked at Mrs. Fritz for help, but she was apparently not willing to risk another glare from the table by whispering to me.

The woman went on. "We can't just give our land away to people. If we give these people our land, everyone will want some."

Bill Lyons could stand no more. Without rising, he said, "It's not your land; it's a right of way."

But it was clear that now they were at a stalemate. I didn't know it then, but this was already the third hearing on this trivial issue, and the Lyons family was living in a trailer waiting to build their house.

Seeing the problem, she had caused, the unknown woman council member offered a solution. "Let's sell it to them for, oh, I think five hundred dollars."

I heard Lyons say to his wife, "That's not bad. It costs $600 to file for a variance. It's a deal."

Heads bobbed up and down on the council table. Gerry called for a vote, and it was approved unanimously. But as the mayor started to move on the next issue, the woman spoke up again. "No, that's too much. Make it $300."

No one said anything. I asked later and was told that indeed the

Lyons paid $300 for a *cul de sac,* even though the council had all voted for $500. I liked that. And Bill Lyons was telling everyone in town that he now owned a *cul de sac.*

But the one thing that impressed me the most was the decorum. Except for the Cagney imitation, everyone was not just polite to his opposite, but almost solicitous. On CSPAN, you can hear one senator refer to another as "my distinguished colleague," only to follow that by accusing him of being stupid and misguided. None of that in Blackjack. I was glad I was here, but now I knew I had better be watching for the devil's arrival if the adult film store should be approved.

CHAPTER 47

Lieutenant Fritzling

Local Lad Promoted to First Lieutenant

"Joe Fritzling, resident of Blackjack, has been promoted to First Lieutenant in the Army, it was announced yesterday. Joe is stationed at Fort Knox, Kentucky..."

— The Blackjack Press, October 3, 1990

JOE ENJOYED FRATERNITY LIFE, although the dean didn't enjoy those years nearly as much as Joe did. Still, he managed to graduate in four years, becoming a rarity in those days, having only served three semesters on disciplinary probation.

He had run out of money by November of his freshman year, got a job, and was talked into joining Army ROTC for the $50 a month he could receive his last two years. The upshot of that was that upon graduation he was commissioned a Second Lieutenant and called to active duty. After his Infantry branch training, he was assigned to an Infantry Brigade at Fort Benning, Georgia. The Army had no idea what it was about to experience.

Joe had matured a considerable amount by now, and he had a healthy respect for the power of the Army legal system. He tried hard to become a model officer, but his old habits died hard.

To make things worse, he had one of the worst company commanders a person could have. Captain Casper would have been known to the troops as "Casper the Ghost," except that his tyrannical punishments for even trivial or imagined infractions, earned him the sobriquet of Captain Blood.

Casper had several criteria for good performance on the part of his officers, and Joe didn't meet any of them. Casper claimed that in an earlier assignment, as the commander of a company policing the DMZ in Korea, that he had gone the whole year without sleeping. He was very proud of this imaginary achievement, and it had become a measurement that he applied to his officers.

Once, they were in the field for a week, during which time Casper called his platoon leaders on the radio at all times of the night and required that they be awake to answer the call. By Friday, all the lieutenants were asleep on their feet. Joe was no exception. The last operation was a road march back to garrison. Casper was in his jeep, leading a column of trucks, piled high with standing soldiers. Joe was in the cab of the first truck. Every time the jeep stopped for some time and then started forward again, everyone including Joe, the driver, and every standing soldier in the back, was sound asleep. The jeep would pull away, and the trucks would remain stopped. Casper got so furious with Joe that he stamped his feet and threw things while chewing him out.

Joe hadn't planned on making a career out of the Army in any case, which was good.

It was in the Army that Joe discovered his talent for public speaking, something officers do most of the time, if you consider a couple of hundred soldiers to be the public. Joe found that teaching soldiers required considerable initiative and showmanship, both of which he had in abundance.

If there was one thing he couldn't stand, it was a sleeping student in one of his classes. He therefore prepared carefully and always included a number of incentives for staying awake and paying attention.

One day, he was teaching a class on hand-grenades, and he was doing this in the barracks due to a hard rain that was falling that afternoon. He felt this required special incentive.

He started the class: "Men, this is a class on the hand grenade. It's vitally important that you learn what I am teaching you today, because someday it may save your life and the lives of the soldiers around you.

"Look up here. I have two grenades, one in each hand. Even though they look identical, they're not. One of them is a live grenade, and one is a dummy for training. I am putting them down on this table now with the live grenade here by my left hand. You'd better watch carefully as I move them around, because at some point in the class I'm going to pull the pin on one of them, and if it's the live grenade, you will have three seconds to get out of range before it goes off. You will have to know which is which."

The soldiers were fairly sure he wouldn't pull the pin on the live grenade and one or two did fall asleep during the class. This truly annoyed Joe, who had thought his bluff would work. He continued to teach, but his mind was wandering as he tried to think of ways to keep the attention level high.

And that was how it happened that he pulled the pin, entirely by accident, on the live grenade and placed it back on the table. Most of the soldiers had watched the movements of the grenades carefully and immediately recognized that they were in serious danger. They had three seconds to get out of the room, and they bolted en masse for the nearest exit.

Joe was just about the only one who didn't know, but when the whole class rose and headed for the exits, it took only a microsecond for him to realize his mistake. He snatched up the grenade and threw it out through the closed window breaking out the glass. Luckily, there was no screen on that window or it would have bounced right back into the room, but it went through the window and bounced about 8 feet away from the barracks before going off. The resulting explosion blew out most of the windows on that side of the barracks, but by a miracle, no one was seriously hurt. Joe did receive a few small fragment wounds on his arms, but he never told anyone about that. It was bad enough without anyone being wounded, even if he was the one who was.

This led to Joe's first meeting with the brigade commander, a colonel, who told him, "Lieutenant, I should give you an Article 15 for endangering the lives of your soldiers and for breaking a bunch of rules and regulations. I'm not going to do that, because I understand what you were trying to do and it was creative and imaginative. I like that in a young officer. But screw up like that again, and you will leave me no choice but to throw the book at you."

Joe meant to be more careful after that, really. Then one of his sergeants told him that he had four anti-tank mines he had stolen from someplace and now he needed to get rid of them. Joe recognized the opportunity to save them for a class on mines. He put them in the bottom of a closet in his platoon arms room and covered them with a box of rifle-cleaning supplies. After all, what could go wrong with that?

That might have worked fine except that a young soldier in his platoon, attempting to set a new record for shiny boots, was burning a base of shoe polish into a new pair of boots one night when a puddle of lighter fluid from the can he had tipped over caught fire. It set off the fire alarm and the fire department responded. The fire was long gone by the time they arrived, and the little fire had been confined to the concrete floor. However, in the time-honored tradition of firemen, they insisted on making sure nothing was still smoldering. They pried open the locked closet and discovered the mines lying about two feet from the place where the fire had been. Had they gone off, that whole end of the barracks would have been destroyed.

This time, the brigade commander was not inclined to forget the incident. He administered "Non-Judicial Punishment" and placed a letter of reprimand in Joe's personnel file.

From then on, Joe really was more careful. He still tried to use dramatic events to keep his classes interesting, and he succeeded in that to the point where he became famous for it. Oddly, once Captain Casper had seen one of Joe's classes, he became enamored with the use of pyrotechnic training aids and insisted that Joe use them in every class.

Joe's increased pursuit of pyrotechnics and simulators for training soon exhausted the supply available through normal supply channels. It was then that he met SFC Brown from the Infantry school. Brown told him he could always get such things from him, but not to tell anyone where he had gotten them. Brown kept a large supply in the old barracks building that had been sitting vacant awaiting demolition. As it turned out, Brown would facilitate that destruction.

Joe continued to employ simulators and pyrotechnics profusely until the fire.

He had trouble getting up mornings, probably because his social life often precluded his going to bed until nearly dawn, so on this particular day, he didn't arrive at the company until nearly 9. He found his Captain Casper in an unusually agitated state and eagerly awaiting his arrival. They had been summoned to the colonel's office.

Colonel MacTavish was in quite a mood himself. He left them standing at attention in front of his desk, instead of inviting them to sit, as he normally would have. Without a hint of warmth, he told them, "Last night, there was a fire in the old division area. An old barracks building burned down. It turned out that there was a large stock of explosives in the building. The fire was like a bad Fourth of July. Rockets and star clusters set five other wooden buildings on fire, and every fire department for miles around spent most of the night knocking down the fires, all the while dodging exploding things and cooking off ammunition. I'm told that it sounded a lot like World War II. An investigation traced the ammunition to a SFC Brown who spilled the beans about his customers, including you, Lt. Fritzling."

That ended Joe's short military career, and in the long run, it probably worked out for the best for Joe. An Army buddy, a Kansan, introduced him to one of the Kansas senators, Bob Hunt, who hired him as his Public Relations assistant. Joe had found his calling.

The people of Blackjack uttered a silent community prayer of thanksgiving. Joe was not returning to town. If he did come back a few years from now, maybe it would be with a wife and a kid or two, and Joe would be a changed man.

Maybe.

CHAPTER 48

The Blackjack Ghost

IT HAD BEEN A long time since I worked day and night to write the Bill Just article. It turned out that I dug up enough material on Bill Just to write a book, I think.

After the article ran, the world stood still for me. Mrs. Fritz was very pleased with it and didn't assign me anything right away because the article that portrayed Bill as a real hometown hero actually caused a little stir. Lincoln and Omaha TV and newspapers called and even sent down reporters and camera crews. The resulting articles and shows were used on other Mid-western media outlets. For a day and a half, I was a celebrity.

Then, just as quickly as it had happened, the national interest died down. I found myself with not a lot to do. If I hung around the paper, Mrs. Fritz would have me doing all the stuff she normally had to do, and I hated that. *I'm a reporter!* So, I made myself scarce around the office.

I was sitting in The Ideal having a big lunch of broasted chicken, now my default daily repast, when I overheard an interesting conversation at a nearby booth. A large woman that I didn't recognize said, "I'm telling you, it scared me half to death. Why! I've never been so scared in my entire life."

Her lunch companion said, "I don't know. It sounds pretty fishy to me. Don't you think you just imagined it?"

Both of the women appeared to be around 40 or 50, and both were wearing dresses, heels, and beauty-shop hairdos. I wasn't sure who they were or why they were so nicely dressed, but I was interested in what this story might be about. I thought I had missed it already, but then I was saved by the arrival of a man who joined them at the booth. He was in jeans and a work shirt, but he sat down and joined the ladies for lunch.

The large woman said, "Karl, did you hear what happened to me the other night?"

"Nope," he said. "I have a feeling I am gonna, though."

"Well, if you don't want to know, that's all right with me, but I was scared out of my mind, and I'm telling you there's a ghost in this town. You just wait, and you'll find out."

"Ghost, huh?" the man replied without apparent surprise or interest.

"Yes," she said. "I was just closing the office, had turned off the lights, and was the last one there when I saw him. He was in a soldier's uniform. Maybe a general, old time, like the Civil War or something."

"Oh, you saw him, did you?"

"Oh, yes! And more than that. I felt the cold from him, and he spoke to me. He said, "I was right. I was right.""

"He did, huh?"

"Yes, he did. There's a ghost in town, I tell you. There's no telling where he could show up next or what he'll do."

I smelled a story. I decided to wait until they were leaving and to follow the woman back to her office for an interview, unless she got into a car, in which case I'd have to get to her before she drove off and ask her if I could talk to her.

She did start to get into a car, so I intercepted her and introduced myself. She was very pleased that a reporter wanted to interview her and told me that she worked in the courthouse in the recorder's office. Now I remembered seeing her there. She told me to come by at closing time, and I might get to see the ghost myself.

Still staying away from *The Press*, I stopped by the fire hall, often a good place to pick up stories of fires, rescues, and accidents. The firemen were always happy to have someone to talk to and loved talking to the new reporter who seemed to eat up their stories. In a small town, where you tell the same stories over and over, new blood, like this new reporter, me, was fair game.

Doug Jones, the chief, saw me talking to the boys out front. That always worried him, since he knew they often exaggerated events in hopes of seeing their names in print. He came out and invited me into his office.

There had only been one rescue call all week, and that one was of little consequence. By chance, I thought of the ghost story and told Doug what I had heard. Doug listened and scratched his head. "You know, a weird thing happened here last night. I don't want to make a big deal out of it, and I don't want to see it in the paper."

"Okay," I said, "tell me anyway." I had my fingers crossed behind my back, hoping it would be good and planning to write the story if it was.

Doug was actually a little man for a firefighter. He was well-trained, though, and had a cool head—both important qualities for a fire chief.

"Well," Doug said slowly, taking his time to think about what he was telling me, "I looked up and found the boys all standing in a line. Bert was wiping a big spill of orange pop off his white shirt—it'll be stained forever—and he looked scared. The others were standing like I was going to make an inspection, but they were dressed in their street clothes. I asked what they were doing. They said someone had ordered them to line up for inspection. Bert said it scared him so bad he dropped his can of pop. We never figured out who said anything to them. Bert says it sounded strange, so strange that he jumped up and spilled all over his shirt."

"Like a ghost?" I asked without cracking a smile.

"Yeah, well, that's what Bert said, but I wouldn't put much faith in that. The other guys said it scared them too, but no one else said 'ghost.'"

At 5 that evening, I talked with Maria Mills, the large woman from the Recorder's Office. No ghosts came calling while I was there, and I learned little more than I had heard at lunch. I went to see Mary Dubchek at the library.

I stood in line while Mary checked out *Lady Chatterley's Lover* to two giggling teenage girls. When I finally got to talk to her, I asked, "Know anything about a ghost in town, Mary?"

"Sure, why?" Mary answered.

"You do?" I exclaimed.

"It's an old story, but of course no one really believes it. Do you want to know about it?"

"You bet I do," I said.

She showed me a book from the Blackjack history shelves. I still hadn't gotten around to reading those, and I made a mental note to do so soon. The book, written nearly a hundred years before, told of a ghost of a Civil War colonel from the town who had been disgraced during the war and was coming back as a ghost to convince people he had been wronged. The colonel's name was J. B. Funk.

I went back to the front desk and asked Mary if she knew any more about J.B. Instead of answering my question, she told me that I should try the county genealogical site on the computer. It took me only a few seconds, once on the site, to get to the Funks, and there he was, old J.B. himself. Of course, the entry had been written by the old guy's granddaughter, so I hardly expected to get the true story.

According to the writeup, J.B. stood for James Bull, but once he reached adulthood, he went by his initials for the rest of his life. That was very much the vogue at the time. J.B. had a farm on the edge of town, and he bred some excellent draft horses there, in addition to raising hay, oats, and barley. He brewed an interesting beer from his barley and sold kegs of it during the holidays. But the thing that made him fairly rich was the drawing power of his horses. At a time, when the West was right at his doorstep and expanding ever westward, he had "horsepower" to contribute.

His "contribution" was for the top dollar only. He didn't waste his animals on cheap jobs, and thereby kept them healthy and rested while filling his bank account. A couple of friends who worked as executives for the railroad helped him get plenty of its business while they were clearing rights of way, and that ensured them a fine place to stay wherever they found themselves working.

When the Civil War broke out, J.B. saw his duty. He raised a regiment from the local area, uniformed and equipped it, and led it to war. He had the misfortune to fall under the generalship of U. S. Grant, a man who was more often than not on the attack and pressing hard against the enemy. J. B. and his regiment reacted with less alacrity than Grant desired, and eventually Grant relieved him from command of the regiment he had raised and named after himself, Funk's Frontier Regiment.

J.B. returned home in disgrace. He lived only a short while after that and died, many said, of a broken heart. Since then, at irregular intervals, he was said to have come back to reclaim his reputation. The irony, of course, was that no one would have remembered him or his disgrace otherwise, so when he reappeared, according to the legend, it reminded everyone of the very disgrace he supposedly sought to undo.

I kept reading the genealogical site. I found that the Funk family had continued to be a force in the community for some time, despite the embarrassment suffered by its patriarch. J.B.'s wife, Vendla, found herself with a farm, a business, and a brewery to run. She could have sold it all and lived on in comfort, but she decided to run it herself instead.

It was highly unusual for a woman to run a business at the time, and especially that sort of business. But she was a canny negotiator and got high prices for her hauling services. The tough men who worked for her learned quickly that they had to be obedient and respectful if they wanted to be hired again. She controlled them by their paychecks, which were generous but carefully apportioned.

The farm had good and bad years, as they all did, but provided fairly good income. Vendla brought in a German brewer for the beer making and later sold the brewery to a Bohemian brewer for a tidy sum.

She was also an accomplished violinist, at least by town standards. She had played even before she emigrated from Sweden as a girl. Everyone in her family back there played, and fiddles were very common in many

Swedish homes. Churches in Sweden seldom had organs; they had choruses of fiddlers.

Her parents, both of whom played well, had taught her at home. They used traditional Swedish church music for teaching exercises, and she had learned to play many of those hymns by heart long before she knew how to read music. In her turn, she used those tunes to teach her students. One year, she took seven of those tunes and joined them together into a sonata. She played it at a town festival and everyone loved it. She hired a composer from Kansas City to help her orchestrate it, and he succeeded in convincing the symphony there to play it. So far as the people of Blackjack were concerned, she was the most famous resident of all time.

I knew I had a great story and went to work on it immediately. Before I could finish writing it, though, Maria Mills had another encounter with J.B's ghost. She believed it was following her home from the courthouse one night, and she rammed through the apparition with the sharp point of her umbrella. That was the last sighting, at least for the present.

The school orchestra, such as it is, annually performed Vendla's composition at graduations. Everyone in Blackjack still loves it.

In fact, Mary Dubchek, who was on piano at her class's graduation, still plays it on her upright Baldwin at home. She told me in greatest secrecy, "When I'm playing her sonata, I can sense the presence of someone who may be Vendla Funk. I even hear her rocking in the rocking chair behind me where I can't look while playing, but when I do sneak a peek, it's not moving."

CHAPTER 49

Nebraska Cuisine

CECILLE PASSED THIS ON to me. It is from some of Bill's papers. It looked as if he might have been planning to write a book about Nebraska eateries.

Nebraska is a beef state, not a corn state, despite the Cornhusker nickname. A large percentage of the grain-fed beef in the United States comes from here, and that means a lot of Nebraskans are engaged in raising beef. We also like to eat it. So, most Nebraska restaurants serve steaks and not much else, and it's fabulous-tasting and easy-chewing. The premier example of a Nebraska steak house is Johnny's, found down by the old stockyards in Omaha. Get a steak or prime rib, and you won't need a knife to cut it.

But eating in Nebraska can be much more varied than a steak and fries menu, if you look for it.

The state has a marvelous mélange of nationalities living in it, and luckily, many think, the nationalities originally tended to cluster together. There were disadvantages to that; for example, some kids didn't learn English until they went to Kindergarten. If the town they grew up in spoke only Swedish, German, or Czech, that was probably the only language kids learned at home.

The good side of that was that some of the old cultures were preserved.

Towns such as Wilbur remained Czech, or Bohemian, as they were called when the settlers arrived. There were German, Polish, and Swedish communities too. Old country traditions remained around for decades, because the population was so sparse that the residents weren't forced to fit into someone else's culture.

Remains of that, in this day and age, are largely found in restaurants, and one has even turned into a large franchise operation spreading across the Midwest. A favorite Russian dish is the meat pie, or pierogi. Descendants of Russian settlers started selling those meat pies in a restaurant in Lincoln and gave them a new name: "Runza." Now they have dozens of Runza restaurants across Nebraska, Iowa, and other nearby states, selling not just Runzas, but also beating out the chain hamburger joints by selling the "best tasting burger in the state."

The most famous burger in Nebraska, however, is the Coffee Burger. It has nothing to do with the hot, dark beverage consumed for breakfast, but is named after a rancher named Coffee who challenged a restaurant in Harrison to fill his workers up at lunch time. The result was a 28-ounce burger served on a standard-size hamburger bun, with meat hanging precariously over the sides. No one can say for certain that it filled the ranchers up, but it has been noted that they leave carrying half burgers wrapped in a napkin. That will probably be their supper. The surprising thing is how good a Coffee Burger tastes. The recipe must be a secret because there are none like it elsewhere.

Sioux Sundries in Harrison is the home of the Coffee Burger. It's a five-and-dime-type store, and to find the food counter, you have to walk all the way to the rear of the store. It happens to be the only place in town to eat, so when I, being hungry and having a ways to go to my destination, stopped in town, I was directed there by the first person I saw. I ordered a Coffee Burger, although nearly put off by the price, which seemed awfully high for a burger. I understood when it arrived at my table.

There aren't a lot of people in Harrison. One of the Coffees has engaged in a little joke by erecting signs on the highway saying, "Harrison Next Three Exits." The whole town lies along a couple of blocks of one street, so there are no "exits" in Harrison, just a turn onto Main Street. In fact, there aren't many people in all of Sioux County.

Within a few minutes of sitting at a booth in Sioux Sundries, I had been identified as a visitor by a couple, who had come in from the ranch to town to re-register their car. Excited to meet someone new, they asked me a lot of questions and eventually told me all about themselves.

John, the husband, told me, "Our daughter is the only elementary school student in the entire county. That's led to problems with the county, since they don't see why they should run a school for one student."

"I can understand that," I said.

John went on, "One year, they closed the school and bussed her all the way down to Scottsbluff. We had to sue to get the school back open. It turns out that state law requires counties to provide schools, so they had to open the school, hire a teacher, and even a substitute teacher, just for her."

I wasn't sure I believed that story, so when I got back home, I went to the library and checked population statistics for Sioux County. The year before 7 people had died in Sioux County, and one had been born. The story seemed plausible.

I got interested in Nebraska restaurants after my experience in Harrison. Up until then, my only real dining experience, outside of Blackjack, was at Misty's in Lincoln before Nebraska football games, and Johnny's, of course, in Omaha. Now I go out of my way to find interesting restaurants.

One day, I found a little seafood restaurant in St. Peter with a sign in the window saying, "If it swims, we serve it." Although I had never eaten fish, I was intrigued. I went in and took a seat. I looked at the menu, and it had little of interest on it, so I waited for the waitress to come to the table. I asked, "Do you have swordfish?" I had read about swordfish in the library and had wanted to eat some ever since.

"Nope," the waitress answered.

"All right," I said, "how about marlin?"

"Huh?" she asked.

"Marlin. It's a kind of game fish."

"No, don't have any."

"How about Chilean Sea Bass," I asked. I had read about that fish and knew it was neither Chilean nor bass, but it was becoming very popular, and he thought it must be pretty good.

"Nope," she said.

"Well, what do you have then?" I asked her.

"Catfish" she said.

"And?" I added.

"Just catfish," she answered.

"But, how about your sign that says, 'If it swims, we serve it'?" he asked.

"I wouldn't know about that. I guess it's the only thing that swims down at the spillway," she said.

I ordered a chicken fried steak.

Later, though, I found restaurants in Nebraska that serve swordfish and even abalone. If you are willing to drive a ways, you can eat almost anything in Nebraska, and I found most of it to be wonderful. Still, nothing beats a Nebraska steak.

CHAPTER 50

Go Huskers!

I WROTE AN ARTICLE about "Go Husker" signs. Mrs. Fritz liked it and ran it on the front page.

It happened that I was trying to do my best Bill Just imitation one Sunday morning. I borrowed a bike and was riding through town and then out on the highway. That was a mistake, so I took some paved back roads, got lost, found myself, and rode back to town.

The scenery was dramatically different outside of town. Pretty much fields of crops dotted with farmhouses and barns. A few feed pens cast their ugliness across their tiny pieces of prairie too, and the smell from them was overwhelming. But one thing was a constant: Signs in most front yards urging the Nebraska football team to victory.

Since I rode for almost two hours, I had a chance to think about that and the oddity of it. I thought, *This is Nebraska. Would anyone want the team to lose? Why do these people feel obliged to put a sign in their yard proclaiming to the world that they are fans of the Nebraska football team? Do they think that anyone who isn't a Nebraska fan will see those signs, or that the team will drive around looking at them for inspiration?*

Sure, there are lots of other colleges in Nebraska, and in fact, the football team everyone is proclaiming support for is at just one of the

University of Nebraska sites: Lincoln. Technically it's called The University of Nebraska at Lincoln, of UNL. UNO, Omaha, is a big university (branch) too, and it has a football team. I didn't see a single sign about that team; in fact, I've never seen one. I wondered if they even have them in Omaha. Probably not. We're not far from Bison with another branch of the university. You would think they didn't even have a team, but they do. I know; I went there.

And, after pondering that, I wondered about the 20% of the houses that don't have signs in the yard. Are they not fans of the football team? If not, why is that? I can think of some reasons and some of them are actually pretty good. For example, they think, as I do, that it's simply useless to put such a sign in your yard. Or, perhaps one or more members of the household attended a rival college, such as Colorado. Or, they couldn't care less about football. Hey, it's possible!

One odd thing about Nebraska is "unity," I'll call it. We are the only state to have just one legislative body. We call it: "Unicameral." I wish I knew what that means, but like most Nebraskans, I'm content to think it means "one body." And, unlike most states, we don't have a Nebraska State University. Kansas, Iowa, Oklahoma, Colorado, and—Are you ready for this?—even South Dakota, to name most of our immediate neighbors, all have state universities.

Believe it or not, I actually visited South Dakota State one time, and they have a football team: The Jack Rabbits. The students walk around in jackets with "Jacks" on the back. I used to get confused when I was watching ESPN2, and they were scrolling football scores across the bottom of the screen. SDS, it turns out, doesn't mean South Dakota State, it means San Diego State. That explains why they play so many California teams.

It's fairly common for the "University of" and "State of" to be bitter rivals, and I mean bitter. Kansas and Kansas State really dislike each other, as an example. This is sometimes a problem for KU, as it turns out. Many if not most of the state legislature comes from the part of the state west of Lawrence, home of Kansas University. Kansas State concentrates on agriculture and technical subjects, whereas the university is oriented toward liberal arts. All those state grads in the legislature tend to vote against increases in state support for the university. A bunch of pinko commies, is their impression. So we're glad we don't have that type of problem in our "unity" state.

Nebraska has a long and storied football reputation, honestly earned. Back in the early days of big time college football, Nebraska went to the Rose Bowl, which was the equivalent of a national championship game. Then World War II broke out, and the Nebraska team went off to fight Hitler and Tojo. A lot of them died, and others were wounded. Still others got too old to play at that level anymore. It was many years before Nebraska could recapture the pre-war excellence. No one remembers any more why that was. It was because Nebraska football players joined up and fought instead of staying home and playing ball. Hurrah for them!

There are a few other Nebraska teams that enjoy national prominence, but in this country, it seems that the only sports anyone cares about are football, baseball, and basketball. Who knows anything about the Nebraska Women's Volleyball team? Just every Nebraskan, that's who. The Nebraska ladies are normally one of the top national teams, and its members populate the U.S. Olympic team alongside California and Texas women, primarily.

Volleyball is a big girls sport in Nebraska high schools. Where all those tall athletic girls come from is a mystery, but I think it's a similar phenomenon to the big, tough football players who grow up here. The pioneers who survived had to be big and tough. These are their great grandkids.

Big, tough people often don't look like the models you see in Vogue or GQ. They tend to work at physically hard jobs, like farming and have the farmers' tans to prove it. But they're the people who make this land great through their hard work and loyalty. And before that, they play football and volleyball.

Go Huskers!

CHAPTER 51

Self-Images

IT WAS BECOMING OBVIOUS that Mrs. Fritz liked my articles. Before I arrived at *The Press,* the typical article was a report on a town meeting or even the opening or closing of a store. Not much of real interest. My articles on the goat man and the ghost were actually selling papers. People heard about them and came in to buy a copy of the paper if they weren't already subscribers.

Needless to say, I was pretty happy about that, and I let it go to my head a little. I was now a recognized man about town, mostly for my Bill Just article, but also for the human interest ones that were now featured weekly. The other day Mrs. Fritz suggested, nay, ordered me, to cover a PTA meeting, and I almost said no. I caught myself just in time, and a good thing too. As Yogi Berra said, "You can observe a lot just by watching. PTA meetings may not be the stuff of Hemingway, but they are full of people, and people are what it's all about.

I sat in the rear, so as not to be expected to participate in any way. There were a couple of young adults there not much older than I, so it was possible that someone might have thought I was a parent and put me on the cookie committee or something.

The president of the Green Acres School PTA, one Mrs. Laura Bush,

"The Democrat," as she always said, was sure full of herself. I asked around at coffee and cookie break and learned that she was a stay-at-home mom, who had a brief working career as a hostess at a now-defunct restaurant. Her *bona fides* as a community leader didn't seem to be too authentic. I'm not knocking her, understand, only a sense of importance that radiated from her like rays from the sun. She thought she was big stuff and showed that by being condescending to all other PTA members.

Then there were statements made by others that got me thinking. One mother announced with great righteousness that she "deplored violence," as if everyone else could barely wait until the brawl erupted so that they could pick up a chair and smack someone. Does anyone love violence? Maybe a few tough guys who usually reside in the "state pen," but most of us prefer to live our lives without cuts and bruises and broken knuckles, I think. So what was the point of saying she "deplored violence?"

I wrote this down and began to see some connection to my own new self-image that I was too big a deal to write up a PTA meeting. The next day, I started watching and observing. It wasn't difficult to discover people's self-images and to observe the impact of those on their lives. In some cases, the influence was positive, and in others, you might conclude it was negative.

Mrs. Stearn, the retired principal of the high school, found it her duty to stop young people on the street and correct their manners or dress. This had become a sort of town joke so that her sense of self was now working against her. Her husband considered himself an intellectual and had to hire people to do the most common household tasks. The town joke was that he hired an electrician to change a light bulb. He delighted in telling people that he didn't know which end of the screwdriver was which, an unlikely story, but he was proclaiming his self-image.

Things were a little slow that day, so once I had written the PTA article, I decided to make some phone calls to former college friends. It was only a few weeks after graduation for most of them, and others had yet to graduate. They weren't easy to find during the day, most having gotten summer jobs, but I did reach a few. I asked them to describe themselves in terms of expectations for careers or lifestyles.

Janey Schwab said she expected to have six children and would bring them up to be "ecologically-minded" saviors of the earth. *A noble goal,* I thought, *for a girl who drove a pickup truck the size of Wisconsin that probably got 2 miles to the gallon.* But that wasn't the point. The point was what her self-image was. She didn't say movie star or super model, either of which she might have aspired to. She said, "Super mom."

She added, "There will never be a Disney toy in my house, ever."

I said to myself, *Good luck with that.*

I was surprised by the number of girls who defined themselves by what they would never be caught dead driving, to wit: a minivan. One girl said, "I will personally, never set foot in an RV." *What a way to place restrictions on the rest of your life,* I thought.

Another student, Carlton Fisher, said he expected to go to law school and run for public office. I could see why. For one thing, he didn't ever do much of anything but talk, and that sounded like politics to me. But I wondered who would vote for him for anything. He might spend his life unsuccessfully running for office and end up poor and with no retirement funds. *A bad choice,* I thought, *but it was his, not mine.*

The kids from farms seemed to be less constricted by self-image. They had learned how to do almost anything and had very short "never" lists. Some said they would never work for a big ag conglomerate, and I would have been willing to bet that they would.

A couple of calls to faculty members reinforced my long-standing impression. Some of those highly-educated but lightly experienced ladies and gentlemen clearly considered themselves predestined to speak eruditely to the masses of ignorant and intellectually-inferior students in their charge.

When I talked to Mrs. Fritz about it, she carefully steered the conversation away from herself, but said, "As a matter of fact, we were discussing something like that at the rotary meeting last month. Employers were saying that since lots of middle management people are now back in the job market, they come in with lofty expectations."

"I suppose it's hard to go backwards," I observed.

"Sure," Mrs. Fritz said, "but here's the thing. They don't know your business, and they still expect to be hired for a big salary and have big responsibilities. They need to start over again and learn the business before they can run it. But, in their minds, they're managers, and anything less would be unacceptable."

All of this led me to wonder about Bill Just's self-image. Since I had never met him, if I was going to find this out, it would have to be by asking others. That train had left the station, though. My article was done, and there was nothing less exciting than yesterday's news.

CHAPTER 52

Joe Comes Back to Blackjack (For a Day)

So, I was the big-shot reporter at the dinky *Blackjack Press*, whoop-di-doo. At least that's how Mrs. Fritz looked at it. She still paid me next to nothing and, worse yet, assigned me the jobs she either didn't want to or couldn't do herself. Still, I was surprised when she announced that she was "recusing herself" from writing up her own granddaughter's wedding, and I had to do it. First, I had to look up "recuse."

The big day was a Saturday, of course, and I was getting to go to the reception. Sometimes being a reporter isn't all bad. Attend a party and get paid! My dream job. I wondered if there would be any girls there even remotely in my age bracket.

As it turned out, there were, or at least there seemed to be. Young women are almost impossible to "age" when they get dressed up and covered with makeup. Crafty thirteen-year-olds adept at makeup can pass for 23 so long as they don't chew gum or run across the room in their high heels. Likewise talented 30-somethings can look 18. It's a tough world for a guy who will lose his hair, grow bigger ears and nose, enlarge his belly, and have bad knees in no time.

The service in the little Presbyterian Church was simple and straight-forward, no real news there. Mrs. Fritz was going to have to fill in all the details about the materials in the wedding gown and all that stuff. If it isn't cotton or wool, it must be poly-something so far as I know.

The reception was in the church basement and that was just one of the reasons the party never got off the ground in my opinion. The other was that the fellow Jennifer was marrying was about to go to seminary in some denomination I had never heard of, and that denomination seriously frowned on drinking. No alcohol was allowed. Of course, those were probably the rules for the church basement anyway.

I was standing in line for some little sandwiches with mozzarella and salami on little triangles of white bread when the guy in front of me turned and introduced himself. He was Mrs. Fritz's middle boy, now in his late thirties, Joe. Of course, Joe was pretty infamous in town, so I was delighted to meet him—at first.

The line was moving slowly, and we had a nice chat. He snatched up a handful of ripe olives and handed me some to tide me over until I could get one of those tiny sandwiches. Then he said, "So, Ralph, don't you think this would all go better with a beer?"

"Sure," I replied. *Honest, that's all I said.*

Joe said, "I'll be right back," and he left.

I forgot about it until maybe a half hour later I saw him walking back into the reception trying to hide two six packs of Miller Lite under the sides of his blazer. Everyone who looked at him knew exactly what he was doing, I hope, because, if not, I'm the bad guy in this story.

I was standing at the table with the non-alchy punch and some big bottles of ginger ale and root beer when Joe walked straight toward me. Apparently he was going to give me one of the six packs. Why? I don't know. Maybe he was giving me my award for Reporter of the Month at his mom's paper or something. Anyway, he tried to set one of the six packs down by my feet, but when he bent over to do that, the bottles came tumbling out of the other pack and hit the floor with an explosion of flying glass and beer. I was soaked up to the tops of my socks in beer and there was a huge puddle of beer all around my feet, and Joe was gone. Gone! I don't know how he did that.

I looked up from the mess at my feet and saw that everyone there, pretty much the town, was looking at me with a combination of shock and amusement. The women mostly looked shocked (*Beer at a party, really!*), and the men looked amused. But the knockout punch came from Jennifer, still in her beautiful, non-cotton or wool wedding dress. She gave me a stare that burned right through my head and out the other side. I felt awful.

So, I did what you have to do in a situation like that, I got busy. I asked where I could get a mop and some paper towels. Then I cleaned up the mess, including all the broken glass, only cutting myself in three places. That was good because the blood evinced a little sympathy, even from Jennifer.

Then I looked for Joe. I found him outside. It was dark out by then, and he was hiding in the darkest part of the yard behind the church, eating a big slice of pizza and drinking his beer. His wife and baby had joined him and that may have been the end of that marriage from the sounds coming from the two of them.

I wanted to tell Joe how he had ruined my reputation in town with that stunt, but he was in so much trouble with his wife that I just left and went back to *The Press* to write as much of the story as I could. I didn't want to have to do it under Mrs. Fritz's gaze the next day.

Before I left, Milton Stohlman came out the back door of the church carrying one of those Styrofoam boxes they give you in restaurants for your leftovers. Joe saw his chance to redeem himself, at least in his own eyes.

"Taking food home from a buffet, Milton?"

"Sure," Milton replied nonchalantly. "It'd just go to waste if I didn't," and he walked off with his pride still intact.

As for Joe's rep, that wasn't worth worrying about. Everyone knew more than they wanted to about Joe's shenanigans, and there was nothing he could do to change that now.

And as for me, as it turned out, Mrs. Fritz was busy with family all weekend, and when I saw her on Monday, all she said was, "So, you've met Joe." That was it. Funny how many other people said the same thing to me over the next few days. Most of them laughed when they said it. My reputation was still intact, just like Milton's, I guess. Ralph Anderson, Star Reporter.

CHAPTER 53

Wind Power

EVERY TIME I SAW Roberta from the Lutheran Church, she tried to interest me in attending the men's breakfast on Tuesday mornings. They met at 7 in the morning, a time when I was almost always sound asleep, so it didn't interest me much, but this day I woke up at 5:30 and couldn't go back to sleep. I went out walking and was passing the church when I saw some of the guys driving up and decided to stop in and see what was happening.

Of course, they welcomed me heartily, and pretty soon I was eating pancakes with sausage, a genuine improvement over my usual sugary Corn Pops.

The pastor wasn't there that morning, so the men decided to just have breakfast and talk until it was time to go to work, which suited me just fine. Maybe I could pick up some news or get some tips on sources. Gee, it seemed I never took any time off from being a reporter now. It was turning into a full-time job, and it was my own doing. I loved the excitement of uncovering interesting stuff.

Karl Opstad, a classic Scandinavian in all respects, asked, "Have you fellows noticed all the wind farms being built around here? They're popping up like mushrooms on a manure pile."

For a few seconds, no one said anything. I guess they were too busy wolfing down the pancakes, but then one of them said, "I think those windmills are bad news."

"How so?" someone asked.

"Well," the first one said, "first of all, I read that it costs more to produce electricity on those things as it does to burn oil. Someday we may run out of oil, then those windmills will be needed, but for now they're a waste of money and energy. Probably costs more energy to make the windmill than it will ever produce."

"Aw, that can't be right," someone opined. "Where would they get the money to build them if that was true?"

"Well, what do you think about ethanol?" another one put in. "I've read that it takes about a gallon of oil to produce a gallon of ethanol."

"Hey, lay off the ethanol, Frank," said a guy who was dressed like a farmer. "The price of corn has gone way up since the ethanol plants started buying all the corn they could get."

That sort of stopped the discussion, since no one wanted to start an argument. I decided to re-prime the pump. I had taken a course in college that had taught me a few things about energy production, so I threw in a question: "What do you suppose happens to the wind after it goes through those big windmills? They take energy from the wind, so what happens downwind of the windmill?"

Apparently no one knew. In fact, what I had learned the year before left me believing that literally no one knew.

"So," I went on, "think of it this way. The windmill, which is anchored to the earth's surface, is being dragged through the atmosphere by the earth's rotation, and it is resisted by the atmosphere. That resistance, which to us is wind, passes through the windmill, where it turns the big blades, imparting a force against them. That force must be transmitted to the earth's surface in opposition to the rotation. What happens to the earth's rotation when there are tens of thousands of windmills opposing the rotation?"

There was a little grumbling around the table while they thought about that.

One guy said, "Why do you say it's counter to the earth's rotational? Doesn't that depend on the direction of the wind? Anyway, everything we do has an effect on the earth."

"That's true," I said, "and we could all think of thousands of examples. But most of them aren't of such a dimension as the creation of a Midwest full of windfarms."

And it was true that the Midwest was turning into a sea of windfarms. I had even seen an advertisement for North Dakota crowing about their "available wind." Not everyone considered cold wind an asset, at least not until now.

"Well," Opstad said, "those things couldn't have much of an impact on the earth's rotation. We've had windmills in Nebraska as long as I've been alive. Small ones, I admit, but they didn't stop the wind from blowing or the earth from rotating."

"That's true," I admitted, "but this is a whole new ball game. Have you ever stood near one of those windmills they're building? They're enormous. About 500 high feet at the top I think. Think of the force that each one is applying to the earth."

"They must know the answer to that," someone put in.

"I can't find anyone who knows," I said. I had been looking into it for an article on the big windfarm going up outside of town.

I went on, "One engineer I talked to said it probably would be a small percentage of something, can't remember now exactly what, but a small percentage change in the earth's rotation could change the world in ways we can't even imagine."

"On that cheerful note," Opstad said, "let's go to work. I hope you'll find out the answers to this and come back and see us next week and let us know," he said to me.

I said I would try. I noted with satisfaction that the wind was blowing as always, so the earth hadn't stopped rotating yet.

Before I got to my old car, one of the men reached out and took me by the elbow. He reintroduced himself as Steve Neil.

"Ralph," he said, "I'm the church softball team coach. I read your great article about Bill Just, and I thought you might be interested in his time playing on the softball team. If you are…"

"Sure, I am," I said. "I don't think the Bill Just story is over, and in fact, I don't want to let it die yet. I have to admit that I never heard anything about his playing sports, and it seems out of character for him. What have you got?"

Steve said, "Although you might not consider four teams a league, Blackjack did. In 1991, representatives of four churches met and formed a church softball league. It turned out to be a challenge for everyone involved, and Bill Just was involved.

"Bill was not an active member of any congregation, but he was doing more and more things with the Lutheran church he had helped build. So, I asked Bill to play on the softball team.

"It was more than a little surprising to Bill, who had never really had a chance to play any sports except at recess or PE in school. He had never been on a Little League team. He told me all of that, and I said it didn't matter; we needed another player. We had nine players signed up, and ten constituted a team. Later, a couple of teenage boys joined the team, so we actually had substitutes, but for most of the first year, all ten players had to play all of every game.

"As you probably know, church league softball is an interesting phenomenon. Our team had exactly one practice a year, which occurred the weekend before the games began. Bill didn't own a glove and had to borrow one, but the other players had somehow acquired all the necessary equipment. We had a small collection of bats—some wood and some aluminum. The wooden bats pretty much just laid around on the ground, with only Bill ever using any of them."

I guided Steve back into the church while he was talking. No use standing outside in the wind, apparently undeterred by the wind farms.

Steve continued, "Bill preferred the wooden bats, because he had never hit with an aluminum bat. It was the third year before he did use one, and he never picked up a wooden bat again."

We sat down at a table in one of the Sunday School rooms. I took out my notebook and pen.

Steve kept talking: "The team looked like a bunch of refugees from an NFL offensive line, except older. I would guess that the team averaged about 250 pounds, and that Bill and I brought the average down to that. The other teams in the league looked about the same. That is because in slow-pitch softball, you hit homeruns and jog around the bases. No need to be able to run fast, even in the field. The batters either hit it out or nearly out. By the time one of their fly balls fell to earth, the fielders could stroll over to the landing zone and still have to wait for it.

"I played shortstop and wanted another fit and younger player at either second or third to help out with the grounders. There weren't a lot of grounders, but it certainly improved our chances of winning if we could field the few there were. As it turned out, Bill could do that.

"He tried second base the first year, giving us one adept player on each side of the infield, and Bill didn't have to make any long throws from second. He threw a little like a girl, having little practice growing up, but I worked with him until he could make a decent throw from third and moved him there. Bill played it deep, back on the outfield grass. Those big guys hit everything hard, and you could get seriously injured by one of their line drives standing too close. Everyone tried to tell Bill that he needed to move up, but he didn't. Those big guys couldn't out run a grounder, and it didn't matter how far back he was, he could get the ball to first before they got there."

Steve was definitely on a roll. I decided to just let him talk as long as he wanted. I wished I had my tape recorder handy, but I could always talk to him again for lost details.

Steve went on, "When he first started to play, Bill choked up on the wooden bats and tried to punch the ball out of the infield. It worked fairly well, except that there was a "short fielder" playing somewhere behind second base, so he had to miss the shortstop and the short fielder with his slap shots. At the end of the season, I went back over the games we had played and calculated Bill's batting average at .620—not bad for a guy who had never really played baseball.

"One of the big worries in the league was heart attacks. Every time one of those huge guys hit a homerun, everyone watched him trot around the bases, hoping he would make it to home before having a coronary. Sometimes, one of them would stop on second base to get his wind before going on.

"Base running was a challenge too. If Bill got a hit that looked as if it could be run into a double or a triple, he had to think about whether there was a runner on base, and how far said runner might actually run before stopping.

"One season, a woman joined the team. She wasn't very good, but it was a church league, so everyone was nice to her, and she played in every game. Once in a while, she got on base by drawing a walk. In fact, she rarely swung at a pitch, but throwing strikes in slow pitch is an art that not everyone can master. Once when she was on first base and Bill hit a ball that was going to roll between the two behemoths in left field, Bill figured it for at least a triple, maybe a homerun. As he rounded second he looked at third, and there she stood, gasping for air. He was tagged out trying to go back to second base."

I said, "Boy, I bet that frosted him."

"Nah," Steve said. "I never saw him riled. For Bill, magic happened the day no wood bats were brought to the game. It was in his third year on the team, and his hitting had really improved. He reluctantly picked up the aluminum bats and found one that felt good to him. He abandoned his usual hitting style and swung away at the first pitch to see what would happen. The ball rose majestically in the air, came down in a gap between the outfielders, and rolled beyond them so far that he had been standing at home plate for nearly a minute by the time the ball came in. Now he was another big hitter on the team."

"So," I interrupted, "you had another homerun hitter."

"Not right away," Steve said. "He tried going back to his slap shots, but with the aluminum bats, he was hitting fly balls to the outfield. They had previously dropped in front of the outfielders, but were now easily caught. So he swung for the fences. Well, there really weren't any fences on our field. The idea was just to hit it so far that the big, lumbering fielders took so long to field it that you could jog around all of the bases.

"The games were fun, and it was a study in comparative religion to play in the league. The personality of the teams reflected their beliefs. Bill was amused when some player who had been sanctimonious for much of a season became outraged by an umpire's call and resorted to unexpected and inventive profanity.

"The Baptists had the most players of any team in the league, and most of them were good. They were perennial league champs, at least until Bill started hitting home runs. Then their tags became vicious; they argued more calls; and their previous extreme politeness disintegrated. Many on Bill's team considered that to be some sort of victory in itself.

"After four years, Bill had sustained enough little injuries that he decided to retire. The team now had plenty of players, most of them better than he was, and he wouldn't be missed. He donated the glove and aluminum bat he had bought, and he walked away happy for the experience."

"Wow," I said. "I never would have guessed. Steve, I'm going to save this for the time being. Sometime in the future, it will come in handy, and I will give you a call for a refresher when that time comes. Don't leave town, as the cops always tell suspects."

"I was born here, and I will die here," Steve said. "Unless the earth stops rotating because of the wind farms. Then I may have to move to Mars."

CHAPTER 54

Big Bob

I HAD MET SOME control freaks in his life, but none who could hold a candle to Big Bob.

Big Bob walked purposely into the newspaper office, one rainy day, shook off his raincoat with visible annoyance at the weather, and asserted that he needed to talk to Mrs. Fritzling right then. Since she wasn't in the office, and wasn't expected back for over two hours, Bob became annoyed. He lashed out at the poor part-time secretary, a high school senior taking the secretarial course and working at the paper as a part of her program at school. Bob inferred that she was totally incompetent, though he had just met her and knew nothing of her abilities. He should have known that newspaper people had to leave the office fairly often, and if he called ahead, he would have been able to make an appointment.

Mary Lou explained this to him as calmly and patiently as she could, but unfortunately, it came across to Big Bob as patronizing. Big Bob did not like to be patronized.

He said, "You'll hear about this as soon as I see Mrs. Fritzling, young lady." And, with that, he stormed out, forgetting his umbrella, for which he had to return a few minutes later.

I came in later, and Mary Lou was crying. I sat down at her workstation and asked her what the problem was. She told me about her run-in with Big Bob. I thought the best thing I could do was to listen to her and to tell her not to worry about her job. Mrs. Fritz certainly knew this guy, whoever he was.

Mary Lou was pretty sure she knew who he was, though he had failed to tell her. She told me, "I know him by reputation. Two of my friends at school are his daughters, and although they pointedly do not tell others about their father, that would be too embarrassing, just describing events in their lives give most of us a pretty good idea of what goes on in their house.

"For starters, he says he works for 'the government,' but no one knows which government. He doesn't seem to work for the city, and there are no state offices in town that anyone can think of. So far as anyone can figure, he must work for Canada or Mexico. He isn't telling. And the fact that he apparently has a job, but no one knows what it is, is a part of his control. He'll decide who knows what, and that is that.

"My best friend, Rosalee, is the vice president of the class (her father chews her out for not being the president), an editor, but not the editor in chief of the school newspaper (her dad's not happy), writes the column for *The Press* on high school activities at her father's insistence, which is probably why he came in today, and she pulls an almost straight-A average, but not straight A's, which results in many detentions and groundings. Her father recently declared that he would not pay for college unless she had a 4.0 by the end of the year. These things we all know because of all the punishments and demands on her."

Mary Lou felt better at that point, and I suggested she go home and do her homework.

I was interested. For starters, Big Bob seemed to be a classic bully who uses whatever means he has to cow others and bend them to his will. I had the misfortune to grow up with someone like that and was often the target of his malevolence.

My newly-found reportorial instincts were aroused. I knew I couldn't write a story about this guy, but maybe I could write something general about abusive parents.

I asked around town, and it was easy to find out a lot about Big Bob. For example, there was the boat. Bob went to a boat show one weekend and came home with a little runabout. It cost around a thousand dollars with the 25-horse outboard and the mandated safety equipment. He started towing this boat to little lakes within an hour's drive, and it immediately became a passion with him. Some say that was because he was captain on his boat, and everyone else was a galley slave.

He instructed his daughters on how it was to be washed and polished each Sunday evening, and then he supervised this task, seldom finding satisfaction in their work. He required the entire family to go boating with him, even when they didn't want to, which became the norm. He was an absolute tyrant on the boat, screaming orders at his crew, who had no idea what he wanted and seldom could figure out what to do. The girls learned to hate that boat and all of its kind.

After a few years of this, Bob bought a bigger and more expensive boat. At this point he declared that all of his income would go toward the boat, and that Jane, working for peanuts at the Piggly, would pay all household expenses. The impact on his family was profound. Jane could barely afford food on her part-time job. For some odd reason, Bob didn't complain about the food he was served, which got more and more meager, so long as he could afford gas for the boat.

The really odd thing, though, was that most folks in town only knew Bob superficially and thought he was a nice guy. He was always polite and never showed his tendencies in public. He was a stalwart in his church. His family was too well trained and too frightened to reveal much. Only those who knew his family well had any clue.

There are so many possible angles I could take with this story, all involving some research. What makes people behave that way? Is there a cure for it? How do you live with a person like that? I wonder where the family members could find a hitman in Nebraska?

In asking around town about Bob, I came across a story that seemed to have spread throughout the town. If you live in New York City and do something stupid, you are pretty safe. The other 9 million people really don't care. But in Blackjack, any bit of amusing stupidity goes around town in minutes and keeps going around for years. So the way Big Bob was famous was for this story.

He had, it seemed, yearned to be included in a golfing group in town, although he didn't play golf. He looked at the big bellies on the best-known golfers in town and decided it couldn't really take an athlete to play it. He has never been much of an athlete himself and had let his body deteriorate badly for years.

He decided that he wanted to join a group that spent a week at Fort Robinson every year, but after a few years of hinting for an invite, he decided to take matters into his own hands. He saw Lars Engebretsen in The Ideal one day and told him he was coming on his annual golf trip. Lars called Nils who said, "Why not, seems like a decent guy." So Bob bought a set of clubs from the thrift shop. Unluckily for him, they were right handed, and he was left-handed. He went out to the driving range and hit a few buckets of balls until he got his drives to actually go through the air for 40 or 50 yards, although not necessarily where he intended.

At the Fort, he joined Lars, Nils, and Crow, the Navajo pro, on the course. Nils explained that they played for a dime a stroke. Bob hadn't realized that he would be playing for money, but he wasn't really worried. He actually thought his drives were works of art.

Lars, who had started on the Nebraska offensive line for three years, hit first and his drive went out low and gradually rose as it went down range. It was a beautiful shot, the likes of which Bob had never seen. The first hole was a par five, because it was so long, but Lars's drive went so far that he could chip up onto the green from that lie. Nils hit one that wasn't that pretty, but it still left him with a chance to birdie, and Crow likewise. Bob's first shot dribbled off the tee and came to rest after about 30 yards. It was at that instant that he started to realize that he was completely out of his league.

A few strokes later, he was still trying to reach the green, but it was stuck behind a large tree. He kicked his ball out to a place where he could get a better shot. Nils saw him do it. They watched him closely as he totaled up his strokes for that hole. They had counted 12. Bob wrote 8 on the scorecard.

On the third hole, they caught him cheating again. Crow explained that no matter how badly he played and how well the others played, the most he could lose at a dime a stroke was maybe 10 bucks. It wasn't worth cheating was the message.

He was caught cheating on the 9th hole, and by now, they were pretty sure he was cheating on every hole. They told him they didn't want his money, don't even keep score. But Lars was fuming. He told Nils and Crow that he would get this guy and soon.

When they came off the course, Lars said he needed a candy bar and asked if anyone else wanted him to get one for them from the vending machine. No one did. But when Lars returned he had a handful of Baby Ruths. He asked, "Does anyone want one? The weirdest thing happened. I put in a quarter and pulled the handle and two bars came out along with my quarter. So I tried it again, and the same thing happened. I did it once more, so I paid nothing and got six candy bars."

A few minutes later Bob excused himself "to go to the men's room," he said. Lars and Nils exchanged knowing smiles. Bob returned a few minutes later with a handful of Baby Ruths himself. He said, "I put in my quarter, pulled the handle and I got one bar and no quarter. I did it again and again and never got my quarterback. And the worst thing is, I don't even like Baby Ruths."

That evening Nils asked Lars if he had actually gotten two bars and his quarterback each time, and Lars said, "Nah. I knew he'd fall for it, though. The guy is as greedy as they come."

Now that I knew some things about Big Bob, I was alert and paying attention the next day when he came strutting in to wreak havoc and exert control over an enterprise that was just beyond his grasp, *The Press*. He marched up to Mrs. Fritz's desk and stated sternly, "Your office is a shambles, that young girl who was working here yesterday was incompetent and rude, and I need to talk to you about some important matters."

Mrs. Fritz had heard about his visit the day before, and she listened calmly to this introduction until Bob paused for breath. She was a lemon that day, dressed completely in bright yellow, and her attitude toward Bob seemed a little lemony too. She held up her right hand in a "stop" gesture and, exuding patience, said, "Bob, you cannot tell me how to run my newspaper or my office, so you can march out that door just like you marched in." Then she picked up the phone and started dialing a number.

Bob fussed at her, but she just turned her back to him and started talking on the phone. He stomped out, and as soon as the door closed, she hung up and went back to what she had been doing before he came in. There were three people in the office: me, the pressman, and Harvey Bangert, who was editing his weekly hardware store ad. All of us stood and applauded Mrs. Frtiz.

I filed this away in my storehouse of ideas for future articles, and I might have written the story the next week, if things hadn't suddenly changed so dramatically.

CHAPTER 55

Blackjack High Reunion

Mrs. Fritz apologized for the late assignment, but she was having trouble with her back again and couldn't cover the reunion at the high school as she had planned. She said it only occurred every four years and was lightly attended, so there might not be much of interest but to get some good pictures of the grads, especially those who didn't live around here anymore.

I hurried back to my room to change clothes, not that I thought it would be a dressy affair, but because I wanted to be as inconspicuous as possible. As it turned out, people were dressed in every imaginable way so my nicely-pressed, open-collar shirt and clean and pressed khakis were almost a perfect middle ground.

There was a great deal of laughing going on at a table with five couples seated around it, all around 40 or so years old. That looked like a good starting place. I sauntered over and just sat down at the next table with the goal of listening in. That ruse didn't work for long.

One big guy introduced himself as Cliff Montgomery and his buddy as Pete Rose. Neither of them was actually named that as their wives patiently explained later. They were, legitimately, Cliff and Pete, though.

It was fairly easy to get them talking about their exploits and adventures, which is probably what they were laughing about when I got there.

Cliff said that there were a grand total of three boys in his grade-school classes, the same three, of course, from kindergarten through 6th grade. One of them was Pete, and the other was a notorious troublemaker who was not at the reunion. Cliff said that the three of them pretty much did everything together, even though they had very different personalities. He, for example, was the straight-laced scholar and boy scout. Pete was, by his own admission, just a tag-along, and Herman was the bad seed. Herm always had fireworks, especially around July, whereas Cliff wasn't allowed to have any, so he had to use Herm's.

One day, the three of them were walking downtown, and Cliff noticed that there were an unusual number of people on Main Street, so he asked Herm for a cherry bomb. He lit it and tossed it into the cavity of an old dead tree right in the center of the little business district. It made a wonderful sound in the hollow tree trunk and almost everyone turned to see what the explosion was. The boys chuckled at the success of the thing and continued walking toward the swimming pool, their original destination.

It wasn't a particularly warm day, so after a half hour of swimming and turning blue, they decided to give up on swimming for the rest of the day, and besides, they had heard the fire siren go off and the sound of the sirens on the fire trucks and thought there might be some excitement somewhere in town. Usually the fire calls were for burning barns, but it sounded like the fire trucks went a short distance.

When they got back to Main Street, they were surprised to see the tree where Cliff had thrown the cherry bomb burning brightly with flames actually coming dangerously close to several stores. The firemen were working feverishly to prevent the stores from burning. The boys stayed around long enough to see the firemen pull the dead tree down and drag it away from the buildings.

Cliff noticed that many of the watching adults pointed to them, in particular at Herm, with knowing expressions. It was clear that Herm had already been tried and convicted in the court of public opinion. Cliff knew he was the culprit, and it bothered him. When his father came home that night, Cliff asked if he had heard about the fire. His father said he had and asked if he had been involved. Cliff said that he was the one who actually lit and threw the firecracker, not Herman.

His dad asked, "You know what you have to do, don't you?"

"No," Cliff said.

"You have to go to every house in town and tell people it was you and not Herman," his dad said.

So on Saturday, when most people wouldn't be at work, Cliff went to all 81 houses in town and confessed his guilt. Cliff told me, "It didn't change Herm's reputation one bit, but suddenly I was George Washington.

"And," Pete added, "he still is."

One of the wives said, "Tell him about the jail breaks."

Now we're cooking, I thought. *This is great stuff.*

Pete took over, apparently having outgrown his "tagalong" past.

"Around the time we were in high school, our little town was discovered by a fraternity at Bison State. It was probably because of our great town bar, even though most of them couldn't get served there. They would find a way to get their hands on a few bottles of bourbon and a case of Cokes and would set up in the town park. They always had lots of pretty girls with them, so things got a little out of hand with the guys having to show off for the girls, and vice versa."

"Hey!" said one of the wives. Pete ignored her.

"While hanging out in the park, they observed, somehow, that the town's only stoplight, which was set on blinking most of the time, could be controlled from a box on the pole. Someone had seen a town employee change its setting, and they decided that they could do it too. So for fun they set it on a permanent red light on Main, tying up traffic and never changing. The town employee came back out and reset it, but as soon as he was out of sight, they changed it again.

"After the third time, the sheriff was called. When he arrived, he found one of the college students standing at the pole examining the switch, arrested him, and threw him in jail. As it turned out, that student hadn't actually been involved, he was just curious to see what his buddies had done. So his buddies went to the sheriff and pleaded for the release of their innocent brother, but the sheriff wasn't interested in their claims of his innocence. He had caught him at the scene.

"The frat brothers returned to campus and got up a large mob of students to surround the jail and protest. This quickly came to the attention of the State Police, and a riot squad was assembled in the nearest barracks, which was over 30 miles away. Before the riot police arrived, the students had managed to break into the jail, but they hadn't been able to find a key to the cell. Their imprisoned brother exhorted them to leave him alone. They were only making things worse, but the alcohol, the presence of pretty girls and pressure-pumped teenage testosterone drove the guys to irrational decisions. Unable to unlock the cell, one of them produced a gun, which he fired at the lock on the cell door. By some miracle, he didn't kill himself or anyone else in the process, but he did get the cell open.

"The prisoner refused to leave, so they dragged him out to return him to campus. As they were leaving, an armored convoy of riot police arrived and managed to re-arrest the innocent student and put him into the other cell."

"That's some story," I said, wondering how much of it might be true.

I took their pictures, got their real names, and moved on. None of the other stories were nearly as good as those. Now I hoped that I wasn't the only one in town who hadn't been told those stories a hundred times.

I got some pictures, especially of the still-pretty women, and Mrs. Fritz was well pleased. I actually relaxed and enjoyed the party for another hour or so. Not a bad night. And it was to be the last night for a long time that I was able to relax and enjoy it.

PART 2
SAVING BILL JUST'S NAME

CHAPTER 56

Bill's Other Life

SEVERAL NEBRASKA NEWSPAPERS PICKED up my Bill Just story, and it seemed that Bill was now getting his fifteen minutes of fame. KFAB TV did a short feature on him that was seen by network producers. Bill was then mentioned several times in the national press and once on *Sunday Morning*. Millions of people around the country now learned about the "Angel of Blackjack."

I was ecstatic, of course, since I was also mentioned and had been interviewed three times on television. My article had been reprinted in over twenty other periodicals. I made more money that month than I could have dreamed of, and better yet, *The Press* made money too. I believed my future in journalism was now assured.

I was basking in his sudden fame and good fortune, when Mrs. Fritz called me. She said, "Ralph, I just got a call from a woman in North Carolina who said she needs to talk to you. I gave her your cell number, so she should be calling any minute." As soon as I disconnected with her, my phone rang again.

The woman on the phone said, "Ralph, I am Cindy Kraft, and I'm a reporter for the *North Carolina Star-Post* in Raleigh. How are you today?"

I was anticipating more plaudits and possibly a job offer, so I said I was "just peachy," a phrase I had borrowed from my father.

Cindy went on, "I've been doing a story about a young man in our community, and it appears that he may be the son of your Bill Just, or Bill Larsen, to use his real name. Do you know anything about that?"

"The son?" I blurted. "No, I never heard of anything like that. Are you sure?"

"Not yet," Cindy said, "but that's what I've been told. I'm just starting my research on this, and if you would like, I'd be happy to have you join in."

I said, "Sure," and then added, "Well, I work for a really small town paper. There's no money for something like that. Would I have to come to North Carolina?"

"Maybe not," Cindy said. "Let's think about this. Maybe you could do some calling from there. I'd like your views on this as it unfolds, since you're the expert on the man."

It was the first time anyone had ever called me an expert on anything, and I was thrilled. "I'd be happy to do anything I can, Cindy. If I can do it for free, such as calling from my cell, count me in. Otherwise, I'll have to talk with my publisher. What do you have now?"

Cindy filled me in with some background. She was working a story of a soldier who had been severely wounded in Afghanistan by a Taliban explosive device. The soldier had told her that he was the son of an Army veteran and had given her just enough information to cause her to believe that the father could be Bill Just. A few questions revealed that he probably was. Still, elements of the story seemed strange. She wanted to talk to the boy's mother, but had not succeeded as yet. She needed to fill in some blanks in the story, but as of yet hadn't succeeded.

Cindy's editor was willing to support her research for another day or two, but frankly, there wasn't much interest in North Carolina for the story about a Nebraska man. The only reason he let the story go on was that both the son and the mother were probably still in his state.

After that phone call, I went in to see Mrs. Fritz. I found her in the back room, helping the printer move huge rolls of newsprint. Whether she was actually helping or not, she was making an attempt, which was more than I had been there to do.

I said, "Let me do that," and took one end of a roll and helped wedge it out through the tight storage room door.

A little winded from the exertion, I entered Mrs. Fritz's office thinking, *I really need to get into shape.* I needed to discuss the new development.

"Yeah, I got that much from the girl down in Raleigh," she told me after I told her about Cindy's call. "What do you make of it, Ralph?" She really didn't care what I thought of it, but she was always checking to make sure I thought about things, and that was a good idea.

"It sure would make a good story if it's true," I said. "And, it would be of interest to the national press too. We need to beat them to it."

"I don't know," she said slowly, while she pondered the implications. "I'm not in the business of trying to scoop CBS. I'm running a small town paper. Sure, we'll put more ink on this than they will, but if they want to use their budgets to ferret it out, why not let them?"

My new journalistic instincts, developed over the last few weeks, were kicking in big time now. "Well, for starters, it's our story, our guy. And for another, the answers may be found right here in Blackjack."

I didn't really believe that last part. I just used it as an argument, and she saw through it.

"Oh, really? And what makes you think that?"

"Right now it's just a feeling. Can I spend a couple of days asking around? I can work it in with whatever else you have for me."

"That's a reasonable offer," she responded. She would take all the free work she could get, and the kid would be learning things. Maybe he'd actually find some local news in the bargain. "Go for it," she told me.

I called Cindy back. "I'm on it, Cindy. I'll start here in Blackjack, and you can let me know if you need me to make some calls."

Next, I called Cecille at work. She was usually not willing to talk during working hours, and today was no exception. I told her, "Cecille, there's a story about a wounded soldier who claims to be Bill's son," I exaggerated. "I need to talk to you about it."

Cecille's answer surprised me. She said, "Do you remember our first meeting? I told you, 'Check the VFW.' Have you done that?"

"Uhh, not yet..." was the best I could come up with.

"Well, I'm not talking with you about this, so you'd better do what I suggested."

"B-But..." I stammered, "check with who, er, whom, about what?"

"Ralph, I'm not going to do your job," she said and hung up. I was getting the impression that she didn't like me much, despite my great article about her, uh, lover.

Nevertheless, I was excited. If what Cecille said was right, I could find answers right here in town.

First I had to find the VFW, which wasn't in town at all, but out on a county road, more or less centrally located between three different small towns. I wondered how many veterans ended up plowing into trees on the long way home from this remote place after having a few beers at the bar. Come to think of it, that might be a good story.

Then I had to gain admission. The door was locked and operated, I guessed, by some sort of card reader. Of course, I had no card, so I banged on the door. In a few seconds, it buzzed, and I pulled it open. I entered a short hallway that led into a large room with a bar and some tables scattered around. The bartender was watching me come in, and I figured he must be the one who had buzzed me in. Now I had to establish why I was here.

"Hi, I'm Ralph Anderson from *The Press*. I'm the one who wrote the story about Bill Just, and I'm doing some follow-up on that story. I was told I should ask around the VFW, and that's why I'm here."

The bartender smiled and asked, "What are you looking for?"

"Well, I'm not real sure, to tell the truth. There's something in Bill Just's past that I can't explain, and I was led to believe I might find it out here."

"Oh, Bill's past. Yeah, I suppose you would like to know about that. He was a great guy, and you wrote a good article about him. Kind of got famous too, didn't you? Why not let it be?"

"Something's come up. It wasn't my idea, but if I don't stay involved with the story, there's no telling what might end up in the news." I was grasping for straws.

"And where might this have come up?"

I was trying not to reveal what I had, but decided I had little to lose if I did, and that no one was going to help me unless I gave him a reason to. I said, "A soldier has recently been wounded in Afghanistan, and he may be Bill's son, at least he's making noises like he is. The North Carolina papers are already on it, but they want me to work with them. I can't keep it under control unless I have information."

The bartender wiped two glasses until they sparkled without saying a word. Then he said, "The guy you want to talk to is Eddie Starnek. He usually comes in about five, five thirty. Try again then."

Again, I was thrilled. I drove back to Blackjack in a daze. My journalistic career was taking off again. I detoured to Bison "on the way back" and stopped for a Runza and a malt. Might as well have a full stomach if I was going to be hanging out at the VFW drinking with Eddie Starnek, whoever he was.

CHAPTER 57

Eddie Starnek

I WAS BACK AT the VFW banging on the door at 5:30. This time, a member showed up a second later and opened the door, letting me in. It was Pete Thorson, who had been thinking of me, with whom he had been favorably impressed at the library, he said. I didn't immediately remember Pete, but he looked familiar, so I asked him if he knew Eddie Starnek. Pete pointed me toward Eddie, who was just sitting down at the bar. Pete asked me for my name, handed me a business card, and said, "Give me a call." Neither Pete nor I knew why, but I was hot on the trail of a story and thought it might be in connection with that. It turned out that I was right, but it was just a coincidence.

I turned my attention to Eddie. I decided that I needed to buy him a drink, so I told him who I was and offered to buy. Eddie said, "Sure, man, I'm drinking beer. And not that light crap. Real beer."

I walked back up to the bar and asked the keeper for two beers. The barkeep asked, "Bud or Bud Light?"

"Buds," I answered.

They cost me 90 cents. I made a mental note to ask Mrs. Fritz for reimbursement, since I suspected Eddie would have more than one. I picked up the beers and joined Eddie at a table.

When I told Eddie who I was, Eddie grinned broadly. "That was a great article about Bill, really great. You know, he really was a super guy, just like you wrote."

"Yeah, I know," I said. "How did you know Bill?"

Eddie tilted his beer glass up and drained it in what seemed to be one gulp. He belched loudly and took a second to think, during which time I grabbed the glass and took it back to the bar. I returned a couple of minutes later with a pitcher and two glasses. They cost me $3, and now I was sure I was going to ask for reimbursement.

Eddie began, "It was just a coincidence at first. I was in the recruiter's office joining up myself when Bill came in and enlisted. I had never known him before that, because I lived on a farm out in the county then and had dropped out of school, so there was no way we would have met. But, since we signed up at the same time, we went off to basic together. We traveled together to Fort Jackson for basic.

"During basic, Bill talked me into volunteering for jump school, so after AIT…"

"AIT?" I asked.

"Oh, yeah, that's Advanced Individual Training. We went to Fort Bragg together. After jump school, we were assigned to the same battalion but different companies in the 82d. We hung out together some, but Bill was real serious and after awhile, we kind of drifted apart. I'm probably the only one who knows his deep, dark secret, though. When he was court martialed, he came to see me and we talked."

"Bill was court martialed?" I asked, incredulous. Jailbird? This paragon of virtue? This hometown hero?

"Yeah. Well, he got off, and better yet, he got out of the field and into a job where he learned stuff he needed to know when he got out. All I learned was how to be a rifleman."

"Tell me about that," I prompted.

"I guess I can tell it now that he's dead. I never told nobody when he was alive."

"Nice of you," I said.

"Well, he was a good guy. Of course, I heard most of this from him, but I'd believe him if he told me the Pope was a Mormon. That's the kind of guy he was. Hey, are we drinking here? I'm running low."

"Oh, sure, in a minute Eddie," I said. "I would like to hear about this court martial thing first, though."

"Oh, sure," Eddie said without enthusiasm. Maybe he did need more beer. "Well, his company commander was one mean SOB. He was charging lots of his soldiers with crimes and sending them to the stockade for the slightest things.

"One night, Bill was on guard on main post. There weren't many soldiers on main post, so the Division grunts had to pull guard duty there. In the morning, the guard detail had to clear the guard barracks they had used during the night, and the Corps Sergeant Major inspected. He never passed no one on the first inspection. So they flunked, of course. The sergeant of the guard left Bill behind, his best soldier, and told him to take care of it. He also left him a jeep to get back to his company.

"Before he got back, the company discovered his rifle missing, and before you know it, the FBI was there and about half the MPs on post. They were scared that guys were selling arms to bad guys, and I knew some guys who were too. I remember this one guy..."

"Eddie, how about Bill?"

"Oh, yeah. By the time Bill came back, the company commander was convinced, for some reason, that he was stealing the rifle. It was signed out to him and everything, so it was ridiculous, but the old man pressed charges."

"That does sound ridiculous," I interjected.

"You bet it does," Eddie went on. "At the trial, Bill told his story, but the company commander had testified that at reveille that morning he had made an announcement that whoever had the rifle should bring it back, no questions asked. Of course, Bill wasn't there at reveille, but that somehow made it larceny."

"Ah, yes, 'intent to permanently deprive...' " I quoted from the Uniform Code of Military Justice. I had liked that part of ROTC the best. *Maybe I ought to go to law school,* I thought. That would put off having a job for another year or two.

Eddie went on, "The court found Bill not guilty, and one of the officers on the court decided he liked Bill and he would rescue him from the company. He asked for him and put him in the personnel shop where he became an expert clerk. So it all worked out great for Bill. Hey, you know what he told me? He said that when he parachuted, jumped, we said, he had a typewriter in his bag. What did we call those bags?"

I made a mental note to file that story away for later. Now down to the business at hand.

"Did Bill have a girlfriend at Fort Bragg?"

"Yeah, he did, as a matter of fact. Fran was her name. I don't know why I can't think of what those bags were called. You jumped with them and then let them down before you landed. And he had a typewriter in his! Isn't that funny?"

"But Eddie, were Bill and Fran serious? Did they get married or anything like that?"

Eddie had gone through three glasses of beer already, but he was still alert. "Why, what have you heard?"

"Eddie, it's not what I've heard. The reporters in Raleigh are onto something. They think a soldier who was wounded in Afghanistan is Bill's son. This thing could hit the national press tomorrow. They've asked me to check around, which is why I'm here. Understand, if it comes out, it could be big, and if I don't get them the right story, there's no telling what will hit the street. It could make Bill look bad, real bad."

"Jesus!" Eddie blurted. "Make Bill look bad? You must be kidding! Bill has done everything he could for that kid and for Fran too. It's just that she's a mess, a real mess."

"Tell me about it," I said.

Eddie drained the pitcher and pushed it toward me, but I ignored it. I wanted to hear what Eddie had to say before either of us got any drunker.

Eddie continued, "Well, it was a sudden thing. Fran worked in the Education Center on post. That's where they met. She was gaga over Bill, just nuts. She got pregnant right away, and Bill, he thought he had to do the right thing, marry her and all. He offered, and she was thrilled of course.

"There was a guy in Bill's company who had some kind of degree that made him a preacher in some made-up church. You know, he bought it from an ad in a magazine for twenty bucks. Anyway, he said he was allowed to marry people and would marry them for twenty bucks, that way he would be even. Twenty for the certificate that made him a preacher, and twenty for the wedding, even-Steven. Bill asked me to be the best man, and naturally, I said yes. So this guy, I think his name was Smith, maybe Jones, married Bill and Sally."

"Wait a second," I interjected. "Who's Sally?"

"Oh, geez, did I say Sally? That was a girl I knew down there. Oh, man, Sally. I'll tell you about her…"

"No, please," I blurted out. "Tell me about Fran."

"Yeah, Fran. Well, Fran's family was Catholic. When she told her parents that she was married, they had the marriage annulled. Or at least they were going to have it annulled, but it turned out North Carolina didn't recognize Smith's certificate, and they said the marriage was illegal and all."

I said, "So they never were actually married?"

"Yeah, that's right, but Bill, he was such a great guy, he felt he was responsible for Fran and the kid. Yeah, it was a boy, now that I think about it. Bill told me that later, after we were both back here in Nebraska again. Bill wanted to marry Fran again, but her parents wouldn't let them marry, and Fran, well, she turned out to be kind of nuts anyway. She's a sad case."

I was writing furiously. I now carried and remembered to use a small notebook.

"How do you know she's such a sad case?"

"I guess 'cause Bill told me. Listen, if he told you something, it was so. Take it to the bank."

"Can you tell me what was so sad about her?"

"From what Bill said, she had trouble keeping a job with the kid to raise, let herself go, drank a lot, smoked like a chimney, and pretty much went to pot. So Bill, guy that he was, he sent money and tried to see his son. She wouldn't let him though. She said she was afraid he'd kidnap the boy, and he might've too. He wanted to do right by that boy, and he knew he wasn't learning good stuff with his mother."

"So, what happened?"

"That's about it, really. Bill spent the rest of his life trying to help her and the kid out, but he kind of thought it was like pouring money down a rat hole. She just spent it on booze and cigarettes. You know, as far as he was concerned, he was married to Fran, and he didn't care what North Carolina or Fran's parents thought. But, that was just stupid, 'cause he should have married that lady who he lived with out here. She's something special."

"Do you know Fran's last name?"

Eddie scrunched up his face in thought, but Ralph could see that the beer was now taking its toll. "Geez, you'd think I could remember that. Let me think about it," he said.

I paid for another pitcher of beer, but I was leaving. As I left, I gave Eddie another prod: "It's important to clearing Bill's name. If you have anything that will help, any letters or a diary or anything like that, please look for it, or just try to think of it. We need to find her."

I walked quickly out to my car. I knew I had something now, but I wasn't sure what to do with it. I would talk to Cindy and see how they could handle it. Whatever we did, I felt that we had to save Bill Just's reputation, even though I had never met Bill Just.

CHAPTER 58

Discovering a Past

AFTER I TOLD CINDY what I had learned and was certain that she was going to try to see it from my point of view, I called Cecille again. I began by telling her that I had located Eddie Starnek.

"That's who I was supposed to find, right?" I asked.

Cecille was still playing coy with that information. "Did you learn something important? If so, that should answer your question."

I retorted, "Look, Cecille, I appreciate all you've done for me, and I respect your privacy or whatever it is you're protecting now, but I have to tell you there's one piece of information I couldn't get out of Eddie, and you can probably help me, if you will. I think it's important. I'm trying to save Bill's reputation, and I need your help."

"And what might that information be?" she asked.

"I need to find Fran. I need her last name and any other information you might be able to give me. Eddie doesn't remember her name."

Cecille answered carefully, "You might suspect that Bill didn't talk about Fran with me. By the way, this is off the record, and I mean it. I don't want to find my name in something you write saying, 'Cecille Gadd said...' Are we clear on that?"

"Sure, Cecille," I answered.

I was starting to feel a little funny about calling her by her first name. She was a full generation older than I was and a successful business-woman, while I was a wet-behind-the-ears kid just out of college. And, she was so important to my place in this new story that I didn't dare get on her wrong side. Well, get even more on her wrong side. I had already gotten on that side and was still trying to recover.

Cecille mused over the phone, "Maybe there's something I can find in Bill's address book. If I find it, I'll call you."

When I hung up, I was sure she'd find it, so I now felt pretty confident about my story. I called Cindy back and brought her up to date. She said, "Ralph, we're running out of time. My editor thinks this is too good a story to keep under wraps. He wants to get it into tomorrow's paper. There's not much I can do to stop it. We need to coordinate on the content. I'll email my draft to you as soon as it's done, okay?"

Ah, nuts! I thought. *This isn't working out.* I went to talk to Mrs. Fritz for guidance.

CHAPTER 59

Finding Fran

A LITTLE LATER, I got a call from Pete Thorson. I was tempted to tell him that I was too busy to talk, but Pete said he wanted to meet for a drink. I needed to eat someplace anyway, so I said I'd meet him at The Matador, famous for its burgers.

Pete was his usual gruff self. The conversation was stilted, Pete not saying much and I not sure what to say. Then a man came over who acted like he knew Pete. "Hey, buddy," he said loudly, "long time, no see. How ya hangin'?"

Pete almost jumped to his feet in anger. "Can't you see I'm here with someone? What do you mean by barging in where you're not invited?"

The guy slunk away, mumbling about not needing to yell, just saying hello.

I had seen similar behavior back at school. Some of the less articulate linemen used to act that way too. I had figured out that they were trying to avoid conversations with students who were taking actual academic courses. If your course load consisted mainly of kinesthetics (blocking and tackling) and sports officiating, talking to a poli-sci major or, worse, a physics major, could prove embarrassing.

Without thinking, I said, "I have you figured out."

"Oh, you do, eh?" Pete grumbled.

"Yeah. You're not the mean guy you pretend to be. You're just shy."

Pete grinned. "No, I'm not shy. I jumped right into that guy's face, didn't I? I'm just bashful."

"Well," I began, not knowing where I was going with this, "I hope you're not bashful with me."

"Nah," Pete answered. "The first time I saw you in the library, I kind of took a liking to you. You seem like a nice kid. And it turns out that maybe I can be of use to you in this story you're writing about Just. Or are you through with that?"

I was surprised. "No, I'm not. How can you help with that story?"

Pete looked around to see if anyone was listening. The couple in the adjacent booth was too quiet for his taste, so he glared at the woman, until she started talking to her husband, just what Pete wanted.

"I used to run into Just in some of the little towns around here. He was selling insurance and mutuals, and I was selling cleaning supplies. I introduced him to a lot of potential customers, and after a while, we started taking some sales trips together. I knew people, and he didn't. I helped him a lot. So we got to know each other pretty well, him and me."

"And?" I prompted.

"And, well, I got to know some things about him that I guess you don't, that's all."

"I'm all ears, Pete," I said.

Pete thought a second. "I don't know what you might need. I'm not going to sit here all night telling you his secrets. Ask me something."

I did. "Did you know he had a son?"

"Yep."

Well?"

"Well, I knew that."

"Okay..." I sighed. "If he wasn't married, how did he have a son?"

"He got this girl pregnant down in South Carolina..."

"North Carolina," I interjected.

"Hey, if you know so much about it, why are you asking?"

"I don't know some things, and I'm hoping you do. Do you know the kid's mother's name?"

Pete stared at the ceiling for a minute. "Fran, I think."

"Right," I said, "but Fran what? And what is the kid's name?"

"You know, I think the kid's name is Larsen. When Bill joined the Army, he had to use his real name, which was Larsen. People in town don't know that. He was running away from his family, and he didn't want them to find him, and then, when he didn't need a fake name, everyone already knew him as Just."

"Remember the kid's first name?"

"Umm, no, but it may have been William after his dad. William Larsen, I think."

"But you don't know the mother's last name?"

"No," Pete said, "I don't remember if I ever knew it. I assumed she called herself Larsen."

"That's what I need right now, the mother's name and location. But, since you don't know it, tell me about these business trips. Were they day trips?"

Pete smiled, apparently thinking about the old days. "Yeah, mostly. We'd call ahead and make some appointments. He'd go his way, and I'd go mine. Sometimes we'd meet for lunch, and sometimes we'd just drive out there together. It saved gas and gave us something to do while driving. I'd tell him about the town. You know, there's some funny towns around here. We got Czech towns, Polish towns, German towns, Swedish towns…"

"You mean like Wilber?"

"Exactly," Pete said. "Wilber is the Czech capital of Nebraska they say. Those guys mostly do business with each other, so you got to get to know them before you can sell them anything. You might not guess it, but that's what I'm good at."

I laughed. I didn't mean to, but Pete Thorson, the Grizzly? "That is hard to believe, Pete."

"Yeah, I suppose it is, but I had to make a living, so I had to learn how to get to know my customers. I did all right. I sold nearly all the schools from here to the middle of Kansas their cleaning supplies. I sold to the Czechs, the Poles, you name it, I sold 'em."

"Maybe I ought to look into these towns some time for an article. Would you help me?"

"Kelly," Pete said.

"What? I asked.

"Fran Kelly, just came to me. Lived in Winston-Salem. I think."

I was so excited that I forgot to eat supper. The beer I had drunk in The Matador, on top of the beers at the VFW, were making me sloppy. My first act was to head for *The Press,* and on the way, I called Cindy on my cell phone.

"Look for a Fran Kelly or Larsen in Winston-Salem. I think one of those is the mother's name."

Then, I called Cecille. "Find anything?" I asked.

"Didn't we just talk about this, Ralph? I haven't had a chance to eat my supper yet."

"I know, me neither," I said. "I learned that Fran's name might be Kelly if it isn't Larsen, and she might live in Winston-Salem. That might help you find the address."

"Okay, Ralph, I'll look for the address book."

I stayed on the line. She returned to the phone in under 5 minutes. "I found the address and a phone number."

I immediately called it to Cindy, who was still at work. I got her to promise not to let the story run the next morning, and I told her I would see if I could go down there.

Then I called Mrs. Fritz. "I've got information on Bill's wife, well, the woman he tried to marry and the one who had his kid. I think I need to get down to North Carolina to be part of this story, or there's no telling what they'll do with it."

Mrs. Fritz hadn't expected that. "Well, this is a surprise, and I don't have any money in the budget for travel halfway across the country."

I said, "It's clear that Bill did father this child, who is now grown up and a soldier, a wounded soldier. I've given the reporter in Raleigh enough clues so that she will probably find the mother tonight or tomorrow. I've asked her not to publish anything on this until I get there. I'm trying to protect Bill Just's name here. If you let me go, I'll drive my car and only ask for gas money and maybe a few nights in a hotel."

Mrs. Fritz paused to think, then said, "I've never done anything like this before, and if it was just about anybody else, I wouldn't do it now, but Bill… All right, you go down there, but keep me informed every day and get back here as fast as you can."

Then I told her she owed me for two pitchers of beer. Six dollars. I stopped at the cheapo gas station on the way out of town and spent $12.95 on a road atlas and $6 for a sandwich and a pop.

It was already dark, and I wasn't even sure how to get to Raleigh or, for that matter, where Raleigh was. I headed east and decided I'd figure it out later. Passing through Missouri, I had to stop for gas, and while the tank was filling, I looked at the atlas. I was doing all right so far, but I was now impressed with how far I still had to go. I went into the station and bought a huge cup of coffee. I would be driving all night.

I was happily surprised at the lack of traffic on I-70. I set the cruise control at 79, reclined my seat a little, turned up the radio, and just sailed. Every hour, I mentally clicked off another 80 miles. At this rate, I thought, it won't be long.

Boy, was that wrong!

CHAPTER 60

Road Trip

I WOKE UP WITH a start when my tires hit the rumble strip as I left the driving lane. I carefully re-entered the lane, passing over the rumble strip again. That had scared me. I must have been sound asleep to drive off the highway. I tried to think back to the last thing I could remember, and I couldn't think of anything since I had finished the coffee and tossed the cup to the floor of the car. I looked at the clock and thought that might have been as much as 20 minutes earlier. I pulled off at the next exit and looked for something open. I found a gas station with a Burger King attached and got more coffee and a burger.

I had brought the atlas into Burger King, and now I studied it some more. I had to get south pretty soon or I would have a hard time getting to Raleigh. I had to head for Nashville. *Boy,* I thought, *I wish I could stop there*. But, I couldn't.

Back on the road, I was still fighting sleep. It was now almost 4 a.m., and I thought I might start waking up soon. But after only another 20 minutes, I hit the rumble strip again.

At the next exit on the west side of St Louis, I looked for a cheap motel. I found one that reminded me of an Army barracks in old war movies. As I trudged up the stairs, my footsteps resonated like I was walking on a drum. Same thing in the hallway. A baby cried in one room and a couple was fighting in another. I checked my watch: 4:45. *Who fights at 4:45?* I wondered.

Now I couldn't sleep. Why didn't the coffee that was now keeping me wide awake, keep me awake when I drove? I gave up after an hour, opened my laptop, wrote the story I had been thinking about, while I tried to sleep, and e-mailed it to Mrs. Fritz. At least the WiFi worked in this place. She might be writing it herself, but I had nothing else to do since I couldn't sleep or drive, it seemed.

I looked at the atlas and calculated how far I had come and how far I had to go. I was not even close to halfway there. If I left now, I would still drive all day and not reach Raleigh.

I dozed off while lying in bed, looking at the atlas. I awoke at 9:45 when the maid knocked on the door. I grabbed my computer and hustled down to the car. I remembered that the clerk had said there would be a continental breakfast, but it was too late. I found half a stale donut, filled my big coffee cup that I had tossed to the floor of the car, and headed for Nashville.

Things got slower on the highway. I couldn't make 80 miles an hour anymore, and I was seeing a part of the country I had never seen before. I would have slowed down on my own to make sure I could check the countryside if the traffic hadn't slowed me down. I reported to Cindy.

She told me, "Go straight to Fort Bragg. Billy Larsen has been released from Walter Reed and is an outpatient at Fort Bragg, pulling duty with the 82d from his wheelchair, while waiting for a medical board. I want you to talk to him with all you know about his dad. He seems to be emulating his dad as much as he can. Perhaps you can do some male bonding. We need the story from his perspective, and I think you're the one to get it."

"Will I be able to get into the fort?" I asked.

She said, "When you get to the gate, tell the MP who you are. I'll make sure the PIO, that's Public Information Officer, knows you're coming."

"Roger," I replied. I had been in ROTC for two years and had learned a little bit about the Army. I took a lot of ribbing from some of my dorm mates about wearing my uniform on drill days, as I was required to do. After I dropped out of ROTC, I found out that the guys who were teasing me were the campus protest squad. They were thrilled that they had teased me out of ROTC and tried to recruit me for their next protest, against fur coats, as it turned out. I kept my distance from them after that, but I never rejoined ROTC. Now I wondered how my life would be different if I had. Maybe I would be stationed at Fort Bragg and jumping out of airplanes instead of in Blackjack working for peanuts.

I only made Charlotte that night, but I was glad I did. I drove around the city and was impressed with the downtown area. *A nice place to live,* I thought. And, I was just hours away from Fort Bragg.

The next morning, I got my wakeup call at 7, as I had asked, and had a decent breakfast for a change. I had splurged and stayed in a Holiday Inn Express. I was on the road to Fort Bragg at five after eight.

The problem now was that there were no more Interstate highways on my route. I was making my way through the North Carolina countryside on good roads, but slowing down for towns and the occasional stoplight. Finally, out of Laurinburg, I picked up 401 headed right for Fayetteville and Fort Bragg.

As I got nearer I encountered more military vehicles and a few soldiers apparently on duty nearby. About 10 miles from the fort, I saw a formation of Air Force planes in the sky, and I pulled over to the side of the road when paratroopers started coming out. I watched fascinated as the chutes opened and they drifted downward. When they were all down far enough so that trees blocked my view, I got back in the car and drove on, a little excited by what I had just seen.

I turned onto All-American Highway and followed the signs to Fort Bragg. I had to stop at the gate and fill out paperwork for a temporary pass. The guards inspected my car thoroughly, even looking under it with mirrors. They directed me to the Public Information Office for XVIII Airborne Corps.

I was surprised at how nice it was on the post, with lots of large, grassy spaces, perhaps parade fields. I even found a place to park near the entrance to the building where the PIO office was. It seemed too quiet to me, somehow. I had no idea that I was one or two miles from the airborne division, part of which was deployed overseas at that time anyway, and from Special Forces, most of which was deployed. Things *were* quiet on Fort Bragg.

When I entered the large, brick building, I found myself in a long corridor with no idea what to do next. An officer came out of an office and noticed my confusion. He asked, "Can I help you?"

I said, "I'm supposed to go to the PIO."

"Oh, sure," the officer replied, "I'll show you."

He led me down the hall and around a corner to the door to the PIO. I thanked him and entered the office. I found a secretary working on a computer. She said, "Mr. Anderson?"

"Yes, that's me," I replied, still surprised at how normal it all seemed. The officer who had led me to the office was wearing a combat uniform, otherwise I might have thought I was in a civilian business. That, and the bulletin board in the hallway. I remembered from my two years of ROTC that the Army has a passion for bulletin boards.

Now another civilian came out to greet me. She introduced herself as Mrs. Haas, the assistant to the PIO. "Cindy called and said you'd be coming. I hope you got through the gate without too much trouble."

"Sure did, thanks for taking care of that. Please call me Ralph"

"That's our job, Ralph. Now, Cindy said you wanted to interview Specialist Larsen, and you can do that this afternoon. He'll be coming to our office at 1400. Oh, that's 2 p.m."

"I knew that, but thanks."

Mrs. Haas smiled as if we were old friends. "We'll let you use one of our press rooms. We have two, and no one else is here right now, so you won't be disturbed. If there's anything else we can do to help, please let us know. There's a coffee pot in the outer office, and you are welcome to help yourself. We have to buy the coffee, and if you want, you can drop a quarter in the coffee can next to the pot, but don't worry about it."

I said, "If I am going to have to wait until 1400, I'd like to find something to eat."

She thought a few seconds and said, "It's a little before eleven now, so you have some time. You can eat at the club, and it's not far from here, or at the PX, but you'd have to drive to that. The club is pretty nice, and they won't check for a membership or anything. It has a cafeteria. You might try that."

I was a little annoyed that I would have to wait so long, but it was a nice day, so I walked slowly over to the club, formerly the Officers Club. I guessed that it had been converted to a club for everyone. It sat on the side of a big golf course and right in front of a line of generals' houses. I wondered how the generals liked golf balls coming through their windows.

I had never played golf, but I was interested in it and hoped to learn to play someday. I stopped and watched a foursome teeing off on what seemed to be the first tee. All the golfers appeared to be over fifty—in other words, retired.

Nice, I thought, *fifty and retired playing golf. Was ROTC so bad?*

Lunch at the club was pretty ordinary. That was disappointing, but the price was right. I still had plenty of time before my interview and decided to call Cindy for guidance.

"Ralph, we're going to run a story tomorrow, so call me as soon as you've talked to the kid. I need as much as you can give me. Then drive up here. I'll send you directions by e-mail, and you can help me write it. We've got to move fast on this," was all the guidance she gave me.

"As much as you can give me" was pretty vague.

CHAPTER 61

Sp4 Larsen

WHEN YOUNG LARSEN ARRIVED, he found me waiting in the office set aside for the interview. Larsen seemed surprised to find a young man, perhaps as young as he was himself, casually dressed and looking out of place on an Army post. He probably noted that I was scruffy in many ways. Hair was unkempt, or perhaps just unruly. It would have been cut so short that it wouldn't matter in the Airborne. Shirt was rumpled, though clean. Same with my slacks. The final touch was a pair of dirty running shoes. Larsen was not favorably impressed, and he showed it.

I, on the other hand, was very impressed with the young soldier. I noted that, though confined to the wheelchair, the kid was wearing a camouflaged combat uniform, had his hair cut down to his scalp, and the shiniest pair of jump boots on his now useless legs that I had ever seen.

I jumped up and walked quickly to the wheelchair as Larsen maneuvered it through the too-narrow doorway. Larsen quickly waved me aside saying, "I can do it, sir."

"Can't I help?" I asked.

"No, sir, please don't. I have to learn to take care of myself without the help of others. I can do it, but it may take a little longer."

When he was in the room and pulled up to the table, Larsen stuck out a hand and said, "Specialist Four Larsen, sir."

"Yes, I know," I responded, "and I'm Ralph Anderson. Please don't call me sir."

"I'll try, Ralph," Larsen answered. "Please, call me Will."

"Someone just told me you were Billy," I said.

"I'm trying to become Will. Sounds more mature, don't you think?"

"Sure does," I said.

I explained the background of my involvement in the story along with my admiration of Larsen's father. As I did so, I realized that I probably shouldn't have done that since it might bias what Larsen would tell me, but I was trying to establish rapport.

Larsen told me, "As you know, I was raised by my mother and never met my father. When she talked about him, he seemed larger than life to me. He was a paratrooper in the 82d, after all. I guess he turned out to be my role model, even though I didn't know him."

"Why do you think you never met your dad?" I asked.

"My mom kept him away from me, but I really wanted to know him. As soon as I could, I enlisted, volunteered for the airborne, and followed in his footsteps. That turned out to be, a, well, maybe not what I expected. Here I am in a wheelchair. I may be able to walk again, but it's going to take some time."

I asked him about how he was wounded.

"I wish I could make it a grand and glorious story, but you know how these things are happening with the terrorists. I was out on patrol in a Humvee when we were hit by an IED. The Humvee was blown almost to bits, and my legs were crushed. I've had seven surgeries so far and more to go."

We talked some more about Will's life up to this point and his plans for the future, which were vague. I was impressed with the young man's courage and forthrightness. It was obvious that he held his father in high regard and had tried to pattern his own life after his father's. He didn't know that his dad had been a personnel clerk in the 82d, and I didn't tell him that.

When we finished, I called Cindy and read her my notes. Then I drove as fast as I could to Raleigh and found *The Star-Post* offices.

I had never seen Cindy, of course. So up until now, I had just been entranced by her voice and her professionalism. But oh my gosh, Cindy was a striking young lady and younger than I had expected. I guessed that she was maybe a year older than I was. She had dark brown hair pulled back in a French twist, wore little makeup, but was quite pretty without it. She was a small woman, but had a presence that made her seem much bigger. I was instantly in love. I guessed that most men who met her were likewise smitten.

After a minute of small talk, Cindy said, "I'm writing the story now and have it almost finished. I need you to help finish it up. Have you had anything to eat?"

"No, didn't have time," I answered, since it was now well after suppertime.

"Okay, I'll call out for some pizza. What do you like on yours?"

We went to work on the story right away. I was confused by what I found already written. It was a story of a boy who idolized a father he had never met, went to war, and was wounded. It was a "dog bites man" story. Most boys follow, or try to follow, in their fathers' footsteps. Where was the big story here?

We worked until after midnight, and the story didn't get much better. Finally Cindy told me to go find a motel and get some sleep. She said she would handle it from there. She pointed me toward a highway intersection where there were several motels.

Since I had come all this way, the next morning, I decided to try to see a man I had learned about from Eddie Starnek. A person who had been a positive influence on Just in the Army, Plato Smith, lived on a mountaintop just across the state line in Virginia. I called Smith, and he said he would be delighted to see me, so I headed his way.

I already knew he was black and had retired from the Army as a warrant officer and moved back to rural Virginia. I couldn't fathom why a black man who had achieved so much in life would go back home to a place where he might be, probably would be, considered a second-class citizen.

There are so few blacks in Nebraska that I wouldn't know anything about them and racism, except that most of the football players and all of the basketball players at Bison were blacks. Some of them were good friends of mine, and they spoke openly of white prejudice. I didn't think I was prejudiced so they pointed out to me how I sometimes gave them less respect than I did to my white friends. It was a learning experience for me. I was going to put that learning to use in dealing with Plato Smith.

Smith had given me explicit directions, which was essential since the last half mile was up a steep slope on a rutted dirt road. I had left early in the morning, because I wanted to have time to continue work on *The Star-Post* story, if I would be permitted to contribute, but driving on secondary roads made it a slow trip.

I reached the top of the mountain to find five houses. Two nice-looking cottages, an old, weather-beaten shack, and two spiffy trailers. It was the trailer on the very top that I was headed for.

I was walking around to what I thought was the front door when I heard a voice behind me saying, "Come on in here." I turned around and saw a lady who I guessed was Mrs. Smith. One glance told me this was a classy lady. She was smiling and beckoning me to the kitchen door.

As I entered, I was immediately impressed with the interior of the trailer, and in fact, blurted out, "This is no trailer! It has a fireplace!"

Mrs. Smith introduced herself as Karen and told me to come on in. Plato was over at his sisters' house, at which she pointed, and she would call him and tell him to come home to talk to me. Then, she asked me if I wanted a glass of tea.

Plato Smith showed up in a few minutes. He was as impressive as his wife and his "trailer." He was tall, handsome, and well built. He was a hard man, I guessed, without a trace of fat anywhere on his body.

I had told him what I was doing, and he knew I was there to ask about Bill Just, or Larsen as he knew him, so we got down to business quickly. I had to ask the question that had been nagging me, though. Why would he, a black man, who presumably could live anywhere, choose to live on a dirt road in rural Virginia?

Plato said, "This is my home. I was born here, raised here, and I inherited this land. It's where I belong."

The story was that his mother, a single parent, had to go down the mountain to find work, leaving Plato and his sisters with their grandparents who lived in the old house I had seen. They farmed the small open area and lived mostly on what they raised, supplemented by what money his mother could contribute.

Plato, the oldest child, worked the farm as soon as he was big enough. He told me about carrying bags of grain on his shoulder down the mountain on his way to school and dropping them off to be milled. On the way back home, he would pick up the flour from the mill and carry it back up the hill. By the time he got to high school, he had muscles of iron in his legs and became the star running back on the football team. That led to a college scholarship. Since my car could barely make it up the mountain, I marveled at his ability to carry heavy bags of flour up by himself as a child.

He spent 26 years in the Army and worked in the defense industry after his Army retirement for another 12 years, while his wife, Karen, was teaching school. They both retired and moved "home."

Plato spoke very fondly of Bill. Considering how many soldiers must have worked for him over his 26 years, I had to believe that Bill was very special to have been remembered.

Plato said he always tried to teach his soldiers three qualities. First, they had to be competent at their jobs. Then, they had to be reliable in any situation. This was the Army, and even though they were personnel clerks, they might be called on to fight. Finally, he told me, and they must preserve their dignity. Someone was always trying to take that away, and it was up to the individual to remain dignified in spite of that. I could tell from my short meeting with him, that he was very good at what he preached. I assured him that Bill had learned his lessons well.

Too soon, I had to leave to get back to the city to find out how the story was going, or if it was going, for that matter.

As soon as I got back into North Carolina, I found a copy of *The Star-*

Post. The headline on the front page read, "Supposed Hero Abandoned Out-of-Wedlock Son."

CHAPTER 62

On the War Path

NORMALLY, I STAY REMARKABLY unperturbed no matter what, but for some reason this betrayal of trust pushed me right over the edge. I almost didn't read the article to see what it said, but halfway to town, I decided I needed to. I pulled into a rest stop and read:

> The small-town Nebraska folk hero, Bill Just, featured in several national news stories in the past few weeks, has turned out to have another side, previously unknown. *The Star-Post* has learned that, while a soldier at Fort Bragg, he fathered a child out of wedlock and subsequently abandoned the mother, never to see the child he fathered.
>
> The son, William Larsen, now a soldier at Fort Bragg and seriously wounded in Afghanistan, said yesterday, "I never knew him." Larsen admitted that he was following his father's footsteps by enlisting in the Army and joining the 82d Airborne Division, but now feels that was a tragic mistake.

I was too angry to read the rest or to drive for the next ten minutes.

Three times, I dialed Cindy's cell phone, only to hang up before she answered. I wanted time to think, but I also wanted to get to the paper as fast as possible to force a retraction or correction.

Mostly, I was angry, because I had been used to defame Bill Just, and my interview with the young Larsen was now part of that defamation. I had been played like a sucker by Cindy—used and abused. I had fallen for her and let down my guard. Why hadn't I realized that there was no story there for the Raleigh paper? If they were going to run it, they would have to change it. And, boy, had they changed it!

As I drove toward the city, I realized I had little leverage to use against a major newspaper. I was just a kid reporter from a small-town paper 1400 miles away. *The Star-Post* was looking for national interest, and this story might get it. Their reporter had broken the story, and they would get the credit. I had to take that away from them. But how?

When I reached the lobby of *The Star-Post* building, I was prevented from entering by the guard. I was tempted to just run past him, but I would have to wait for the elevator anyway, and the guard would catch me there, if not before. I called Cindy's cell—no answer. Not even a voice mailbox. What was going on?

With no better ideas, I called Mrs. Fritz.

"Mrs. Fritz, something awful has happened, and I don't know what to do."

Mrs. Fritz calmly responded, "Tell me about it, Ralph."

I blurted out the story and then read her the article in *The Star-Post*. She listened silently until I finished.

"That's pretty low, isn't it? Well, let's think of what the damage is, and if we have to do something about it. Let me think out loud, and you chime in when you want to. What's the damage? Bill's reputation has been smeared unjustly. Does that matter to anyone?"

"It does to me," I said with sincere emotion.

"My, I guess it does, and I agree. He's our town hero and the hero to a lot of our friends and neighbors. So, what can we do about it?"

I was thinking more rationally now. "I would guess that you're going to get a lot of calls from around the country for information and reactions. That's our chance to tell the truth."

Mrs. Fritz mused, "Yes, but won't it sound like a coverup or rationalization on our part? We have to be careful not to give them anything they can use to make us look bad, taking Bill down with us."

"Are you saying there's nothing we can do?"

"No," Mrs. Fritz said patiently, "just that we have to be careful. I think the best response would be something like this. 'Bill did not abandon anyone. He was prevented from seeing the child by the mother's family.' And then, we will prepare a counter-story. If we do get calls from the big news guys, we'll give them that. Meanwhile, Ralph, can you get back here fast? How long will it take you?"

"The best I could do getting here was over two days. Is that fast enough?"

"No, but it would probably be hard to get here any faster even if you flew. Go ahead and drive, but I'll need you IM-ing me for at least an hour a day. Get started right now. Stop somewhere and get me on the computer at about 5, and let's see what's going on by then."

I wrote a terse message to Cindy about betrayal, handed it to the guard, and headed for my car.

I drove as hard as I could without attracting every state trooper along the way. My strategy was to drive 9 mph over the speed limit and stay in the right lane as much as possible. It worked. I passed lots of troopers and cars pulled over for speeding, but no one was interested in me.

At five, I pulled into a Marriott Courtyard and sauntered into the lobby. The clerks at the desk were too busy checking people in to pay any attention to me. I hoped I could get on their WiFi in the lobby, and I did. At least I got onto someone's; I wasn't sure whose.

Mrs. Fritz wrote, "It's hit the fan. Calls from CNN, NBC, ABC, etc."

I asked, "Strategy working?"

"So far, so good. I have ?s." She sent me seven specific questions, and I answered six of them. I had no idea about the other one.

"Back on the road," was Mrs. Fritz's signoff. I grabbed a burger and Coke at a nearby Burger King and was back on the Interstate, driving into the night.

At a quarter after 10 p.m., my cell rang. I answered and was surprised to hear Cindy's voice. "Ralph, I know you're mad, and I don't blame you. You cannot repeat anything I say here. Do you understand?"

"Yeah," I answered coldly.

"Listen, Ralph, they made me do that. I had no choice."

"You always have a choice," I said and was surprised at myself. Since when had I become the ethicist?"

"You know what I mean. They would have run it that way anyway, with me working here or not, so I had to stay to see if I could make things better."

"How can you do that?"

"I don't know yet. What are you doing? In fact, where are you?"

"Cindy, I really liked you, but you've betrayed my trust once, so I know better than to tell you anything."

"I'm trying to get back onto your side, Ralph. Really, I am. I liked you too, and I think we did your guy dirt. I want to help."

"Yeah, well, it's a little late for that. You have to earn back my trust, and it won't be easy."

"I know. I expected that. And, by the way, my editor isn't sure about my loyalty to him on this, so he kept me in the dark all day. I'm sure they were talking to the networks all day, but I was kept out of it. I have to get back in their confidence again before I can do any good."

"Well, Cindy, it sounds like I'm on my own then. Little Ralph from Blackjack, Nebraska, against the big bad press."

"May I call you if I learn something?"

"Sure, Cindy, that would be a good start."

She hung up. I was thinking that except for the 1400-mile problem, Cindy and I just might hit it off.

At 2:30 a.m., I pulled into a Holiday Inn and got a room for the rest of the short night.

The next day, Mrs. Fritz sent me the counter-story she had written with my help. I agreed with it, but I thought it paled in comparison to the story broken by the Raleigh paper. I couldn't see how it would help. I drove on, still thinking.

CHAPTER 63

Call to Quarters

BACK IN BLACKJACK, MRS. Fritz was of the same opinion as I was. *The Press* story wasn't getting a lot of ink or face time on TV. The networks liked the bad-news story better. They were busy digging up all the dirt they could, and if they didn't find anything, they speculated about what they might have found. Things were still going downhill. She decided it was time to play her trump card, something she had never done before. She called her prodigal son, Joe.

Joe wasn't at his desk. He wasn't even at his office. He was in the Pentagon. He only went to the Pentagon for one thing: the Athletic Center. How he had managed to talk someone into letting him become a member of that was something he held very close. He hadn't even told his first or second wife, and his third had never asked. He wouldn't tell her either.

He played handball at the POAC, as it was called, because originally it had been a club for officers, the Pentagon Officers Athletic Center. The POAC was, as far as most handball players in the area believed, the ground zero for competitive handball, and Joe was very competitive. He had first learned the game from Pete Thorson back home, when Bill Just had added that to his character-building and tire-Joe-out course.

When Joe played, he played until he staggered out of the court from exhaustion. Whatever he did, he did it as hard and fast as he could. After each game, he went out of the court to change his shirt and gloves. He had to do this, because after every game, his shirt was completely soaked with sweat, as were his gloves. The purpose of handball gloves is to keep the ball dry, so wet gloves don't cut it.

When Joe pulled a clean shirt out of his bag, he heard his cell phone ringing. He normally wouldn't have answered it in such a situation, but something told him to answer it now. He was surprised to hear his mother's voice on the phone, and it was apparent that she was in a tizzy, something she never was.

She was talking so fast that Joe was having trouble understanding her so he said, "Hang on, Irma. I'm going to move to a quieter spot." He told the guys in the court to go on without him. A new player promptly took his place.

He walked to the door and went outside to escape the noise of the POAC. Here he had to deal with the traffic noise from Hwy 110 and flights in and out of National, but it was still better than inside. He dodged a couple of joggers coming back from a run across the Memorial Bridge, and put the phone back to his ear.

"Okay, Irma, I'm here. What's the emergency?"

Joe knew about the Bill Just story, of course. He had been sent a copy by his mother, and then when it hit the national news, he made more copies and handed them out to friends. He learned now for the first time about the outrageous story in the Raleigh paper.

"God damn it, that's awful!" he shouted.

Three more joggers who had just come in from long runs and were now stretching, turned and looked at him. "I'll tell you what, I'll take care of it," he asserted.

The joggers looked away. If he could handle it, we hadn't just invaded another country.

"No," Mrs. Fritz said, "I'm taking the helm on this one, Joe, but please help me. I need to get to the national press with this before tomorrow morning's papers and morning shows. By then, they will have seen the

Raleigh article and their nose for scandal will be twirling like a whirlygig. I need your help to get it to them."

"I can get to most of them for you, but not all. What am I going to get to them?"

"I'm just thinking that through now, but I'm thinking we need to give the TV guys something pictorial, so I'm thinking we make a video. We combine it with an article of our own like a press release. But it won't be; it will be like an article in a special issue of the paper."

Joe thought for almost a full minute. "You know, Irma, these days you can send all of that electronically, so you have hours to get it done. But can you do all of that in something like 15 hours? And I mean do a professional job? You can't send them something amateurish."

Mrs. Fritz didn't know how, but she knew she could and would.

Joe gave her one last piece of advice. "That video. Make sure there are some short soundbites in there. They'll need things measured in seconds, not minutes."

Joe gave up his handball game and went back to his office. He thought he would tell Senator Hunt about the problem and enlist his support.

Mrs. Fritz continued making calls. She called Ken Jackson and had him pull out of class at the community college. She told him he had to make the video. Ken was eager to help, and by the time he got back to the classroom he had made it into a project for his class.

Cecille said she would gladly state that Bill had done all he could for his son, even though she really knew very little about it. She told Mrs. Fritz about Eddie Starnek, the Army buddy usually found at the VFW after 5. Mrs. Fritz called Pete Thorson and asked him to bring Eddie over to *The Press*. Then she called the fire hall. It took two more calls to hook up with chief Doug Jones, who said he would be happy to help.

When Mrs. Fritz called Sheriff McBean she didn't know what she would encounter. Jackie said she would be delighted to tell of the good work Bill had performed for the town and its residents.

Lastly, she called Mary Dubchek at the library. Mary had just learned of the Raleigh article and said to count on her.

Mrs. Fritz notified everyone to meet at the community college at 5.

In the interim, she would work on her article for the special issue and get the printing of that started. She put her advertising "manager" to work getting some ads for it. She dashed out an outline of the video the way she would like to have it go. Ultimately, Ken Jackson would control that, but she wanted to make sure all the best points were covered. She would have something to say about Bill's influence on her boy, Joe. The outline read like this:

DID NOT ABANDON
    Eddie Starnek
    Cecille Gadd
TOWN HERO
(don't rehash Ralph's article)
    Me
    Doug Jones
    Mary Dubchek (?)

She decided to let Ken control the taping. She suspected he would interview the witnesses, but that was his business, and she knew less about that than she did running a newspaper. When she was ready, she went home and changed into a bright red suit with matching shoes. She climbed into her bright red Caddy and drove to the community college.

CHAPTER 64

The Video

THE STARS OF THE video showed up at different times, as could have been expected. Ken and his class, at least the members of his class who had chosen to participate in the project, had planned their recording in such a way that it didn't matter. As each one came in, they took them to a classroom and went over the questions they would ask and the answers they could expect. A little coaching as to how to act when being recorded was given too, such as how to sit. It seems that normal sitting positions were not favored by the videographers. They want their subjects sitting up very straight, perhaps even leaning forward slightly.

Mrs. Fritz had been the first to arrive and was also the first to be recorded in the studio. She spoke about the work Bill had done with her son, and she actually made it sound as if he was the youth leader for the community in general. The shoot was done twice, once with her on camera, and a second time showing Ken asking the questions. As soon as her recording was completed, the recording was hustled to an editing room where a few short segments were selected for inclusion in the final product.

Doug Jones went second. He exaggerated Bill's role in the fire department so much that Ken stopped him and started over again after

310

cautioning him that *The Press* might be around to check on his assertions. He told the story of the firehouse fire with Bill as the man who saved the town.

None of this was core to the story Ken and Mrs. Fritz felt had to be told, however. The key would be a convincing story of how Bill had attempted to marry Larsen's mother and to remain in contact after the sham marriage was dissolved. And the key figure in that would be Eddie Starnek. Mrs. Fritz was praying that Pete had snagged Eddie before he had a chance to drink some beers.

Pete and Eddie rolled in around 6:35. Pete told Mrs. Fritz, "I grabbed him the minute he walked in the door of the VFW, but he was dressed in dirty work clothes. I took him home to change, but he doesn't have many nice-looking clothes that fit him. I guess he doesn't dress up very often. I had to take him to my house for a clean shirt and a tie."

"It's all right, Pete," Mrs. Fritz said. "He looks just fine. In fact, I've never seen him looking as good."

Eddie was a tough interview. He talked and talked despite the coaching he had gotten in the classroom. Mrs. Fritz was watching in the booth, and she wasn't happy. She told Ken, "He stunk it up, didn't he? We'll have to reshoot him."

Ken, on the other hand, was unconcerned. "We can make a good piece from all of that, don't worry." Ken was thinking he might be editing all night, but it didn't matter. Whatever it took was all right with him.

Cecille arrived late from work. She had actually gone home to change clothes and redo her makeup. She looked great. Mrs. Fritz worried about that. She asked Ken, "Do you think we should use Cecille? She looks great. Maybe too good. We don't want *The Press* to think she's a femme fatale, do we?"

Again, Ken was confident. No problemo.

Mary was the last to arrive since she had to close the library. So when she did arrive it was after 9. The filming had been going on for over three hours. Mary hadn't bothered with dressing fancy or makeup, so the college girls went to work on her. She looked nice and came across well on her brief shoot.

Ken asked everyone to be prepared to come back if needed. He said he wouldn't be certain before midnight, so if everyone would stay available until then, it would be appreciated. The only one visibly disappointed in this was Eddie, who had planned to go to the VFW and regale his buddies with tales of stardom. Ken took him by the elbow as he walked out to Pete's car. "Eddie, no drinking tonight, just in case. Okay?"

"Ah, yah, okay…," Eddie said dejectedly. That promise lasted until about 10:30 when he decided that one little beer couldn't hurt.

Ken and the students went into the booth to call up all the edited material. They had an outline they were working, with timelines. Now all they had to do was fit it all together. One of the students, a tall, blond kid was chosen to be the narrator because of his rich, resonant voice. He was given a working script to practice while the editing proceeded. A final script would be prepared from the final version, but it would be close to the one he was practicing.

Ken superintended the whole process. Now the most important things to accomplish were getting it all together in something not over two minutes long, while still telling the whole story. He constantly referred to the story Mrs. Fritz had written for the special edition, still being printed, to be sure that the video supported it and didn't contradict anything in it.

At 1:30 a.m., Ken recorded the narration and added it to the final version. They finished at 2:15 and called Joe for instructions.

Joe had actually told everything to his mother earlier in the evening, but Ken wasn't sure he could trust Mrs. Fritz's recollection, especially since it sounded to him, speaking with her on the phone, that she had been into the Scotch.

Joe gave him contacts for the major networks, including CNN, and the major news bureaus. He included specific addresses for some of the biggest newspapers, *The Times*, for example, and the *North Carolina Star-Post*. The last one was to be sure they had it early in case they wanted to print a retraction. Ken used the Public Television facility for transmitting the video. The only glitch was that he had long ago lost his key to the station, but since it was always open, when he went to it, he didn't need one. When he came to the locked door, he realized he had a problem.

He had to awaken another producer and arrange to borrow her key. She wanted to know what was going on, and he said he'd tell her later that day. He figured she'd have it figured out by then.

All of this I had learned when I called Mrs. Fritz from the road. I was still hundreds of miles away, so she told me to stop for the night. I would get there the next day just in time for the reaction, if there was one. She told me, "Call your honey at the Star-whatever it is and tell her what we're doing. Tell her we're going to show that their story is wrong, and if they don't want to look stupid, they should have something in the morning paper saying they were wrong."

I gladly called Cindy. I was excited by the defense my little town had mounted so quickly, and I also wanted to stay in touch with her. There was still something about her that I couldn't shuck off. Cindy was surprised and appalled. Her loyalty to her paper kicked in before her disgust at what they had done.

"And just what do you think that will accomplish?" she asked petulantly.

I had a ready answer for that, "Restore the good name of Bill Just," he said with an enthusiasm he even wondered at.

"While ruining the good name of *The Star-Post!*" she retorted.

"Hey, Cindy! *The Star-Post* did that to itself."

"We could attempt to preserve both of our jobs in all of this if we tried," she said, sarcasm dripping from her voice like drops from a melting icicle, and with just about as much warmth. The tone of her reply didn't give me much encouragement about a future *rapprochement*. Still, we were talking to each other, and buoyed by optimism, I treated myself to a night in a Holiday Inn Express. From Mrs. Fritz's mood on the phone, I deduced that she would gladly pay for it.

At 3:20 ("a.m. in the morning," the community college students boasted to their friends), the last transmission of the video went out and the special edition of *The Press* had been posted on their website. The URL had been sent to a long list of addressees Joe had provided. He had already alerted them to be looking for it and promised that it would be worth waiting for.

Everyone in Blackjack was in bed trying to sleep by 4, but most of them were too excited for that.

I slept well. I had a dream involving Cindy. Cindy, on the other hand, spent the rest of the night at *The Star-Post* with her editor writing an unapologetic article presenting a different version of the Sp4 William Larsen story. It admitted no wrong-doing on their part, but revealed that new information had been discovered.

CHAPTER 65

Headlines

ALL HANDS WERE ON deck early the next morning. Mrs. Fritz was at *The Press* offices by 8 and reading the wires services. Mrs. Fritz had subscribed to a bare-bones wire service for years, and this was one of the first times she had actually used it. She was joined by Ken and three of his students. One of them, Thor, was on the computer checking papers around the country. Both of them found articles on the Bill Just story, and all of them were obviously based on the material they had sent out. The portable TV Mrs. Fritz had brought in was on NBC and *The Today Show* showed a few seconds of their video and reported the story exactly the way they had hoped: Bill was not at fault here and remains a hero in the eyes of his hometown.

All in all, it was an amazing triumph. A tiny Nebraska town had defended one of their own against an assault by a powerful newspaper… and had won.

I was in my car driving west, and asked on my cell phone if they had pulled up Raleigh's *Star-Post*. Thor tried and got only the day before's issue online.

"Have you gotten it online before," Mrs. Fritz asked.

"I don't think I've ever tried before, but it's after 9 there now and I should be able to read it."

"Why don't you call your honey there?" Mrs. Fritz asked.

I felt my face go hot. I wanted to debate that description of the "relationship," but once I felt the blood rushing to my face, I simply said I would, so I picked up the phone and called her.

Cindy answered her cell phone after quite a few rings.

"Yeah...?" she murmured into the phone.

"Cindy, it's me, Ralph."

"What time is it?" she asked.

"It's almost 8:30 here, so it must be 9:30 there."

"Ralph, I was up all night. Please, let me sleep."

"Sure," I said. "Just tell me what your paper said about Bill Just today."

"Good guy," she said. "Call me after noon, okay?"

I relayed that information to Mrs. Fritz. Total victory. Bill Just was now, if anything, even more of a hero than before. The revelation of his attempts to take care of his son despite the roadblocks thrown in his way, made him look even better.

As I drove, I thought, *It doesn't matter, really, what anyone outside of Blackjack thinks of Bill Just, especially now that he wasn't even living, but this is a sweet victory for the little town anyway. I'm certain that reporters from Kansas City, Denver, Lincoln, and Omaha for both papers and television will visit over the next few days, and images of Blackjack will be seen all over the central plains.*

I smiled, thinking, *Once again, Bill's story is being told, this time to a much larger audience.*

I set my cell phone to alarm at ten after twelve. I would call Cindy then. We had a lot to talk about, I hoped.

CHAPTER 66

Back Home

I DROVE INTO BLACKJACK mid-afternoon, feeling both elated and a little sad. The reason for the sadness was that when I had called Cindy, I had gotten her answering machine. I tried her work number and got her voice mail. It seemed to me that she was avoiding my calls, and that made me very sad. Why couldn't I get her out of my mind? She was half a country away. But then I thought of her eyes looking into mine. I was a goner.

I went to my room as soon as I drove back into town and changed clothes. I had been wearing the same shirt and pants for days, and it felt good to put clean clothes on again. Then I went to *The Press* to congratulate Mrs. Fritz and perhaps get some strokes for myself. If not, I had some good story ideas to work on, garnered from my interviews with the goat guy and the county agent.

I had called Mrs. Fritz when I was about 100 miles away, so she would know I was coming and would probably be waiting to see me. So, when I walked through the door, I wasn't surprised to see people in the office, but the number did surprise me. I saw Joe Fritzling sitting with his mother at the editor's desk, and Ken Jackson, sitting on the corner of the desk and talking with Eddie Starnek, Bill's Army buddy. Mary Dubchek was standing next to Ken, talking to Cecille, who was beautifully dressed, as always. The little room was packed.

Everyone looked up as I walked in and gave me a round of applause. I was very embarrassed about this and was sure I was blushing like mad. I returned the applause and said, "*You* did it! I'm applauding the real heroes of this story."

At that moment, the pressroom door opened and Cindy walked in. Everyone looked at me to see my expression, which was a Cheshire Cat grin from ear to ear, they tell me. No wonder Cindy didn't answer her phone! She must have been flying in, which would take all day at least.

Cindy ran up to me and gave me a big hug. She didn't flinch when I held her for another minute. Life was good now! Real good.

CHAPTER 67

Postscript

LIFE IS VERY DIFFERENT after the Battle of Bill Just. For one thing, I am now known by almost every citizen of Blackjack and the surrounding countryside, although I can only call maybe a hundred of them by name. And, all of those who know me seem to think of me as a local hero, although in actuality I am neither a real local nor any kind of hero. The real heroes stay quietly in the background.

Another thing, I now have a love interest. You can guess who. Cindy quit her job in Raleigh, probably just in time to avoid being fired, since it was known that she had sided with us against her editor. She has a job in Kansas City, and we visit each other as often as possible. Of course, she has to do most of the driving, since my car can't stand that much travel.

For a guy who hardly ever had more than three dates with the same girl before, this is a new experience and has taken some learning on my part. Cindy is patient with me, for which I am grateful and for which I love her even more.

My "fame" hasn't resulted in riches, but job security is assured. I still live in a rented room with the Lindstroms. This makes it impossible for us, Cindy and me, to meet in Blackjack, so we find places between here and Kansas City to meet. So far, it's been fun, but we'll have to decide what we want to do in the longer run.

The most amazing thing happened a couple of days ago, though.

Cindy called me and asked if I could take on an assignment with her for her Kansas City newspaper. She is writing for their Sunday magazine, so she usually has a week or two to research a story and get it ready for publication—sometimes more, depending on the lead time. Her Kansas City paper seems to have plenty of subscribers up here in Nebraska, for some reason.

I told Mrs. Fritz about the offer, and she said "Sure, as long as we get to publish it too." Cindy got permission for that, and I drove down to meet with her and her editor.

There's a new and somewhat surprising politician on the Western Nebraska scene these days: Tim Adams, a rancher from the Sand Hills. Given the fact that he lives about 10 miles from his closest neighbor and probably only speaks to about 20 people a week, and the same 20 the next week, you wouldn't expect him to be a canny politician, but he is. People out in the western parts of Nebraska and Kansas are looking at this guy as their next great hope. A new Chuck Hagel, it seems.

We were asked to interview him and his mother, who is still alive and living on the ranch. The editor had already contacted Adams, and he was willing.

I wasn't really excited about the prospects for making much of a story out of this; after all, those Sunday supplement magazines are pretty much fluff. But they pay really well, and Mrs. Fritz doesn't. Cindy and I both need the money.

Cindy had a new GPS in her car (the joy of working for a real newspaper in a big city, I guess), and it led us right to the ranch, the Double A. Cindy had never been in the Sand Hills, so it was making quite an impression on her. For me, it was boring driving. We drove through Scotts Bluff and headed north, passing through a few towns now nearly deserted. Some of those towns were just a post office and a bar.

We had been warned that ranchers work hard, and we would be lucky to get an hour of Adams' time, but his mother was a better prospect. She likely had little to do. Both of those turned out to be wrong.

Adams met us as we drove up to the house. I was surprised at the size of the house. I knew that the most family that ever lived there had comprised four people, two of whom had been children, until they grew up and left home. It appeared to be about a 10-room house, so it could have had as many as six bedrooms. The huge barn had what appeared to be a bunkhouse built onto one side. I wondered why so many people would want to sleep out there.

Adams was a big man—not huge, but big enough to handle a steer. He was dressed Western, as everyone in this part of the state was, except for his footwear. He was wearing shoes that most resembled sneakers, but they were brown high-tops.

My first question was, "Tell me about the shoes."

Adams laughed and took Cindy by the arm, leading us both onto the big porch, where he had a pitcher of lemonade sitting on a table and his mother was sitting there waiting to pour it into glasses. Next to the pitcher was a plate of homemade cookies.

Adams, in the tradition of politicians, insisted that we call him Tim. His mother was Helen.

Tim said, "Okay, first about the *boots*." I had called them shoes. "This is what passes for roping boots now, and doggone it, they actually work better. Drink up that lemonade, Ralph. We're going to ride."

"Horses?" I gulped. I had never ridden a horse and didn't want to do so in front of this rancher who might be a United States Senator in November.

"Well, we actually still have a couple of old horses on the ranch, so if you insist…"

"No, no, I'd rather not, actually."

"Me too," Tim said. "But if you need to take a picture of me on a horse, I can saddle one up. Remember all those pictures of Ronald Reagan on his ranch? That old boy was from Illinois. Never saw a ranch before he went to Hollywood."

I grabbed a couple of the cookies as he led me to his Jeep, and we started on a driving tour of the ranch. Cindy was getting the inside scoop from Tim's mom and the help around the house.

In that part of Nebraska, it takes a lot of land to support one head of cattle, so we rode pretty far before we had seen much of a herd. Windmills sucked water out of the aquifer, I now knew so much about, and pumped it into large stock tanks. Most of them overflowed, and the excess water soaked back into the ground and eventually found its way back into the underground sea, which I now knew was actually being depleted. The cattle seemed to stay within a short walk of a stock tank.

As we drove, we passed probably 12 or 15 workers engaged in all manner of jobs around the ranch. I realized that Tim was an employer. Each one waved to us, and if we stopped, they eagerly came up to talk in friendly and respectful terms with Tim. You could tell they admired him greatly.

After what must have been about an hour of riding the range, Tim said, "I have something I want you to see. It's an important part of my life and philosophy."

He explained to me that every Friday and Saturday there was a cattle sale at a sale lot, which happened to be on his ranch, since his father had donated the land to the grange for that purpose.

The sale lot was the first one I had ever seen. It was under a large, corrugated steel roof, but open on the sides. Inside were perhaps ten pens, connected by runways between the pen fences. One pen was "the theater" as Tim called it, or the sale pen. Each lot of cattle was brought into that pen to be sold and then returned to a holding pen. The holding pens were mostly occupied by cattle, either sold or up for sale. Tim told me to watch carefully how the whole operation worked.

A call would go out for a lot number, and a few seconds later that bunch would come into the sale pen where the bidding would begin. The efficiency and order was amazing. Tim explained that back in the lot, workers were stationed to open and shut just the right gates at just the right time. If a steer got mixed in with a group of cows with another bull, there would be big trouble as the two bulls sought to gain ownership of the females. Each gate had to open and shut at exactly the right time, or chaos would ensue.

When the sale was over for the day, Tim led me over to meet the sale pen boss, a guy named Snake. Snake had a huge snake tattooed on his right arm, and in that hand, he held a bullwhip. I had noticed that once during the sale, a bull had started to get out of control, and Snake had stepped in front of that 500lb snorting piece of fury and cracked the whip beside the bull. The bull looked at him for a couple of seconds, and Snake held the coiled whip up by the bull's face. The bull walked calmly away and caused no more trouble.

"Snake here taught me more about life than anyone else," Tim said. "He doesn't get mad or scared or excited, he just gets control and keeps it. My brother and I worked for him when we were in high school, and it was the best lesson we ever had. I would like to take that kind of lesson to Washington. Maybe I'll even take Snake with me."

"You just go there by yourself, Tim," Snake said. "I'm stayin' here."

I couldn't get over the stark differences between Western Nebraska, which reminded me of an old Western movie set, and the part of the state I knew best. The contrast made even more of an impression on my Carolina cutie.

We went back to our respective homes and cooperated by email on the story, which ran in the Kansas City Sunday supplement two weeks later. Both of our financial statuses improved when the checks came in.

The other day, we had both gotten the same two days off and were meeting in Marysville, where there really isn't much for a visitor to see or do, but that was just fine with us. We found this little complex of a motel, gas station, restaurant, garage, general store, and deer checking station all wrapped up into one place called the "Top, Plop, Slop, and Shop." The food was okay, the gas was expensive, but the motel room was dirt cheap.

We were out walking when my cell phone rang. It was Mrs. Fritz.

"Ralph, where are you?"

"We're out on a hiking/biking trail near Marysville, Kansas," I answered.

"Can you get back here in two hours?"

"Maybe. Depends on how long it takes us to walk back to the car. How about three hours?"

"Well, that might be okay. I need you, and bring Cindy with you, okay?"

I thought that was a little strange. In fact, if Cindy was to go back to work the next day, she would have to drive her car to Blackjack and then back to Kansas City. I doubted that she would be enthused about doing that, so I asked her.

"Sure," she said cheerily. "Let's go."

I was fairly sure something was going on that I wasn't in on at this point, but no amount of questioning brought forth more information. We made it back to the motel in about a half hour and were on the road to Blackjack in under an hour.

The roads in this part of the world are straight as arrows in all three dimensions. The biggest problem is falling asleep at the wheel. Twice, Cindy honked at me as I started to leave the pavement.

I pulled up in front of *The Press* offices and the two of us walked in. Mrs. Fritz was there in one of her all-red pantsuits. Today her nails were blue—fingers and toes.

She said, "I don't have time to explain, but here's the short version. Today, the first Bill Just Award is going to be presented. The ceremony starts at 7:30, so you just have time to change into some nice clothes and get there. Cindy, can you take some pictures for us?"

"Sure, Mrs. Fritz," Cindy said with a smile. "I brought my camera. I'll take it in with me."

"Fine," Mrs. Fritz said, smiling benevolently at Cindy, like a mother-in-law. "Ralph, you take notes. I'll be there too, but I'd like you to record impressions for a human-interest angle. I'll see you both at the Lutheran Church in an hour."

We were hustled out to Cindy's car. We changed in my room, and I was surprised to see that Cindy had brought a cute little dress. Normally she lived in jeans and blouses, and this was going to be one of the few times I had seen her in a dress.

"What's the occasion?" I asked.

"I thought Mrs. Fritz said it was an award presentation," she answered innocently.

Hmmm... I thought.

We stopped for a quick snack at The Ideal and arrived at the church to find more than a few cars jostling for parking spaces. Cindy grabbed her large camera bag from the trunk, and we made our way in through the crowd. I guessed there were between a hundred and a hundred and twenty people already in the church. Mrs. Fritz took my arm and pointed me to the front row, where there was a vacant seat next to the mayor. I wanted to protest, but Pastor Jansen was asking everyone to rise for an opening prayer. After that, the VFW honor guard presented the colors, and everyone recited the Pledge of Allegiance. First impression: pretty formal ceremony.

Ken Jackson came forward and stood facing the audience, now numbering at least 150, and he said:

"Most of you know that we're here to make the first-ever presentation of a brand new award called The Bill Just Award. An anonymous donor has endowed the award, and he named it in honor of one of his heroes, also one of ours, Bill Just. Although he wishes to remain anonymous, a wish we must honor, please join me in a round of applause for this generous gift. This year's recipient will receive this beautiful plaque and a check for $5000. From now on, the monetary award will be $2500, but this first time it is for twice that.

"This award is presented to a person who best exemplified the ideals and service of Bill to our community over the past year. I'm sure we all agree that encouraging more Bill Justs in our community is a good thing."

I was writing furiously while observing the audience as much as possible. As I looked around, I saw several people I thought would be great candidates for the award. Mary Dubchek the librarian, for example, who taught me so much about not just Blackjack but the entire area. Ken Jackson himself, but it wasn't likely going to him since he was MC-ing the affair. Doug Jones, the fire chief and town council member, would be a good choice. Just looking around I picked out these and others.

Ken went on.

"Interestingly, the award committee chose for this first award a relative new-comer to our community. Given the dynamic nature of the settling of this part of the country, that seems very fitting. A mere hundred and thirty years ago, few folks had lived in this town for more than about 15 minutes. That has changed lately, but it's fitting to recall that historically it has been the case."

I tried to think of any new-comers to town who had done anything meriting the award and decided that somehow I had missed the individual about to be honored.

Ken continued. "The first presentation of the Bill Just Award goes to Ralph Anderson!"

I was still writing, and it actually took me a few seconds to realize what he had just said. *Me? What had I done? Was this a big joke at my expense?*

No, everyone was standing and applauding. Cindy was by my side hugging my arm, and my mom and dad appeared from someplace and came over to give me a hug. Tears edged out of the corners of my eyes.

Ken stepped down and guided me up to the pulpit. He then read a long and exaggerated, I thought, account of my articles about Bill and the fight to save his reputation. That fight was made by Mrs. Fritz, Ken, Joe, and others while I was driving around the country. Suddenly, I realized that I was alone at the pulpit, and everyone was seated waiting for me to talk.

I don't think I had ever talked to that many people at one time before. Looking back, I wasn't nervous. I was too overwhelmed to think. I stammered through a little speech, saying that I was sure I was low on the list of people who should have received this award. I saw my mom make some gestures to me, and she was mouthing words reminding me to thank everyone for coming and especially thank the donor of the award and the committee that had chosen me, no matter how inappropriately.

There was a brief closing ceremony, including the retiring of the colors and another prayer by Pastor Jansen, in which he thanked God for people like me. I'm sure God was amused. Then we all retired to the social room for the usual punch and desserts.

Lots of people came by to shake my hand and tell me that no matter how humble I was, there was no one better deserving of this award. I remained stunned and in disbelief. I still thought there must be someone from *Candid Camera* around, recording this for my ever-lasting embarrassment. But they all seemed so sincere. It still made no sense to me.

Now, though, I understood why Cindy had a dress with her. So she had known. Obviously, my mom and dad had been told, as well as Mrs. Fritz. My reporter's instinct, as new as it was, wanted to know who the donor was. Everyone I asked said they didn't know. Well, someone did, and I would find out who. It shouldn't be hard. How many guys in town were rich enough to endow an award paying out thousands of dollars a year?

Over the next few weeks, I checked out the wealth of the families in town. Not surprisingly, those who had sold large farms headed the list. There were a lot more of them than I would have thought. Most of them hardly knew me, and I didn't know them. Mary at the library was no help. I was fairly sure that Ken Jackson knew, and I bugged him several times, but he swore that he didn't know. Joe Fritzling said he didn't know, as did his mom, my boss. If Mrs. Fritz didn't know, who did?

Weeks of prying yielded nothing, until Mrs. Lindstrom, head of town gossip, dropped it one day while I was eating my bowl of Corn Pops. "Imagine," she said, "a fellow like Earl Farris having so much money. Why, the man lives like a tramp or worse. Nutty as a fruitcake too. Where did he get money for an award like that?"

"You mean he endowed the Bill Just Award?" I asked incredulously.

"Well, I can't say for certain, but I'm pretty sure he did. I was talking to…"

I was already out the door and on my way to Earl's goat farm.

As before, the approach was the most dangerous part. I stopped my car within sight of Earl's shack and honked the horn. I was already in negotiations to buy a used Pontiac from one of the firefighters with the $5000 from the Just Award. I had been going to pick it up that day, and now I was glad I hadn't done that yet. Earl might not recognize the new car, but I was pretty sure he would recognize my old one.

Apparently he did, because no one shot at me. Eventually, I saw Earl coming around the house. He paused to look at me waving to him, decided I was all right, and waved for me to come in.

He greeted me in the yard, strewn as always with junk and goat marbles.

"Why might you be callin' on me?" he asked, although I suspect he had a pretty good idea.

"Just want to talk, Earl," I said, and he seemed to accept that.

We talked for about an hour about this and that, not mentioning the award. Finally, I said, "I do have a question, Earl, and I promise you I won't mention a word of this to anyone. It's just for my information and not for anyone else's."

"How 'bout that fancy new girlfriend of yours?" he asked.

"Okay, I might tell her, but she doesn't live here and probably never will, so that's the same as not telling anyone," I promised. "But how do you know about my girlfriend?"

"Saw her at the award ceremony," he said.

I let that pass for the time being.

"So, I guess you've decided you know who paid for that award and for some reason you think it's me."

"Yep, that's it exactly," I said, "and I'm deeply grateful to you, but what I can't figure out is how you got enough money to do that. I've been doing a little math, and I figure it this way: It's supposed to pay out $2500 a year, every year, forever I suppose. To do that, the endowment must have around $60,000 in it. And since you already paid out $5000, make that $65,000 you would have put in. Now, Earl, where would you get $65,000? And the reason I want to know is that I don't want you going broke on this deal."

"Well," Earl said slowly, "let's just say I was the guy, and let's say I put in $68,000. I think what you really want to know is why I live like this if I got that kinda money."

"Pretty shrewd, Earl," was all I could think to say.

"If I had did that, and I had that much money to do it with, and more besides so's, I'd never have to worry about that 68 thou, I'd still live just like I do, because I like the way I live. Doesn't everyone tell you I'm nuts?

Because maybe I am. Whether I'm nuts or not don't have much to do with whether I got money, don't you agree?"

"I suppose, but you have to admit that people who are nuts usually don't get their acts together well enough to make that kind of money, nor do they do such sensible, public-spirited things with it," I opined.

"Just so we're straight on this, I don't think I'm nuts. Eccentric, sure. Dirty, yeah. Lazy, darn right. I always been that way and expect to be that way for the rest of my life. I don't see no point in cleanin' up for people I got no use for. This way, people leave me alone, except for you, that is. You're gettin' to be a regular pest around here."

"Aw, c'mon, Earl, twice is all I've been here in my whole life," I said.

"Yeah, but you've only knowed me for 6 months!"

"That's true," I said, "but you started it this time, you gave me the award."

"True enough," Earl observed. "How'd you come to the conclusion it was me?"

"I heard it from someone who knows things around town, and I came out here to check. I think you've confirmed the rumor."

"Can't have people knowin' I've got some money. You have to keep it quiet, Ralph, and I'm real serious about that."

"You have my word on that," I said, and I meant it. "You haven't told me where you got it. So far as I can tell you don't make a penny."

"Yeah, and they think I'm nuts! Let's just say I inherited this old farm from my folks. You're looking at about 3 acres here in this goat pen. You probably think that's the whole farm. Most folks think that, and that's the way I want it, so that's part of the deal too. No one can know."

"You've got it," I said earnestly.

"I've still got 20 acres, and maybe someday, I'll show you the big parcel where I have the meat goats. I have close to 200 goats out there sometimes. There's a guy comes here from St Louis a couple of times a year to buy goats for the Greek market there. I get a good price for them, and he comes to me. I just tell him which ones he can take. So I make money every year without doin' nothin'. Nuts? Yeah, crazy like a fox!"

"And," he went on, "some years ago I sold off 33 acres for a lot of money. I went to Bill Just and asked what I should do with it. He set it up for me to put it into a mutual fund. Before I took out the 68 thou, it had growed to $361 thousand, which I don't need. Bill was the fairest guy I ever met. He didn't take advantage of me, which he surely coulda done. He took care of me good. That's why the award is named for him, and you got it, because you told the world what a good guy he was. Now, that's pretty sane, I think... Don't you?"

"Absolutely," I said, and I meant that too.

I went back to town and bought the car.

I think about that award a lot, and Cindy and I talk about it. We think about our lives together without having to drive hundreds of miles, even with the "new" Pontiac. We've never said marriage once, but it seems that's where we're headed except that her job's in KC and mine is in Blackjack.

I can see why most of the kids with gumption leave the little towns and go to the cities. I can't make much money at *The Press*, because there's not much money to pay anyone with. I couldn't support the two of us on my salary, and I wouldn't want Cindy to support me.

Up till now, there wasn't much chance of me getting a newspaper job in a city, but with the award... Who knows? I love irony, and that's just the kind of irony I love. What if the award, Earl Farris's award, made it possible for me to get a good job and, consequently, have to leave Blackjack... the little town I've grown to love?